P9-CNC-974

DATE			

LIFE AT THE
ZOO

LIFE AT THE ZOO

BEHIND THE SCENES WITH THE ANIMAL DOCTORS

Phillip T. Robinson

COLUMBIA UNIVERSITY PRESS   NEW YORK

Columbia University Press
Publishers Since 1893
New York   Chichester, West Sussex
Copyright © 2004 Phillip T. Robinson, DVM

Library of Congress Cataloging-in-Publication Data
Robinson, Phillip T.
    Life at the zoo: behind the scenes with the animal doctors / Phillip T. Robinson.
      p.   cm.
    Includes bibliographical references and index.
    ISBN 0–231–13248–4 (cloth : alk. paper)
    1. Zoos.   I. Title.

QL76.R64 2004
590.73—dc22

2004043893

Columbia University Press books are printed on
permanent and durable acid-free paper.

Printed in the United States of America

c 10 9 8 7 6 5 4 3 2 1

CONTENTS

PREFACE

Zoogoing is one of America's favorite pastimes. In fact, more Americans are reported to visit zoos and aquariums annually than attend all major professional sporting events combined, with present numbers approaching 140 million. Worldwide attendance at zoos and aquariums is estimated at 600 million people. The motives of zoogoers range from simple curiosity and amusement to educational and spiritual growth. Americans are fascinated with animals. This is clearly reflected in our annual expenditure of billions of dollars to purchase pets, supplies, and animal medical care. Cats, dogs, birds, ferrets, lizards, snakes, and tortoises have become common household companions for people, causing a huge growth in the pet industry worldwide. Television programs involving animals are at an all-time high, representing one of the most popular segments of the communications and television entertainment industry.

Perhaps no area of veterinary science is as intimidating or demands as much versatility as the practice of zoo animal medicine. At times it requires a taste for the kinds of body slams, physical and mental, that might be found elsewhere only in the World

Quagga in London Zoo, 1870

Wrestling Federation. After all, zoos are made up of both animals and people—and people usually bring the most uncertainty to the running of a zoo.

The evolution of zoos is ongoing, at times painful, and fraught with some lingering anachronisms involving purpose and ethics. Along with the public's growing awareness of environmental degradation and species extinctions, the expectations of zoos have risen steeply. In addition, animal welfare concerns have placed zoos under the public microscope, questioning the care and conditions of animals under their stewardship. Responding to these influences, the zoo profession has undergone a steady transformation over the past thirty years, changing many of its values, priorities, and programs.

Given the global urgency to protect wildlife and wild places, some people look with optimism upon the capabilities of the new zoological gardens to help provide security for the survival of nature. The quagga, a now-extinct relative of the South African plains zebras, epitomizes a dwindling population of creatures that escaped the grasp of modern civilization. In 1873 the last, nameless, individual died in captivity at the Artis Zoo in Amsterdam, Holland. While the collective capacity of zoos and aquariums to offset the steady losses of animal species in the wild is far too small for the global problem at hand, zoos' contributions to conservation biology are significant, and growing. Zoos have enormous potential to educate the public about environmental conservation and are collaborating in the field and the laboratory to help address problems of animal extinctions.

My purpose for writing this book is to share some hard-earned insights into the dynamics of caring for and conserving wild animals in captivity, as well as to consider a few broader implications for how we view nature and animals in our society. Truthfully, when I left zoo work I never had an exit interview, and, in part, this book fulfills that exercise. This book will not tell you how to run a zoo, but it may give you a better idea of what to be pleased or perplexed about when you visit one in the future. It is written from my personal perspective as a staff veterinarian at the San Diego Zoo, a university research veterinarian, a wildlife biologist, and a nature lover. The experiences described are mostly my own, but the insights and knowledge therein have been honed by my fortunate association with many talented, dedicated professionals throughout my zoo career. I have filled in some of the blanks with supplementary research about zoos, which becomes hard to attribute in detail without citing sources like an academic treatise. Comedian Michael Wright put it this way: "To steal ideas from one person is plagiarism; to steal from many is research."

This book recounts some of the thinking and thoughts that go through a zoo veterinarian's mind when visiting animal patients in a zoo. My focus, as zoo medicine should be, is more on keeping animals healthy than on the technology of treating preventable conditions. In sharing my experiences and ideas about zoo people and zoo animals, I have struggled to balance the inclusion of personal opinions and the cataloging of esoteric facts and diseases; I am not always sure which prevailed.

Most of us in the zoo-doctor profession believe that it takes a quirky combination of science, art, and good fortune to practice successfully. My own experiences corroborate just that—especially the quirky parts. Through their dedication and perseverance, zoo veterinarians have advanced the knowledge of animal keeping, health, reproduction, and conservation, as well as the humane well-being of wild animals in captivity. In doing so they have fundamentally altered the course of zoos, bringing them along—sometimes kicking and screaming—into this new millennium.

It may be the blend of art, science, and pragmatism of zoo medical practice that makes it a unique and rewarding career, but it is the romantic fantasy of working in a zoo that somehow captures everyone's imagination, including mine.

Family, friends, mentors, and associates have all helped me over the years on my zoo and conservation journey, and, thereby, in the preparation of this book. I am sincerely grateful to them all. My lively, loving mother, Marge Robinson, has always encouraged me to pursue whatever occupations or projects inspire me, but she never anticipated that she would end up referring to me as "the monkey doctor." Several individuals in particular have actively encouraged, tolerated, and assisted me in refining my efforts to articulate my thoughts on the written page, especially Katherine and Shane Robinson, Dr. Rollin Baker, L. James Binder, Donn Stone, and Dr. Duane Ullrey. Marvin L. Jones provided helpful comments on the final draft. I also have been fortunate to benefit from the skills of my helpful editors at Columbia University Press.

As a veterinarian, I have often been joined in my efforts to improve the lives of zoo animals by the generous collaboration of zoo directors, curators, keepers, biologists, physicians, researchers, and architects. While only a few of them have been mentioned by name, many of them have made significant contributions to the field of zoological medicine and deserve the public's gratitude and admiration.

LIFE AT THE
ZOO

INTRODUCTION

In every generation there are restless souls who cannot be made to fit the common mold. A few of these are valuable in keeping their communities and professions in a ferment by their constant challenge to the existing order of man's thoughts and actions.

—Memorial to Dr. Richard C. Cabot (1868–1939), the Ella Lyman Cabot Trust

I opened up a cardboard box that had been taped shut and tucked away in a storage closet. When you move on to a new position, it is easier to set up housekeeping in your next office from scratch than to salvage aging supplies from your old desk. After a while, most of the objects in a desk become so invisible to the consciousness that one unthinkingly pushes familiar things aside while hunting through drawers to find an item that you know is in there somewhere. I fumbled past a stack of old business cards, a little metric ruler, a favorite calculator to convert ounces to milligrams, and a broken ostrich egg that could be shaped into an interesting tie tack some day—if they should ever return to fashion. I wondered where that nifty paper wheel gadget was from the horsemeat company that could be used

1

to calculate the pregnancy due date of anything from an aardvark to a squirrel. Struggling to make sense of the forensic remains of my own zoo career in this box of junk, I also wondered whether, if a volcanic eruption smothered my house in ash, an archaeologist in the next millennium could figure out what I had done for a living, or would simply write me off as an eccentric pack rat.

A small cupful of paper clips looked like a mini-museum collection in itself; their variety reminded me of the curious displays of "Barbed Wires of the Old West" seen hanging on walls in country restaurants and southwestern tourist traps. These little fasteners had been detached from letters sent to me over the years from all over the world. Wide boxy types (Dutch, I think), funky colored plastic clips, vinyl-coated ones, a circular model, and some foldable, silver-foil discs originating from a private animal collector in Switzerland. The least pretentious ones of the lot were thoroughly rusted, attesting to their humid equatorial origins. I doubt that any cheaper paper clips existed; these were from Nigeria, where recycling has been practiced since time immemorial.

Comatose pens clogged with ossified ink filled an old pencil box, and the only one that still worked was a lonely Bic ballpoint—a stark contrast to the Nigerian model of quality control. I rediscovered the old fine-point Rapidograph pen that I had used to mark labels with indelible ink for a collection of small-animal museum specimens during my graduate field research days in Africa. In the bottom of the box languished a few unused paper museum tags with strings still attached—their unemployment bore witness to the spared lives of several obscure tropical rodents, whose less fortunate relatives now resided within white steel cases at the Michigan State University Natural History Museum, mothballed into perpetuity.

Next, I spied a rubber leg and a head from a small desktop model of a horse—a heartfelt gift from a graduate of Beijing University veterinary school. The rest of the horse, mounted in a standing position on a lacquered wood base, had strayed off somewhere else. Little red dots on its body labeled with Chinese script identified the useful acupuncture points to remedy lameness, colic, and equine liver ailments. I remain impressed that the horse has merited centuries of neurological research.

Finally, digging into a manila file folder, I extracted a long-forgotten letter that I received while I was the director of veterinary services at the San Diego Zoo. It was addressed to "Chief Veterinary Doctor, Zoo Hospital." The undulating penmanship detailed a most peculiar and dangerous medical condition that the writer's doctors were "too incompetent to properly diagnose." The patient was confident, however, that it could easily be remedied if I would personally intervene on his behalf. He pleaded, "Doctor, I have a live rattlesnake inside my stomach and without assistance from a serpent expert like you, these people are sure to kill me when they try to take it out!" The return address was: "Psychiatric Unit, Veterans Administration Hospital, Salt Lake City, Utah." The archaeologists are going to have their work cut out for them. But first, let me start toward the beginning.

As I made my way down the tree-covered lane toward the San Diego Zoo hospital for the very first time, I came upon the peculiar spectacle of two medieval-costumed swordsmen engaged in a heated battle near the hospital's front steps. They briefly emerged from their Shakespearean characters, shifted to the roadside to let me pass, and resumed their bloodless encounter. Strewn around the perimeter of this cul-de-sac were fragments of a stage set for the Old Globe Theatre's production of *Hamlet*. Moving past the actors and through the tall iron gates, I entered the equally surreal world of wild and exotic animals at the San Diego Zoo.

Just a few short weeks before, clutching my freshly inscribed veterinary diploma, I rushed home to pack after June graduation ceremonies at Michigan State University. With all my worldly goods secured in a horse trailer, minus the horse, I hooked it to my car and headed for California. After climbing over the Rockies and gazing into the Grand Canyon, I angled southwest across the Sonoran Desert through a blur of creosote bush and ocotillo. With the car's temperature gauge in the red zone and the heater on high—my last-ditch effort to keep the coolant from boiling over—I impatiently switchbacked up the grade from the desert floor and entered the coastal mountains of eastern San Diego County. Little did I know that this fifteen-month internship would take me fifteen years to complete.

Earlier in the year, I had received the welcome news that I had been selected as the new veterinary medical intern at the San Diego Zoo. It was pure serendipity that I had ever learned of this opportunity to begin with, since it was a new program—the only zoo medicine internship in the world. My zoology academic advisor, Dr. Rollin Baker, director of the MSU Natural History Museum and a colleague of the zoo's curator of mammals, had learned of this opening in correspondence. I applied immediately.

My longstanding goal was to work in wildlife conservation research in Africa, a career for which I had learned Swahili and completed BS and MS degrees in wildlife biology. I had no occasion to use my Swahili-language training on the opposite side of the continent, where I spent most of a year doing field research in the Republic of Liberia, a destination for freed American slaves in the nineteenth century. There I trekked through rainforests with native hunters and lived in remote villages while studying the habits of the pygmy hippopotamus for the World Wildlife Fund. I made recommendations for its conservation in the wild. Thirty-five years later, I am still attempting to implement them.

I grew up in Grand Rapids, Michigan, which hosted a small municipal zoo that I rarely visited. The only zoo of any real size was near Detroit on the opposite side of the state. I had always been put off a little by what I had seen and read about zoos, with their closely confined animals and circus-like atmospheres. After returning from Africa I combined my wildlife biology interests with veterinary medicine and was accepted into veterinary school at Michigan State. I expected that San Diego would be but a brief educational detour on the way to other places.

As a student, I had several zoo experiences, but nothing vaguely resembling those awaiting me in southern California. In veterinary school, I went on rounds with an MSU faculty member to the Potter Park Zoo in Lansing, Michigan. The most memorable medical cases involved problems with lice on donkeys at the zoo's farm exhibit and roundworm parasites in their bobcats—but at least that was a start. In the winter of my senior year in veterinary school, I ventured to Chicago to work with the staff at the Lincoln Park Zoo. There I encountered a whole new level of zoo medicine. I began on the first morning with a previously arranged meeting with the zoo's director, Dr. Lester Fisher, at the baby animal nursery, where the zoo's longtime veterinarian and administrator had stopped by to check on his charges en route to his office across the park's grounds. Well-spoken and well-dressed in a smart suit and tie, he carried himself as if he were the mayor of Chicago, and he probably would have made a splendid one at that.

In the morning, Dr. Fisher worked as a zoo veterinarian, then shifted to the role of chief administrator and afternoon host of a local radio program about zoo animals. He often ended the day at fundraisers and meetings with civic leaders and politicians. Today he listened to the heartbeats of a baby tiger, checked the rectal temperature of an infant chimpanzee with a cold, and chatted in a fatherly manner with the nursery staff about the magical little creatures in their care. Several zoo visitors stood outside in the cool, misty drizzle, straining at the window in hopes of getting a mere glimpse into the exotic little world inside. I couldn't help but beam internally because I was on the more interesting side of the glass.

Dr. Fisher thoroughly enjoyed his limited, but continuing, hands-on contact with the animals. Dr. Erich Maschgan, however, saw most of the cases that surfaced on a daily basis, dividing his time between his own private pet practice in Chicago and the zoo. We visited his patients in the lion house, monkey house, reptile house, and various behind-the-scenes locations on the zoo grounds. I was awed by the unassuming, competent manner with which he evaluated and treated animals that showed up on the sick list. A monkey had been in a tussle, and its ear was split by a bite. After a dose of an anesthetic, he scrubbed the ear clean and neatly trimmed away a hopelessly dangling piece of skin and cartilage, returning the animal to a holding cage for follow-up antibiotics to be administered by a keeper. I didn't realize it then, but I would see many monkey injuries in the coming years, the results of squabbles over food, females, sex, and resting space.

Dr. Maschgan was a kindly, modest man who genuinely liked animals. He had warm relationships with the animal care staff, many of whom had been doing this unusual work for years in the heart of Chicago, serving a zoo that had been open to the public since the 1870s. I wondered if every medical case in a zoo veterinarian's career was different, since no two hours were alike during my entire visit there. It was a mystifying place, in the sense that living bits of animal nature from all over the globe had been assembled into a synthetic jungle. They carried on with their immigrant lives on foreign soil, through hot Chicago summers and icy winters, entirely dependent upon humans for their health and well-being.

As I watched the large carnivores and apes, I speculated on how heavy the cage hardware was and if these contraptions would really hold a powerful animal if it became excited or vexed. I examined the widths of the moats required to contain dangerous animals and the precautions that employees took when they came close to them. Who really knew whether a Jim Thorpe, Mark Spitz, or Michael Jordan of the animal kingdom might defeat barriers that were designed for just-average animals? An impala antelope in the wild can clear an obstacle eight feet high and forty feet wide, but zoo enclosures half as large are meant to contain the same animal in captivity.

Studying the padlocks, I imagined their crumbling inside from age and corrosion and the cage doors falling off one day, liberating their feral inhabitants. In fact, in the years to come, several cage locks did fall apart in my hands. As with an aging airplane, how do you know when to replace this stuff? In the interest of safety, zoos often adopt a two-lock design on the most dangerous doors, just as aviation mechanical systems provide for engineering redundancy. Such things are learned by good and bad experiences that have become part of the practical lore of zookeeping, learned the hard way by animal escapes, lumps, bumps, bruises—and a few plane crashes along the way. Yet, whereas the planes had operation and service manuals, no books existed then on how to run a zoo.

During my zoo career I would meet countless veterinarians, doctors, dentists, nurses, and other professionals in my attempts to diagnose and treat problems in zoo animals. In comparing and contrasting our professions, I usually asked the physicians to consider the following scenario: Your patient has a badly broken leg. It attacks you when you try to approach, refuses to tell you anything about its injury, resists all of your efforts to examine, x-ray, and diagnose the problem, requires you to forcibly sedate it for surgery, tries its best to tear off the cast that you put on their fractured limb after the surgery, and, finally, when awake, attempts to flee from the hospital, threatening the life of anyone who comes near. This is the nature of medical practice in the zoo. In some ways, I suppose it is like specializing in providing medical care to demented maximum-security prisoners.

Because of the scope and novelty of their work, zoo veterinarians have the pervasive sense of never having quite enough medical or surgical expertise to tend to every possible injury or disease in their practice. Indeed, it is their everyday job to discover and assemble solutions for these uncertainties on a case-by-case basis. A zoo veterinarian must be part epidemiologist, surgeon, ethologist, ecologist, detective, and shaman. Coping with these complexities is the fundamental conundrum that pricks the imagination and enthusiasm of individuals who make it their career.

No matter how humble the zoo's staff or facilities, veterinarians must provide the 911 responses to all emergencies and be prepared to cope with any catastrophe that arises. They are the paramedics, anesthesiologists, trauma surgeons, and midwives. And when these efforts fail, they become the priests who administer last rites.

San Diego Zoo Hospital and Biological Research Station, c. 1930

1. INTERN AT THE ZOO

An Eclectic Orientation

The San Diego Zoo originated as a commonplace menagerie—a by-product of a small, temporary animal display that had been assembled for the 1915–16 Panama-California Exposition in the city's spacious Balboa Park. The exposition commemorated the impending prospects for international commerce brought about by the newly completed Panama Canal. Its inaugural event was a grand midnight concert attended by fifty thousand people on New Year's Eve in 1915, and its centerpiece attraction was the world's largest musical instrument, a massive pipe organ, which had been installed in the new outdoor Spreckels Organ Pavilion. Newly caged but zooless animals listened nearby in the darkness to a musical performance that aptly began with Haydn's *The Creation.*

A makeshift arrangement of enclosures had been erected to exhibit this hastily gathered hodgepodge of wolves, bears, leopards, and bison. They were displayed like a circus sideshow for the amusement of the visitors. The exposition ran for two years instead of the scheduled one. In 1916, as it began winding down, the idea of installing these animals, and more, into a permanent facility in Balboa Park took root with the birth of the nonprofit Zoological Society of San Diego. Dr. Harry Wegeforth, a local physician, scanned the dry, brushy hillsides and canyons in Balboa Park and envisioned animals from all over the globe living in a tropical garden. As a teenager Wegeforth had had a passion for animals and circuses and slipped away from San Diego for a time to become a tightwire walker with the Barnum and Bailey Circus.

Wegeforth's initial zoo efforts drew upon his connections in city government and the business community to expropriate building materials and solicit donations and sponsors for animal acquisitions. He funded his passion a nickel and a dime at a time. Almost single-handedly, Wegeforth organized a plan to create his notion of a world-class zoo, and in 1921 the city of San Diego was finally persuaded to provide the permanent property for the zoo in the park. Thanks to innate wisdom, or, more likely, thanks to the protective leadership "Dr. Harry" wielded, city politicians seldom succeeded in meddling significantly with the zoo's management or budget. This remains the case even today.

On the first day of my veterinary internship, I anxiously sought out the Zoo Hospital and Biological Research Station, a classic piece of 1920s Spanish revival–style architecture, built through the philanthropy of Ellen Browning Scripps, an heir to the Scripps newspaper fortune. Balboa Park had evolved into a grassy fantasyland of exotic eucalyptus, jacaranda, orchid, frangipani, and fig trees sprinkled around botanical gardens, reflecting ponds, fountains, and museums with quaint Spanish facades. The zoo hospital was completed in 1927—a simple, picturesque two-story building cloistered away on the zoo's perimeter, now adjacent to the backstage entrance to San Diego's Old Globe Shakespeare Theatre. Dr. Harry's oversized head, cast into a commemorative bronze, rested on a pedestal next to the staircase inside the front entry hall. Later, as I learned more about him, I couldn't help but think that it was inconsiderate to locate him so far from the hustle and bustle of the zoo entrance, where he would be pleased beyond his imagination at the income-producing queues at the ticket booths.

Roaming the zoo grounds on my own for the first time, I encountered weathered cement relics of generations of exhibits for the big cats, bears, and great apes. These antiquated structures were moldering reminders of the zoo's rustic beginnings. There was a surprising absence of actual buildings of any consequence, aside from the restaurant, reptile house, gift shop, and administration offices. Scattered here and there, tucked inconspicuously behind exhibits, were various "keeper shacks"—small, makeshift workstations where animal foods were prepared and daily diaries logged. The animals I saw, all strangers to me then, would gradually take on names and personalities as I tended to their medical dilemmas in the coming years.

Unlike most other American city zoos in the early 1970s, the San Diego Zoo had become an enviable tourist destination. From a sleepy US Navy town in the 1940s and '50s, San Diego was fast becoming a major, cosmopolitan city. The zoo's annual visitor attendance was approaching three million, making it the envy of other mostly struggling urban zoos. San Diego was exuberantly proud of its zoo—the city's official sacred cow. Its politically provincial and plutocratic Board of Trustees fought to keep it safe from the harm of bureaucratic encroachments and ran the organization like an elite club of civic leaders and socialites. The membership of the Zoological Society has always been regarded primarily as a fundraising base rather than as a democratic, intellectual association. Indeed, for most of the society's history, it has been traditional to pass board positions to close friends, relatives, and other patriotic members of the San Diego establishment, with minimal public fanfare and without extramural solicitations of candidates.

The animal collection in the zoo numbered in the thousands when I first arrived on the scene in 1972. The days of postage stamp–style zoo animal collections were still alive, but numbered. The zoo's sizeable budget and the inclinations of its management had brought together an incredible variety of birds, mammals, and reptiles. The early years of the zoo's operation had been hand to mouth, but with the help of the warm, subtropical San Diego climate, the zoo smothered its arkload of animals with lush plantings of exotic trees and flowers, overwhelming the arid native landscape and concrete animal abodes with an illusion of verdant fertility. Many of the heavy brick-and-mortar overhead expenses of the typical temperate-climate zoo were avoided in this comparatively idyllic setting. Contrary to the more ordinary zoo experience of smelly lion grottos and barred, steam-heated monkey houses, the San Diego Zoo provided a refreshing contrast for visitors. Even winter in San Diego was as nice as it ever got at home for most of the out-of-towners.

Many of the animal exhibits were styled in the form of open, dry-moated enclosures, a concept borrowed from the private Hagenbeck Tierpark, which opened near

Hamburg, Germany, in the early 1900s. Efforts to produce truly naturalistic exhibits would not come to San Diego until the 1970s, however. Carl Hagenbeck was an animal dealer whose new style of zoo began to do away with the rigid separations between people and animals. San Diego's expanded use of spacious, unfenced outdoor exhibits took away the detracting smells and many of the visual barriers. The use of trees and plantings softened hard exhibit structures and concealed the service areas. Some of the initial visitors to San Diego's first open-moated lion exhibit, built in the 1920s, were so alarmed by their unbarred proximity to the animals that they complained to zoo management of its "danger" to the public. Zoos were very different even in those relatively recent times—certain animals that we now expect to see in most moderate to large zoos were relatively uncommon. The first giraffe born in captivity in the United States, for example, lived for only six days at the Cincinnati Zoo in 1889, and even by 1925 there were only five zoo giraffes in the entire country, although they were present in traveling circuses. It was also widely believed then that keeping a gorilla alive in captivity was virtually impossible.

The San Diego Zoo of the 1960s and '70s was as much an emerging international theme park as a zoological garden. Joan Embery, one of the zoo's nursery attendants, with her entourage of zoo baby oddities, had become a favorite guest on TV personality Johnny Carson's Los Angeles–based *Tonight Show,* and she eventually logged more than seventy appearances, only a few short of Rodney Dangerfield. The crowds of visitors at the zoo were regular and impressive in size.

As soon as they entered the main gate, visitors would fix their attention on an aqua lagoon filled with pink flamingos surrounded by emerald greenery. The zoo has always prided itself on the crispness and cleanliness of its grounds. Swarms of paper pickers and sidewalk sweepers constantly combed and ironed the zoo to assure that restrooms and walkways were spotless and wrinkle-free, and that fallen ice cream cones, spent peanut shells, and the dregs of soft pretzels were promptly swept away. Early in the morning, before the arrival of the daily masses, hoses, brooms, and pressure sprayers groomed the entry and exhibit mesas; the glass windows in the reptile house were squeegeed free of noseprints and fingerprints; and the chrome entry turnstiles were cleaned and buffed.

For unspoken but financially lucrative reasons, drinking fountains were far scarcer than snack stands and vending machines. There was no mistaking that this was also a thriving business enterprise, with abundant entrepreneurial opportunities inside the gates for food vendors, popcorn wagons, souvenir shops, and tour bus rides.

Visitors shifted in a politely impatient, gradually congealing queue at the entrance, where they awaited the skyward retraction of the gate that marked the starting line for another day in paradise. The zoo is like a living creature, demanding to be fed, bathed, and nurtured in a daily ritual of reincarnation. Even the animals seem to join in this orchestrated transformation, awaiting the attentions of their keepers, who bring them their daily concoctions of fruits, meats, biscuits, seeds, and alfalfa.

Annual attendance and per capita visitor expenditures were the San Diego Zoo's daily management mantras in the 1970s, just as they are today. The administrative climate of the zoo exuded commerce and competition, and zoo officials intensely followed the statistics of tourist visitations to regional competitors, such as Disneyland, Knott's Berry Farm, Sea World, and Universal Studios. There was no need to track the performance of other zoos, inasmuch as they were regarded as noncontenders. Some of this commercial and animal collecting frenzy, however, was beginning to give more ground to ideas of wildlife conservation activities outside of the zoo's gates.

The zoo grounds and exhibits were laid out up and down heavily landscaped hills between islandlike mesas. At first, it was a disorienting, almost dizzying, experience to wander the grounds. I wondered which of these animals would be my first patients. Dr. Charles J. Sedgwick, the chief veterinarian, was my zoo medicine mentor. "CJ" possessed a singularly strategic sense of what zoo animal medicine should be about, a feat requiring more than an average capacity for both humor and enlightenment. Years later, as we reminisced about our veterinary careers, he observed, "Like you, I seem to have a knack for eventually annoying my boss no matter where I go." Of course, I wasn't quite sure what he meant by the "Like you"—I would prefer to believe that the two of us might just be two of those restless souls referred to earlier in the memorial to Dr. Richard C. Cabot. But, let's face it, at one time or another, most of us have found ourselves talking when we should have been listening.

CJ's first initiation in a zoo job had been in Los Angeles in the 1960s, where he moved the entire Los Angeles Zoo animal collection, physically and chemically, to a new facility in Griffith Park. His diversified experiences included surgically descenting skunks for a Disney movie—at home, but in his garage (on the orders of his wife Shirley). Before this he had been a dog and cat doctor and a NASA veterinarian, preparing monkeys for the early rocket flights that preceded America's great manned space missions.

Philosophically, Sedgwick was much more interested in understanding and preventing problems than in simply treating them. (This trait is not universal among veterinarians, or most people.) He always looked for the underlying, cryptic implications of animal diseases, using every available resource to solve a clinical problem, experimenting with new medical equipment, and recruiting skills from local specialists in anesthesia, surgery, and neonatal medicine. When it became clear that he regularly asked his interns for their opinions and perceptions, I knew that he would come to be regarded as one of the most insightful veterinarians with whom these trainees would ever work.

Supplementing the clinical experiences were the resources of the Pathology Department, headed by Dr. Lynn Griner, the initial supervisor of the zoo's veterinary internship program. Less affable than Sedgwick, Griner was a capable and dedicated zoo pathologist and teacher nonetheless. Never having actually experienced the humility (and occasional humiliation) that comes from practicing clinical medicine, his empathy for yeoman veterinary clinicians was tentative.

The intern whom I replaced, a Canadian, overlapped with me for several months in the beginning. He tiptoed lightly around the pathology office, and he could never fathom whether it was his Canadian accent, personal demeanor, or preoccupation with photographing bird eggs that routinely irked his pathologist boss. On my inaugural car ride to an animal health meeting with the Canadian and the pathologist, who rode in the back seat, the egg photographer received a scathing lecture about cleaning the car after treating animals in the zoo—unfortunately, Griner had sat down on a used hypodermic needle that the intern had left out during the morning's medical rounds.

Perhaps nowhere else could more be witnessed on the diseases of a greater variety of animals. A stygian sign hung in the autopsy room declaring, "All Ye Who Enter Here, Abandon Hope"—a whimsical statement that a clinical veterinarian would be loath to endorse, although not entirely without some historical validity in zoos. Actually, the term "autopsy" is not correct in veterinary medicine; the preferred veterinary term for the postmortem examination of an animal is "necropsy," and that is the one that I will use henceforth.

A lingering stigma of the questionable clinical prowess of veterinarians in zoos, along with the ever-present willingness of many veterinarians to give zoo work a try, may have accounted, in part, for the short average tenure (two to three years) for most clinical veterinarians who had worked at the San Diego Zoo from its inception in the 1920s. Dr. Charles R. Schroeder, one of the zoo's first veterinarians and later its director, was expected to devote time to nonveterinary duties that included developing photos that were made into postcards by night for sale on the zoo grounds the next day. I had missed the more whimsical salad days when the hospital staff occasionally barbecued a postmortem hindquarter of a zebra or antelope.

Nothing impresses medical knowledge upon students' minds more than observing disease firsthand in the necropsy room. Daily lessons were available on cases of malnutrition, infectious disease, parasitism, cancer, and trauma. The causes of zoo animal deaths are as endless as a medical encyclopedia and parallel many human diseases. Eventually, nearly everything that died in the zoo, including feral creatures, was necropsied, from hummingbirds and giraffes to koalas and Komodo dragons. Deceased animals were sliced, stained, and magnified under microscopes to determine the causes of death. The outcomes of all of our clinical efforts were transparent—the pathologist always knew if the veterinarians had screwed up, missed a diagnosis, or made errors in treatment. Pathologists are known in all medical circles as having the last word. The historical staffing priorities at the zoo appeared to place marginal hope in clinical salvation, valuing, instead, the study of death after life more than life before death.

Shortly after settling into my office in the old hospital building and starting a daily clinical routine, I was dumbstruck by the scope of the huge job ahead. Keepers brought sick animals to me faster than I could adequately treat them, and often sooner than I could learn enough about them. The existing medical records amounted to a faint paper trail of fading index cards that were filed in haphazard fashion, accompanied by a few sketchy logbooks of animal treatments. After starting the day with the boxes and crates of sick creatures that awaited me at the hospital each morning, there were house calls to be made in the zoo for animals needing evaluation and treatment. The days often ended with night emergencies at the Children's Zoo Nursery when one of the baby tigers, orangutans, or gazelles had diarrhea, indigestion, or an infection.

The old San Diego Zoo Hospital was a stately but outdated facility consisting of two floors of antiquated laboratory space. Its lofty ceilings and large, double hung windows pre-dated mechanized air conditioning. In the beginning of my internship, there was no veterinary nurse or secretary to support the clinical veterinary staff, and little legacy of enduring clinical medical programs. The old hospital was being used mostly for pathology labs and a few visiting researchers; this latter function was in a state of limbo after several failed attempts at constituting a research center in the 1960s.

In the years to come, however, the long-delayed research vision of the zoo's founder, Dr. Harry Wegeforth, would finally be realized with the successful development of the Center for Reproduction of Endangered Species (CRES) under another talented physician, Dr. Kurt Benirschke. The CRES unit is now a leading research center in the zoo world, with an emphasis on reproduction, genetics, and animal behavior. Its "frozen zoo" evokes futuristic images of Aldous Huxley's *Brave New World*, with a bank of liquid nitrogen reservoirs that house thousands of live tissue specimens—suspended at -196° C—from hundreds of species of animals, including the sperm and ova of many highly endangered creatures. Peeking into one of the heavily insulated vaults through a thick door on the top, a cold fog billows from the stainless steel racks containing rare and endangered DNA. While the technology to utilize this living library fully is still in its infancy, artificial insemination, in vitro fertilization, and cloning technology are being experimented with, already producing panda pregnancies and wild cattle births using surrogate domestic cattle as mothers.

Some years before, the clinical veterinary activities at the zoo were shifted from the old hospital into a series of rooms that had been converted from animal barns. Out the back door and down a few steps, an outdoor compound stretched back some 150 feet in a quadrangle. To prevent animal escapes it was completely covered, top and sides, with chain link fabric, and zoo vehicles entered it through tall sliding metal doors. Surrounding this space were various barred outdoor cages suitable for housing big cats, bears, and other carnivores, and freshwater pools for seals, sea lions, otters, and aquatic birds. Housing for the hoofed animals was out back in outdoor pens, and several indoor rooms were appended to the back of this compound, where birds, monkeys, and all manner of zoo miscellanies were held for treatment or quarantine. Larger animals—rhinos, elephants, hippos, giraffes, and the like—were treated in their more substantial living quarters on the zoo grounds.

The equipment in the old zoo hospital was spartan by any standard and included retired and donated medical tools that had come to rest there over the years. We never did figure out what surgical procedures on humans had employed some of these obscure implements. Our surgical area was located in a room with a wall-mounted gas heater, which had to be turned off to avoid fire hazards when anesthetic oxygen was in use. In the summertime, it was cooled by screened jalousie windows that lined the wall toward the central compound.

We heated the developing solutions for processing X-rays in a tiny dark closet where an ungrounded aquarium heater gave users intermittent electrical shocks. In the heat of summer we placed ice-filled jugs in the tanks to cool the fluids to a workable temperature. In the years to come this would all be corrected with the construction of the Jennings Center for Zoological Medicine, which provided state-of-the-art treatment, radiology, and surgery facilities. But, for now, this was a fire-engine style of medical practice by anyone's estimate—and there was smoke in the air.

Trimming lion's claws at London Zoo, c. 1880

2. TOO EARLY FOR THE AUTOPSY

Fitting in at the Zoo

Zoo veterinarians have undergone a vigorous evolution in the past century through the process of successive approximation. More simply put, they have become more competent by learning from their mistakes. Initially, they brought relatively little to the table clinically because of the lack of a knowledge base on diseases, animal husbandry, and restraint techniques for exotic animals. Though woefully unarmed with useful sedatives, medications, vaccines, antibiotics, equipment, and facilities, they steadily improved their clinical capabilities over time. To begin with, veterinarians acquired a lot more experiences than understanding. Like the stepsisters' struggles to fit into Cinderella's glass slipper, the early efforts to incorporate veterinarians into zoos were often awkward.

Veterinary medicine as a professional discipline dates back to Egyptian times, but formal training did not begin until 1761 when the first veterinary school was founded in Lyon, France. Zoos as we know them today originated in the 1800s after a flurry of scientific exploration and discovery. Following the lead of natural history museums, botanical and zoological gardens came into being as living public collections for the display of newly described species. Advances in plant and animal classification, including the use of binomial nomenclature (systematic scientific Latin names), devised by the Swedish botanist Carolus Linnaeus in the 1700s, brought order to the descriptions of the earth's biota. His *Systema Naturae,* published in 1735, classified living organisms into the now-familiar system of genus and species. The public came in droves to view these far-flung animal and plant curiosities.

Perhaps the Schonbrunn Zoo in Vienna, founded in 1752, was the first significant urban zoo in modern times, followed by the Ménagerie du Jardin des Plantes in Paris in 1793. The London Zoological Garden, founded in 1828 at Regent's Park, but not opened to the public until 1847, is the oldest public zoo in English-speaking countries. Its parklike atmosphere popularized the zoological garden and sparked the beginning of a wave of new zoos in Dublin (1830), Bristol (1835), Manchester (1836), Amsterdam (1838), Antwerp (1843), Berlin (1844), Rotterdam (1857), and Frankfurt (1858).

The distinctions between menageries and zoos were often somewhat blurred in the beginning, and a number of zoos were derived from these less formal assemblies of animals. Traveling menageries sometimes dead-ended in cities, and through local initiatives they became stationary attractions that evolved into zoological gardens. The traveling circuses that developed in the 1800s frequently added animal menageries as sideshows. Indeed, because of their cramped, commercial nature, "menagerie" became a pejorative expression that implied exploitive and banal values. Zoos, however, out of economic pressures, have always courted the public to one degree or another by staging assorted activities that could hardly be considered zoological in character, such as balloon ascents, concerts, roller coaster rides, pyrotechnic displays, and overt circus-animal acts.

In 1829 London's Regent's Park zoo hired a Mr. Charles Spooner as its first "medical attendant" (veterinarian). His assignment was to "attend three times in each week, and oftener when necessary, to prescribe for and examine all the animals and to keep a record of his observations and practice" for the sum of sixty pounds sterling annually. Spooner's journal entries show an emphasis on postmortem evaluations and almost no surgical interventions, although cases of malnutrition appeared to be common and were treated with various mineral salts. He tended to kangaroos with abscesses, bison with internal parasites, a cape hunting dog with pneumonia, and jackals with bites to the legs, for which he prescribed that "Tincture of myrrh compress to be applied to the parts affected every morning." One of his early observations in avian medicine is this: "Several of them [the parrots] are continually nibbling and cutting off their feathers as they grow. They seem to be troubled with intolerable itching of the skin and keep themselves disgracefully bare." For the feather-pickers he prescribed the following: "R_X Dissolve grains of corrosive Sublimate in half an ounce of spirits of wine—add a half pint of water and with a bit of sponge. Apply a little of the lotion all over the bird."

In 1833, complaining that the workload had increased substantially due to the increase in animal numbers, Spooner requested a salary raise. After an inquiry into the care of the animals at the zoo his request was denied, and Spooner's services were dispensed with. Thus, Spooner had the distinction of being the first zoo veterinarian to be hired, denied a raise, and fired. Subsequently, a Mr. W. Youatt was employed for a higher annual salary of one hundred pounds.

In the United States the first public zoos developed in Chicago, New York, and Philadelphia. Depending on your history source, each of these cities lays claim to hosting the first American zoo, although a zoo history buff pointed out to me that if we consider America in the broadest sense, Montezuma's zoo in Mexico might be the hands-down winner. The Lincoln Park Zoo, for example, considers the donation of a pair of swans in 1868 to mark its founding date, although a zoo director was not hired until 1888. The Central Park Zoo was originally a menagerie that gradually morphed into a zoo; where it crossed the line is a matter of conjecture. The Philadelphia Zoo records its founding date as 1859, when it was first chartered, although it did not open to the public until 1874. Given its initial size and persistence in pressing the point, Philadelphia's claim may seem to pull the most weight, although this hair-splitting has probably served only to diminish this historical distinction. Not claiming first bragging rights in this contest, the Cleveland Zoo unapologetically states that it is the seventh-oldest zoo in the United States. The Roger Williams Park Zoo in Providence, Rhode Island, claims to be the third-oldest. According to the dates that zoos were actually opened to the public (as operations of reasonable substance, whatever that means), America's flock of pre-1900 zoos fledged in the following years:

1873	Lincoln Park Zoo (Chicago), Central Park Zoo (New York)
1874	Philadelphia Zoo (Pennsylvania), Buffalo Zoo (New York)
1875	Cincinnati Zoo (Ohio), Ross Park Zoo (Binghamton, New York)
1876	Baltimore Zoo (Maryland)

1882	Cleveland Zoo (Ohio)
1883	Roger Williams Park Zoo (Providence, Rhode Island)
1887	Portland Zoo (Oregon)
1889	Atlanta Zoo (Georgia), St. Louis Zoo (Missouri)
1890	Dickerson Park Zoo (Springfield, Missouri)
1891	John Ball Zoo (Grand Rapids, Michigan)
1892	Milwaukee Zoo (Wisconsin)
1893	Seneca Park Zoo (Rochester, New York)
1894	Denver Zoo (Colorado)
1896	Como Park Zoo (St. Paul, Minnesota)
1897	Alameda Park Zoo (Alamogordo, New Mexico)
1898	Henry Doorly Zoo (Omaha, Nebraska), National Zoo (Washington, DC), Pittsburgh Zoo (Pennsylvania)
1899	New York Zoological Park (New York), Toledo Zoo (Ohio)

The early zoo veterinarians were usually large-animal practitioners, inasmuch as veterinary medicine began with its principal emphasis on agricultural species and beasts of burden. These veterinarians provided part-time services to zoos and were often called in when animals were already sick. It must have been an awful dilemma for them—unable to treat many animals until they were so ill that they unable to stand. Modern-day veterinarians who have traveled, unequipped, to some remote vacation spot, and have been unexpectedly presented with a sick animal to tend, know the helplessness of having no anesthetics, instruments, X-rays, or capable assistants, which was the norm for these pioneers of the profession. Even worse, these founders had a huge knowledge gap that would take a long time even to begin to overcome. Most basic scientific information about immunology, infectious disease, metabolism, reproduction, and genetics was yet to be revealed. These first zoo veterinarians often arrived too late for any helpful treatment, but too early for the necropsy.

In America, the first full-time clinical zoo veterinarian to be employed was Dr. Frank Miller, who joined the New York Bronx Zoo in 1901. In the same year, Harlow Brooks, M.D., became the zoo's pathologist, simultaneously working on the staffs of several human hospitals in the city. Joining Dr. Miller in 1902 was Dr. W. Reid Blair, who served as veterinarian from 1902 to 1926. The first operation that Dr. Blair performed was to lance several abscesses on an alligator.

Reptile House at the London Zoo, c. 1900.

Miller and Blair encountered some initial resistance from the zoo's director, Dr. William Hornaday, who was reported to distrust veterinarians. When it was proposed that newly arrived primates be isolated for a quarantine and acclimatization period after their arrival, Hornaday vetoed the idea, stating that monkeys could be replaced when needed and did not justify the labor and expense of the proposal. The budgetary needs of the medical staff took a back seat to Hornaday's interests in constructing animal buildings, and the veterinarians struggled along in the beginning with scant facilities, reference materials, laboratory equipment, and even necropsy instruments. Lacking their own microscope, Brooks, the pathologist, paid for the first one out of his annual honorarium. After only two years, Miller departed the zoo to return to a more lucrative private clinical practice in the city, while Blair stayed on as staff veterinarian.

Thus began the first zoo animal–health program at the Bronx Zoo, and the zoo hospital was finally built in 1916. Given the established practice of donating deceased

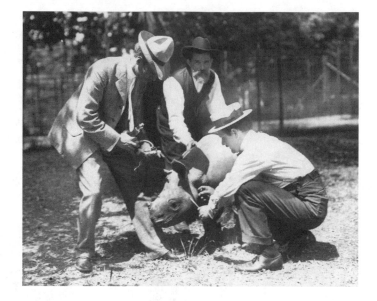

Dr. W. Reid Blair (*right*) treats a rhinoceros calf at the Bronx Zoo, c. 1909

animals to several of New York's natural history museums, there were struggles about priorities when museum curators complained that postmortem examinations were spoiling their specimens. Hornaday settled the argument, informing the curators in no uncertain terms that postmortem exams had first priority over museum accessions. Early work in the medical department focused on ongoing nutritional problems in the zoo's primate collection, most likely the result of inadequate dietary vitamin D and imbalances of calcium and phosphorus. When Hornaday finally retired in 1926, Blair became the zoo director and served for fourteen years in that capacity. Surprisingly, up until his time as director, the visiting public had been banned from taking photographs (a common restriction in European zoos then) in the zoo in order to protect zoo sales of postcards and guidebooks—a Hornaday mandate. Blair soon did away with this practice after he became head of the zoo.

Writing in an article in the New York Zoological Society *Bulletin* in 1913, Elwin R. Sanborn recounted some of the difficulties of handling animals for treatment in the Bronx Zoo:

On several occasions in her younger days the African rhinoceros Victoria required medical attention for an abscess that had developed on the left jaw. She was astonishingly mild tempered, but displayed energy and activity out of all proportion to the estimate of her strength. In the early stages of development of the growth, she yielded readily to the surgeon's knife and subsequent dressings. Several operations at infrequent intervals reduced the swelling, but did not arrest completely its progress, although a perfect cure seemed to be effected each time.

A further recurrence of the trouble convinced the doctor that a more thorough operation was necessary. Elaborate preparations for the operation were made and a force of men was assembled to aid the surgeons and their assistants. It was the first attempt that had been made to secure the animal, and we have never ceased to rejoice in the fact that it was and has been the only one. Seven veterinary surgeons, a professional anesthetizer, a dozen keepers, ropes, patent hopples, mattresses, pails, cotton, a varied assortment of surgical instruments and appliances and two and one half pounds of chloroform and ether were arrayed on one side, and nine hundred pounds of rhino on the other. Victoria fought a noble fight that morning, with malice toward none, and emerged from the anesthesia groggy, but triumphant. Had it been possible, without the slightest doubt she would have returned thanks that the operation was a complete success.

In today's zoo, using contemporary knowledge of chemical restraint, all this might be readily accomplished with several keepers, the veterinarian, and a veterinary assistant.

The first veterinarian to become the director of an American zoo was Dr. William A. Conklin, who directed the Central Park Zoo starting in 1870. Veterinarian Gus Knudson was hired by Seattle's Woodland Park Zoo in 1907 at the age of twenty-six. He was appointed to the newly created position of zoo director in 1922 and struggled for years to convince the Board of Park Commissioners to create a zoo that was free of traditional bar and wire barriers. Frustrated by an unfenced zoo perimeter, ongoing vandalism ("throwing rocks, breaking windows, firing rifles and bee bee guns, using sling shots, poking sticks at monkeys, and even giving them lighted cigarettes and matches"), and a lack of cooperation in local government, Knudson eventually succumbed to the absence of science and the abundance of zoo politics, resigning in disgust in 1947 and making his feelings well known in the Seattle press. Four years later the zoo perimeter was finally fenced. In the 1970s, Woodland Park would start to

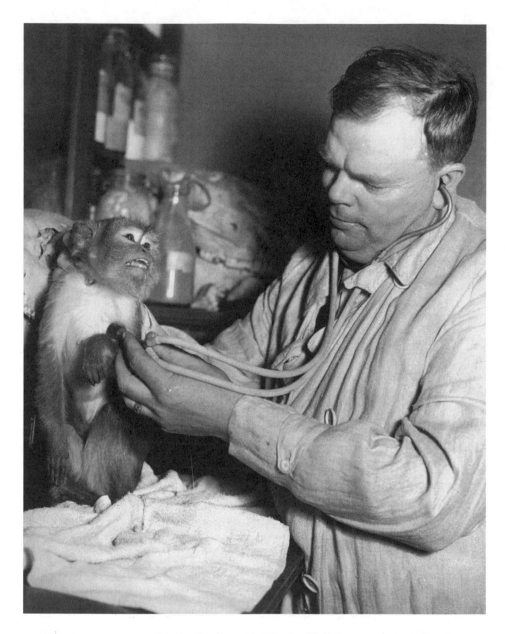

Dr. Gus Knudson of the Woodland Park Zoo

become many of the things that Knudson had envisioned and would help to set new standards for modern animal exhibits.

Dr. Patricia O'Connor Halloran was the first full-time woman zoo veterinarian in the United States. She was employed by the Staten Island Zoo in 1942 and retired from that institution in 1970. It was largely through her initiatives that the American Association of Zoo Veterinarians was formed, and she served as its first president from 1946 to 1957. In 1955, at a time when only scattered bits of literature on the diseases of zoo and wild animals existed, Dr. Halloran compiled *A Bibliography of References to Diseases of Wild Mammals and Birds*. In that same year there were only six full-time clinical veterinarians working in zoos in the United States.

With celebrity zoo animals in yesteryear's zoos, it was sometimes rumored that management's timing of summonses for medical help were calculated to assure that the veterinarian was on the zoo grounds prior to an animal's demise—at least by minutes. After all, it was essential to demonstrate that everything humanly, if not humanely, possible had been done before a publicly beloved beast passed away. Under such circumstances, it was no wonder that zoo veterinarians started out lacking reputations for medical agility, however heroic their efforts. The arrival of the veterinarian in those early days was often an ominous sign in the zoo—something important was often going to die! It would not be until much later that effective clinical interventions, coupled with strong programs of disease prevention, became their modus operandi. Disease avoidance has always been the principal focus of effective zoo medicine programs, as the practical options for medical treatment of feral species are much more limited than in domesticated animals.

Some years ago a revealing obituary was published in *Newsweek* about a recently deceased senior physician with the United Nations World Health Organization, which targets human disease problems through immunization, nutrition, clean water supplies, and other fundamental approaches. This doctor's philosophy spoke volumes about the exponential value of preventive medicine and it is equally applicable in zoos. Described as a person who "gave up a very lucrative clinical practice to help run a global health bureaucracy," his own explanation for his career change was this: "In private clinical practice I could only effect cures on a retail basis, whereas, with the WHO, I have the luxury of practicing medicine on the wholesale level." And so it is, or should be, with zoo animal practice—prevention always offers the greatest overall dividends. Failing to unearth the root causes and attack the instigating factors for a caseload assures that a veterinarian will see the same problems over and over again in a zoo.

Surprisingly, nothing is harder to sell in medicine and environmental management than investments in prevention. This may be so, in part, because prevention constantly enters the realm of subjective opinion and speculation—areas that are flat ground and fair game for both doctors and administrators. Even though we are placing new emphasis on education in the United States to prevent social problems related to illiteracy, poverty, and crime, spending for the military and law enforcement vastly exceeds that for education. The annual cost of incarcerating a person today—at least according to the television commentator Andy Rooney—is $60,000. Because energy, water, and atmospheric problems are often politically ignored and minimized, we may wake up to our environmental dilemmas one morning only to realize that the world was destroyed while we were sleeping.

In a zoo it is difficult to construct clear cost/benefit models to convincingly demonstrate how adding an $8,000 warm-water floor-heating system to the bears' sleeping areas will pay financial dividends. However, any food service manager worth his or her salt could easily argue the wisdom of buying a $4,000 vending machine, by projecting sales and profits and amortizing the costs over its useful lifespan. Decisions in government, zoos, and our personal lives are often made on whim, bias, and ignorance of the seemingly petty, but critical, details.

Even though zoos house a wide range of exotic creatures, relatively little illness, overall, comes from obscure diseases. Many people are surprised to learn this. Even so, zoo veterinarians always have to be vigilant for the possibilities of more exotic diseases such as rabies, Marburg virus, simian B virus, foot and mouth disease, rinderpest, African swine fever, avian Newcastle disease, and the like. These diseases are so uncommon or nonexistent in the United States, that most veterinarians—like physicians looking for anthrax infections in people—have never seen a single case in their entire career. For fiscal reasons, the critical animal-management challenge in most zoos is prioritizing which basic improvements should be made in order to leverage the greatest health gains for the investment. Even small, basic Band-Aid enhancements in animal environments or procedures can drastically reduce the numbers of animal health problems.

Much of the veterinary caseload in zoos is a result of management, husbandry, and logistical failures and the shortcomings of animal facilities. I refer to this large body

Table 2.1 Examples of preventable zoo mortalities

Species affected	Condition	Cause
Hoofed animals	Broken neck	Ran into fence
Sea lion	Gastric ulceration	Swallowed coins thrown into pool
Baby monkey	Rickets	Inadequate ultraviolet light
Monkey	Zinc poisoning	Licking galvanized caging materials
Emu chicks	Gastric obstruction	Eating artificial turf substrate
Zebras / wild horses	Gastrointestinal impactions	Consumed sand / eating off ground
Small parrots	Intestinal worms	Food contaminated with droppings
Cheetah	Anemia / death	Fleas
Parrots	Lead poisoning	Chewing on lead perch bases
Antelope	Peritonitis	Ingesting street-sweeper wire
Swan	Gastrointestinal obstruction	Ingesting plastic coffee stirrers
Duck	Drowning	Sucked into filter intake
Antelope	Broken leg	Caught leg in fence
Tiger	Decompression / death	Aircraft "mishap"

of problems as "diseases of captivity." Table 2.1 is a list of examples of actual fatalities that I have seen that illustrate this point.

A helter-skelter zoo clinical practice is the primary symptom of a failed program of preventive medicine, which should place great emphasis on *avoiding* the typical array of the maladies of confinement. While physical facilities have fundamental bearings on animal health, procedural and personnel factors weigh just as heavily in the balance.

After joining the hospital staff at the San Diego Zoo, I began to equip the zoo hospital with advanced orthopedic surgery equipment in response to the prominent caseload of broken legs that was occurring in the animal collection—my own personal contribution to the pursuit of technological imperatives. As time went by, however, preventive measures in housing and handling techniques began to pay dividends, and we saw far fewer orthopedic injuries, leaving this surgical equipment sitting idle most of the time. Over the years our cases shifted away from broken legs, malnutrition and hypothermia. As husbandry programs improved, the character of our clinical medical practice, and how we expended our efforts, changed dramatically.

In the so-called early days, zoo veterinarians and physicians began to study the causes of death in zoo animals; they had ample material to learn from given the generous supply of mortalities. Dr. Max Schmidt, a veterinarian, became director of Germany's new Frankfurt Zoo in 1858 and served there for twenty-five years before becoming director of the Berlin Zoo. In 1870 he published a handbook, whose German title translates to *Comparative Pathology and Pathological Anatomy of Mammals and Birds,* the first known work of its type. Appointed by Schmidt in 1859 as scientific director, Dr. David Weinland launched *Der Zoologische Garten* (The Zoological Garden), the first journal dedicated to zoo animal management and health. Other studies of zoo animal mortalities began in England with the appointment of a pathologist-anatomist at the London Zoo in 1865.

At the Philadelphia Zoo, founded in 1875, its president, Charles B. Penrose, M.D., led the way in the study of comparative pathology in 1905 with the formation of the Laboratory of Comparative Pathology. Herbert Fox, M.D., became its laboratory director in 1906, opening a long, lonely trail to compiling meaningful data on the diseases of zoo animals. In 1923, Fox published the first English-language book on the study of wild animal pathology, derived from his postmortem studies at the Philadelphia Zoo, entitled *Diseases in Wild Animals and Birds.* Although the Philadelphia Zoo was among America's oldest zoological gardens, it did not hire its first full-time veterinary clinician until 1973, more than a hundred years after its founding.

Pathology studies in zoos have been critical to the development of a knowledge base for clinical zoo practice, and began to define the scope of what *could* go wrong medically with zoo animals. Initially, the prospects for clinical treatment were so dismal that most zoos simply budgeted generously to replace dying animals as needed. Significant pathology programs gradually developed in institutions such as the San Diego Zoo and the National Zoo. Veterinarians in most zoos do their own postmortem examinations and work in conjunction with pathologists at universities and government animal diagnostic laboratories.

It was not until the 1960s that the use of new drugs and improved handling procedures finally allowed animals to be safely sedated for extended diagnostic procedures, treatments, and surgery, but there were still relatively few full-time zoo veterinarians in the entire country. The real advances in zoo medicine and research began to accelerate in that decade. Finally, it was feasible to intervene without a significant probability of killing the patient. These successes began to create a demand for the services of veterinarians as full members of zoo staffs, and the profession expanded sharply in the 1970s and '80s. Safer anesthesia completely changed the rules of engagement, catalyzing rapid progress in zoo clinical medicine and research. In the late 1960s only twenty-five full-time veterinarians were employed in American zoos and aquariums, but by 2004, this number had increased tenfold.

Zoo animal medicine requires skills in identifying the underlying, often cryptic, causes of diseases. Inexperienced veterinarians get sidetracked by concentrating on the business of treating problems, rather than consistently searching for the inciting factors. This emphasis has been due, in part, to a lack of understanding of how to house and feed many species and monitor their well-being. The fundamental goal is to recognize problems early enough to be able to remedy them. The most successful zoo practitioners have an uncommon degree of common sense.

Finding the causes of disease sounds simple, but it is in truth a stumbling block that I, and most others, have tripped over in zoo medical practice. The species *Homo sapiens* is by nature composed mostly of tacticians rather than strategists, with inborn inclinations for picking the low-hanging fruit. Strategists focus on creative concepts and visionary thoughts, while tacticians translate this information into practical applications. These differences in human dynamics affect society's intuitive approaches to medicine in general. As ample proof in our everyday lives, witness the weighted emphasis on treatment vs. prevention in human medical practice. We expend most of our collective medical resources treating diseases, rather than understanding and preventing them.

Society needs both strategists and tacticians—and, on balance, many more of the latter. It is our fundamental nature to deal with the proximate and the tangible, rather than root causes and their seemingly abstract consequences. Today's human healthcare systems provide for expensive high-tech cardiac bypass surgery, but little for prevention, such as supervised exercise wellness and nutrition programs. Strategists tend to go into research, preferring to focus on the "what and why." The best clinicians have a healthy mix of both capabilities.

Holistic styles of medicine—human and veterinary—take into account the whole organism and its environment, rather than simplistic prescriptions. It is the only truly effective approach to a zoo or a human medical practice, requiring insights into behavioral, nutritional, and environmental factors that influence disease. Many veterinarians cringe at the notion of being identified as holistic, because they misconstrue the label as having some connection to quackery or as a narrow synonym for unconventional or alternative medicine, which seem to have hijacked a good word. Eight hundred years ago the medieval Jewish physician Moses Maimonides wrote, "The

Table 2.2	Problem analysis of a zoo animal injury
Diagnosis: Antelope with Broken Leg	
A. Hit fence jumping out of exhibit	
B. Chased by startled exhibit mate	
C. New employee frightened herd	
D. Employee not adequately trained	
E. Staff turnover due to inadequate wages or working conditions	

physician should not treat the disease but the patient who is suffering from it. Treating problems in isolation from their inciting causes and their hosts amounts to insensitive medicine." Without a doubt, Maimonides was a holistic practitioner, as were many physicians before the advent of comprehensive diagnostic blood panels and computerized imaging tools. TV's Marcus Welby, capably played by actor Robert Young, is my romantic notion of what a family doctor should be like. He seemed to be as interested in who someone was as a person as he was in the vitality of his or her gall bladder.

Table 2.2 illustrates an example of problem analysis of a zoo animal injury. Some past zoo administrators have argued that the zoo veterinarian's problem solving involvement should be limited to steps A through C, though I don't believe that veterinarians can be very effective in a zoo if they accept that premise.

This example, similar to chain reaction stories like the Great Chicago Fire, where a cow supposedly kicked over a lantern and started it all, helps to point out the importance of analyzing problems. In the zoo, a diagnosis alone won't explain how a problem arose, how best to treat it, or in particular, how to avoid it in the future. Interpreting information and events, and prescribing solutions, is the subject of many vigorous discussions in zoos. A real doctor, like Marcus Welby, should be just as keen on finding out what is causing a problem and preventing it as on treating it and collecting a fee. Successful zoo veterinarians have to be part sociologist, epidemiologist, ethologist, and detective in order to treat the whole animal.

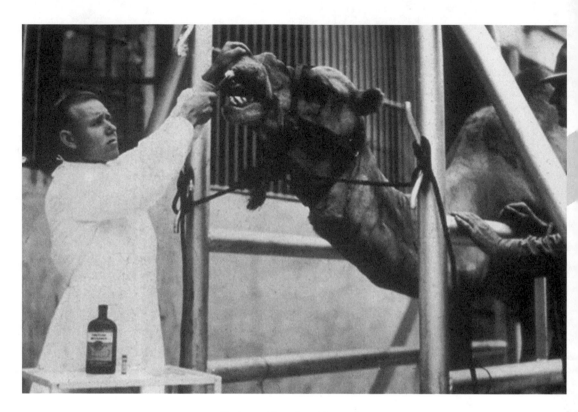

Dr. Charles R. Schroeder with camel, c. 1935

3. GROWING PAINS

Educating the Menagerie Makers

"It's a pretty good zoo," said young Gerald McGrew, "and the fellow who runs it seems proud of it, too." But if Gerald ran the zoo, the New Zoo, McGrew Zoo, he'd see to making a change or two.

—Dr. Seuss, *If I Ran the Zoo*

When they began to arrive on the scene, veterinarians often blended into zoos as readily as oil mixes with water. It was the natural order of things that veterinarians were predestined to impinge upon well-established territories. Veterinarians were needed, revered, and occasionally feared, but seldom were they unconditionally embraced by all of their new employers and coworkers. Some gave up in frustration when it became clear to them that zoo management's receptivity to new ideas and personalities was limited.

Feelings about veterinarians in zoos have ranged from "vexation to veneration." In fact, that was the precise title of a testy little paper that was once presented at a national zoo conference by a frustrated zoo director. He had somehow achieved an overdose of veterinarians, felt that they were a bittersweet addition to the zoo world, and tried to reconcile himself to the reality that they were here to stay. He simply hoped (perhaps prayed) that they would find more gracious ways of fitting into zoo operations, and empathize more with pragmatic institutional and fiscal priorities.

Veterinarians generally feel that no institutional priority should be greater than animal health. What constitutes that, of course, can be a matter of personal bias or opinion, as well as of clinical judgment. The rub comes when veterinarians relentlessly press not just for more medical supplies or equipment, but also for major changes in the quality of animal facilities and husbandry programs. In many zoos it was expected that veterinarians limit their activities to the traditional practice of medicine and leave the aesthetic, ethical, ecological, and economic matters to others on the zoo staff.

Actually, veterinarians were mostly misunderstood. Their priorities focused on creating more objective measurements of animal health and well-being within a traditionally subjective zoo world. In a subculture typified by animal lore and habitual practices, they considered defining reality to be an important part of their job. Veterinarians tend to view the performance of a zoo somewhat like a baseball game where not only the score but also errors are important. If, for example, you were a human anesthesiologist, most people would not be too impressed by the fact that 95 percent of your patients survived your care if the norm exceeded 99 percent. Veterinarians always go after that last one percent. They have an apparently annoying habit of concentrating much of their efforts on the part of the glass that is empty, with a view to promoting changes that avoid repeating mistakes that cause healthy animals to become patients.

The personnel difficulties arise when there are conflicting management priorities about what to change in a zoo. Unlike most human doctors, who ordinarily are called upon to tend only the sick, veterinarians seemed strangely interested in the healthy as well. Some institutions wanted veterinarians simply to concentrate on ill animals and leave the healthy ones to the curators and keepers. Experience quickly taught them, however, that problems ignored or undetected today invariably ended up in their hands as tomorrow's medical cases. The problem with zoo veterinarians, as employees, was that, unlike yesteryear's house-call doctors, they didn't go away after the treatment was finished. They kept looking around and finding more broken things that needed fixing.

A veterinary school classmate of mine once had a fine black Labrador retriever named Bart who was insane about duck hunting. Even though he was deaf from years of field shooting, he lived to hunt. My friend was considering retiring Bart because of one persistent habit: he was such a good bird retriever that he not only brought his master's ducks back to him in the field, but also picked up every crippled bird within a radius of a hundred yards. It was hardly possible to go hunting with him and take the legal limit because Bart regularly brought back ducks downed by other hunters. Just as you thought you were about to reach your car with the legal number of birds, Bart would return from the marsh with yet another duck in his mouth and put you in jeopardy of a poaching citation. I suppose that zoo veterinarians, like Bart, seemed a little overachieving, at least to some zoo directors and curators.

I have tried to empathize with and imagine how the veterinary mentality makes some zoo directors and curators uneasy at times, and how this would play out if the same dynamic developed between me and my physician. For example, suppose that your family doctor literally hung around your house with you and admonished you: "Put down that doughnut, it's saturated with fat and cholesterol! Knock off that third cup of coffee, the caffeine will destroy your heart! Fix those broken steps, someone's going to trip and kill themselves! You should get a little more exercise and drop a few pounds!" The established notion that doctors were supposed to be primarily for the sick set veterinarians off on the wrong foot in some zoos. That's just not what zoo veterinarians do. They believe that they were hired to prevent disease, as much as to treat it. Opinions often differ, however, about what the zoo veterinarian's job should and shouldn't be.

Some zoos have employed veterinarians as zoo directors. This has been one way of assuring that veterinary care was always available, and it has relieved city administrators of many of their lurking fears about safety and animal welfare fiascos. The only way that some zoos could afford both a capable veterinarian and a zoo director was to put them both into one package. I have always been a little ambivalent about this director/veterinarian arrangement because a veterinarian's unequivocal first loyalty should be to the animals, rather than to city hall or the park department, which puts the veterinarian in the position of wrestling with conflicting identities. My concerns have apparently been misplaced, however, since some of the great zoo directors have been veterinarians. Veterinarian zoo directors have served in zoos in Asheville, Brownsville, Chicago, Cincinnati, Cleveland, Columbus, Detroit, Fresno, Los Angeles, Louisville, Memphis, New York, Oklahoma City, Oakland, Omaha, Phoenix, Pittsburgh, San Diego, Seattle, St. Louis, Toronto, and Washington, as well as in European zoos in Amsterdam, Basel, Berlin, Frankfurt, Leipzig, Paris, Whipsnade, and Zurich. When a fiscal crunch arises, I'd like to believe that a veterinarian zoo director would have a cost-cutting approach differing from others who came from management or finance backgrounds. I would expect them to juggle the books secretly so that animals would not feel the budgetary pinches that bean counters impose on zoos. The arrival of veterinarians in zoos challenged both them and their institutions. But, more important, it started to leverage changes in institutional priorities and the lives of zoo animals.

One of the natural conflicts that arose in this new marriage of animal doctors with zoos was the occasional antipathy that characterized the relationships between the animal curators and veterinarians. I don't think it necessarily has to be that way, any more than dogs and cats necessarily have to be adversaries. Whenever I see a dog and cat living together as friends, I think that veterinarians and curators should pay close attention to how they pull it off.

Curators are the key staff members who manage the animal collections and are in charge of buying and trading animals, supervising their daily care, and planning their exhibits. After the keepers, curators have the jobs most of us would want in a zoo. In reality, curators have about as much chance as the president of the United States does to understand and control fully the destiny of their constituents. The ideal management system in zoos is one where directors, veterinarians, and curators have seamless, collaborative relationships. In many zoos the veterinarian was always at the top of the personnel ladder as the most educated person on the zoo staff, including their zoo director boss, although this has changed considerably. Most of the zoo directors in the history of American zoos have not been biologists, and many now come from marketing, management, or administrative backgrounds. Zoo curatorial positions were not typically academically oriented ones either, but often were filled by savvy, trained-on-the-job animal aficionados of highly varying credentials and backgrounds. Zoo professionals have always had to work within the constraints of the economics and knowledge that typify most zoo operations. Perhaps it was preordained that these newly arrived zoo veterinarians would encroach upon resident territorial domains, since many of the solutions to animal health problems lay within the theoretical realm of curatorial influence to correct. Most of the disagreement has come from housing, feeding, and management issues that affect animal health.

Perceiving the complex managerial needs of the zoo profession, several academic institutions now have courses in zoo biology and management. Michigan State University offers a curriculum in zoo and aquarium science. Canasius College, in Buffalo, New York, has initiated a zoo biology program that covers topics on the genetics, physiology, and nutrition of captive wildlife. Numerous zoos now host veterinary internships or residency training programs for graduate veterinarians. The American Zoo and Aquarium Association (AZA), the principal industry professional organization, has offered short courses in zoo administration for many years.

It has been a fitful process to blend veterinarians into the sacred ground of exhibition and daily animal management. Veterinarians correctly perceived these two areas as the wellspring of most of the medical problems that they deal with every day, and, like Dr. Seuss's young Gerald McGrew, they also set about trying to make a change or two.

Today, the management in most progressive zoos has succeeded in integrating the capabilities of the key players on their professional zoo staffs, and transcended a lot of the rough spots along the old road. The best organizational models create compatible team environments in which sharp divisions of job territory have been done away with, or at least blunted. Among the many jobs of the zoo director is the task of balancing the priorities of veterinarians and curators, in addition to those of trustees, donors, and civic officials.

Everyone wants to be a curator, from the trustees, director, and veterinarian down to the zoo docents. This seemingly endless list of aspirants must be a constant source of irritation to real curators. When encroached upon by their superiors, curators sometimes have to hold their breath and humor certain sacred pet projects until a proposal suffocates under its own weight. Such was the case with a proposed exhibit at the San Diego Zoo made in the late 1960s by the zoo's director, Dr. Charles Schroeder. Because of its anachronistic qualities, this legendary story was still fresh in circulation when I arrived as an intern in 1972. In keeping with the heavy emphasis of the zoo collection on African animals, Dr. Schroeder's brainstorm was to build on this strength by adding an anthropological tilt—a human exhibit in the form of an African village. As the centerpiece of this politically incorrect idea, "real" African people would be brought over from the "Dark Continent" and live in a village in the zoo, "just like they do in the bush." (In all fairness, Schroeder did have a contract arrangement in mind for the villagers, rather than a capture expedition.) His proposal continued, "Think of how interesting it would be to watch natives in their natural habitat, weaving baskets, tending chickens, nursing children and all of the other fascinating things that 'natives' do."

In 1906, the New York Zoological Park, where Dr. Schroeder served as veterinarian for several years in the 1930s, had "exhibited" a human African pygmy in the primate house, although Schroeder seemed not to have absorbed the lessons learned by his mentors there. This whole affair became a public relations disaster for the zoo, and it was criticized by human rights groups in the New York press. It can be read about in some detail in William Bridges's excellent 1974 book *Gathering of Animals*. Ota Benga, a male Congolese pygmy, and a pet chimpanzee had accompanied a businessman to America from Africa. When the zoo was approached to house the chimpanzee, Ota Benga stayed on and was "employed" as a helper in the primate house, where he was seen regularly by the public playing with the chimps in their cage. A sign describing Ota Benga's natural history, as well as well that of the chimps, was added to the exhibit. Ota Benga eventually became disenchanted with his zoo life and ultimately made a spectacle of himself, flourishing a carving knife and threatening visitors. One day he came into conflict with a vendor in the zoo when denied a bottle of soda during his break from his exhibit. Benga began to strip naked in front of zoo visitors until restrained by several zoo employees. As a consequence of these debacles, the sign was removed from his exhibit and Ota Benga was immediately retired. He wound up in the Colored Orphan Asylum, the Virginia Theological Seminary and College, and left there to become a day laborer before finally committing suicide in 1916.

In the 1970s, a live human exhibit did come to the zoo world. A creative performing artist offered his services to zoos as a live traveling human exhibit called "Urban Man." For the several zoos that hired his short-lived act, it drew lively media and visitor attention. The Urban Man lived in a small movie-style set, doing what much of urban civilization did best—cooking, cleaning, eating, watching TV, and reading the newspaper. A far cry from an African village, however, Urban Man never had the requisite charisma to be hired at Charles Schroeder's San Diego Zoo.

Gradually, one by one, all major zoos, and most medium-sized ones, employed their own full-time staff veterinarians. Zoo medicine internships and residencies started up in larger zoos and at several universities beginning in the 1970s. The San Diego Zoo had the initial zoo veterinary training program. The first major textbook in this field, aptly titled *Zoo and Wild Animal Medicine,* edited by Dr. Murray Fowler of the University of California at Davis, was compiled in 1978, and its fifth edition was published in 2003. Needed, fast-improving expertise was finally on the way, and the zoo veterinary profession experienced a growth spurt, as did its principal professional organization in the United States, the American Association of Zoo Veterinarians (AAZV), founded in 1946. In Europe, starting in 1958, an annual International Symposium on the Diseases of Zoo Animals has been hosted in various European cities, and in 1961 a group of veterinarians formed the British Veterinary Zoological Society, holding its inaugural meeting at the London Zoo with thirty-six veterinarians in attendance. In 1982 the journal *Zoo Biology* began publication, and its scope includes current findings in zoo and wildlife research, medicine, and husbandry.

Among the shortcomings of zoos, even well into the later 1900s, was the lack of systematic record keeping to enable the accurate collection of animal data on origin, genealogy, longevity, medical history, and pathology. One of the great contributions to correct this problem was the development of the International Species Information System (ISIS) in 1973 through the initiative of zoo researcher Dr. Ulysses S. Seal and Nate Flesness. This database now involves more than five hundred member institutions around the world, and it has facilitated the work of special interest groups such as the Conservation Breeding Specialist Group (CBSG) and their programs to coordinate conservation breeding in captive wildlife. Its MedARKS medical record system is used by the medical staffs in hundreds of zoos.

Shepherded for years by executive director Dr. Wilbur Amand, the AAZV's membership now exceeds 1,200 professionals, and it publishes *The Journal of Zoo & Wild Animal Medicine*, promotes investigative research grants, and has a large annual scientific convention. Its meetings are attended by veterinarians, curators, biologists, and students from zoos, universities, wildlife departments, and research institutes around the globe. What used to be a predominantly male occupation, with several notable female exceptions, now reflects the composition of the veterinary profession in general, and more than half its members are women.

In 1983 a new veterinary organization was founded to certify specialists in the new discipline that had become known as "zoological medicine." Eight zoo veterinarians, including me, were selected by the American Veterinary Medical Association to constitute the founding board of the American College of Zoological Medicine (ACZM), which has grown to more than eighty veterinarians who are board-certified as specialists in zoo animal medicine. In addition, specialty groups have formed in wildlife, avian, reptile, and amphibian medicine. Within only thirty years, zoological veterinarians have become inseparable parts of zoos and the veterinary profession. Much of this had to be accomplished by trial, error, compromise, and intermittent doses of analgesics.

As for the curators today, they, too, are evolving. Their ranks are filling with college graduates and PhDs. The gaps are closing between them and the veterinarians, and some veterinarians are now becoming curators—perhaps what they really wanted to be all along.

San Diego Zoo reptile keeper with Galapagos tortoises

4. THE KEEPERS

Nurturing the Health of Animals

The eyes and ears most closely tuned to the animals in the zoo are those of the keepers, for it is they who have the most intimate knowledge of the animals' daily feeding, toilet, social, and sexual habits. The generation of keepers that I first met at the San Diego Zoo was a lively mixture of transformed ranch hands, circus veterans, retired military personnel, short order cooks, janitors, and former zoo tour guides. Occasionally a keeper from another zoo would break into the system, but San Diego had a clear preference for molding new keepers out of raw, local clay.

Perhaps no frontline job at the San Diego Zoo is harder to come by than that of a zookeeper. Someone once joked that in the event of a zookeeper's death, the prime suspects would be wannabe zookeepers. Just as Hollywood is inundated with aspiring movie actors, the zoo personnel office is always swamped with applications for keeper jobs. Instead of parking cars and waiting tables at local nightclubs, if you were a would-be keeper you would be best advised to start anywhere that would afford you even a little toe in the zoo's door. From there, you would have to rely on hard work, networking, and charm to claim a vacancy that might take years to come.

After you entered the zoo employment system as a hamburger technician or paper picker, you were finally on the inside track to building your credentials and to obtaining the essential contacts needed to edge your way into one of these coveted positions. Working in the gift shop or as a parking lot attendant was second string in this arena of competition—it was imperative that you became a face on the zoo grounds, where you could rub elbows with the animal movers and shakers. After selling perhaps 200,000 corn dogs, you might finally be getting closer. A recommendation from your immediate supervisor, mentor, or lover could make or break your prospects when that opening finally came. You hoped and prayed that your boss had enough leverage to help, and that you had enough personal charisma to prevail.

As time passed at the San Diego Zoo, so did many of the older animal keepers. A few of those who had been biding their time betting on corn dog futures moved up, and the numbers of keepers able to lasso a wildebeest dwindled to extinction. Seasoned farmhands were replaced with zoo-trained urbanites, a few bearing scars of faltered aspirations to become curators or veterinarians. Some of the keepers became a bit cynical when they realized that their expectations fell short of the actual experience—where financial constraints, limited authority, and occasional public indifference diminished their expected impact upon the system.

The integration of this more educated, youthful element of the keeper force, and the experienced older employees, was always interesting to observe. The more senior keepers did not gladly surrender their favorite tasks to these idealistic newcomers—after all, they too had to earn their stripes. Like fraternity pledges, the new kids were often delegated the more mundane tasks, such as hosing, raking, cleaning, and chopping veggies, in the manner of a progressive apprenticeship. One common ground that both generations seemed to share was the mythology associated with their respective capabilities with animals. The youngsters attributed their skills to their higher purpose, their academic search for key biological facts, and their astute observations. The oldsters usually credited their insights to their long, seasoned, hard-earned experiences.

The gradual disappearance of the old keepers' faces caused a loss of the country-bred intuition that some of these former livestock wranglers had brought to their jobs. Among those I missed was cowboy Clyde, the old antelope keeper with a horseshoe-shaped depression in the middle of his face—the price of a youthful encounter with a bronco's hoof on a Texas ranch. Clyde's lip tilted into a drool on one side of his lopsided jaw, and he had a no-small-talk kind of rural demeanor. He got right to the bottom line if something was going wrong with one of his antelope charges. The newer crop of keepers read and studied more about animals, accumulated more technical knowledge, and had more of their own self-learned technical notions about animal health and behavior problems. They belong to the American Association of Zoo Keepers, and many now have college degrees. The older keepers always called me "Doctor," whereas the newer ones wanted to call me "Phil."

The assignment of keepers to various animal groups in zoos varies highly from one zoo to another. Aptitude, experience, seniority, affability, obedience, and loyalty all play a hand in the hierarchy of the keeper rank and file. We would all like to think that this is a perfect process of matching the most appropriate individuals with the most appropriate animals, but—let's face it—the animals don't pick their keepers. Some keeper assignments are, unquestionably, more desirable than others. Raking goat droppings off of a steep hillside or cleaning carnivore stools out of a drainpipe just might not be your cup of tea—more a "reward" for political transgressions. Some zoos with strong labor unions go meticulously by the seniority system, which creates some interesting personnel and animal management dynamics. If you want to be the gorilla keeper, you may simply have to wait your turn.

Zookeepers often put their own welfare at risk to attend the primal needs of the predatory and unpredictable tendencies of the animals in their care. Such injuries that I personally observed the end products of were severed fingers from monkey and tapir bites, a paralyzed arm inflicted by a pygmy hippopotamus, and a hand amputated by the bite of a giant panda. Occasionally, this jeopardy costs them their very lives. Unfortunately, over the years, keepers of bears, leopards, and elephants have lost their lives in the pursuit of animal care at the San Diego Zoo and San Diego Wild Animal Park. According to a 1997 report from the Bureau of Labor Statistics, elephant keepers have the highest risk for fatalities of any other profession in the United States, averaging two deaths per 660 employees.

A recent job announcement for a keeper position in an American safari park is a fair indication of the mental and physical agility expected of a tiger handler: "Seeking an individual to work as a Tiger Trainer. Must be mentally alert and be able to pay attention to all daily duties. Must have quick reflexes and be able to react quickly to changing animal situations. Must be able to walk and run quickly as needed. Will require close contact with large, wild animals. We offer a competitive salary with outstanding medical benefits."

Some of these keeper deaths had the same fundamental dynamic, one that has played out similarly in fatalities in zoos around the world. With dangerous carnivores such as bears and big cats, a weak link in the work routine occurs when one keeper goes off for his or her weekend and another follows the next day to care for their animals. As with aviation accidents, where pilot error accounts for most of the fatalities, so do keeper errors incite most animal-caused injuries. The routine with most dangerous animals is kept standardized for safety reasons, and animals are always, without fail, to be moved between locked cages to maintain a security buffer between people and predators. When the carnivore exhibit area is entered and cleaned, it is critical that the keepers ascertain that no predator is still present and that *every single* animal is accounted for in locked areas. In San Diego, and in other widely removed zoos, keepers who arrived on their Monday to clean a dangerous cat exhibit failed to confirm visually the location of all animals, only to be ambushed after entering the exhibit enclosure. Even though the routine may be to lock all animals into bedroom cages at night—"animal bedroom" is zoo terminology for the sleeping/resting space into which animals are typically confined at night—occasionally an animal refuses to return to the bedroom or holding area, posing a potential danger for the keeper who follows the next day.

All large carnivore exhibits in zoos are built with "safety cages," intermediate, secure spaces at the entry to the exhibit that are to be entered before proceeding into the area nearest to the animals. The typical routine is to unlock the outside door to the safety cage, enter and latch the door behind, and then proceed into the next space after making a conclusive visual inspection to be sure that all is safe and clear. Except when entering or departing, both door entries to a safety cage are expected to be closed at all times. Numerous accidents around carnivores have resulted when an attendant's attention is diverted, allowing the critical opportunity for an animal to reach between or under door frames and bars or through feeding chutes and seize their caretaker, resulting in severe lacerations, limb amputations, and worse.

In 2002, a 350-pound African lion at Busch Gardens near Tampa, Florida, ripped off the arm of a zookeeper standing next to the lion's cage while she was giving a private tour to her family. The attack occurred shortly after the zookeeper had fed the lion pieces of meat during training exercises. In the same year, a twenty-one-year-old female keeper at the Vienna Zoo entered a big cat cage, expecting it to be empty. Within seconds a jaguar lunged at her. Onlookers included the zoo's director, Helmut Pechlaner, who was badly mauled when he went to her rescue. Officials at the zoo said

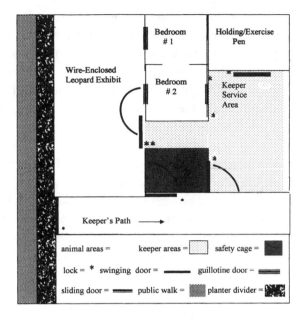

Typical carnivore exhibit layout

they did not yet know how the accident occurred, but they suspected that the three jaguars had burst into the cage through a hatch that had not been locked correctly.

Nearly all facilities with dangerous animals have explicit rules instructing departing keepers to leave concise notes for their relief keeper—always with the caveat that each person must insure his or her own safety by visual confirmation of the location of *all* animals. A San Diego keeper failed to detect the presence of a leopard one fateful Sunday morning and was surprised from behind as he entered the exhibit area to clean. Quickly, surgically, the leopard seized him by the neck, killing him by severing his carotid artery and spinal cord. In parallel circumstances, a female tiger keeper at the New York Bronx Zoo was also killed in an exhibit area, unaware that an unsecured tiger lay in wait for her.

For years after the San Diego leopard killing, the public inquired about which exhibit and leopard was involved. It was impossible to work with animals on the leopard string without the shadow of this event hanging there like a cloud. For some time after the event, visitors walked past the exhibit pointing fingers and gesturing to their companions to illustrate their recollections of the accounts they had read in the newspapers.

Animals that require sedation for examination or treatment may be darted with sedatives from either the public exhibit side (usually before the public arrives) or when the animal is more closely confined in the service area behind. Better-designed holding areas for carnivores have the capability of crating and transporting animals without chemical immobilization, but many zoo exhibits still lack efficient catching facilities. A "crush" or "squeeze" device involves a moving wall, mechanically or hydraulically operated, that forces an animal along a narrowed space and into a holding crate or against a barred area to allow injection with a hand syringe. Naive and calmer animals may allow an experienced person to approach close enough to permit a hand injection, but there still exists the risk that comes with close proximity.

Not all zoos have accepted safety as a fundamental characteristic of employment. The following news report, excerpted from the London *Telegraph,* summarizes the serial mishaps in a private English zoo:

> An experienced zoo keeper was killed by an elephant yesterday at an animal park owned by the millionaire John Aspinall. The park has a policy of not putting down animals that kill humans.
>
> It is the fifth time in 20 years that animals belonging to Mr. Aspinall have killed staff at one of his wildlife parks, where keepers are encouraged to 'bond' with the animals and to mingle at close quarters with even the most dangerous creatures. The elephant, called La Petite, had arrived at the zoo in October from an Austrian safari park. A spokesperson said, "It seems Mr. Cockrill may have trusted La Petite to be as reliable and friendly as the other cows which had been in his care and known to him for seven years." Police and local health and safety officers are investigating whether the elephant killed Mr. Cockrill by accident or intentionally. Mr. Aspinall's wildlife parks have experienced a number of accidents in recent years. Three years ago he went to the High Court to stop Canterbury city council preventing staff entering enclosures in which tigers roamed freely at Howletts Zoo, his other wildlife park, after a keeper was killed.
>
> The keeper was mauled to death in 1994 by a Siberian tiger. Visitors saw the animal pick up Trevor Smith, 32, by the neck and head and carry him in its mouth to a shed in the compound. In 1993, Louise Aspinall, 30, Mr. Aspinall's daughter-in-law, needed 15 stitches after being bitten by a tiger cub at the same park.

Ten years ago, two-year-old Matthew McDaid had his arm ripped off by a chimpanzee at Port Lympne. He was awarded £132,000 damages at the High Court. Four years later, the same animal bit off the finger and thumb of Angelique Todd, 25, a student working at the park.

In 1984, Mark Aitken, 22, a keeper at Port Lympne, was killed when an Indian elephant crushed him against railings. In 1980, keepers Brian Stocks and Bob Wilson were both mauled to death by a tigress named Zeya in separate incidents at Howletts. Zeya was later shot by Mr. Aspinall.

Apparently, the Aspinall zoo had a less lenient policy for serial killers. But, fortunately, most injuries are minor by comparison. One keeper at the Los Angeles Zoo was described as "The Tastiest Zookeeper in America" because of his greater than average propensity to sustain various animal-related injuries, such as those described in these official accident reports:

> I collected the feeding pans from the previous day and was exiting the bobcat enclosure when the female bobcat in the far corner of the exhibit jumped on my back from the side and dug her claws in to my left arm, shoulder and back. The animal ran off immediately after the attack and I was able to get out of the exhibit without additional injuries.

> Bitten by a coatimundi on the left thumb while providing behavioral enrichment.

> Scratched while carrying and weighing a koala.

Meanwhile, his keeper colleagues were having encounters with other creatures:

> After tube feeding a scarlet ibis, the ibis jammed his beak up my right nostril, causing bleeding for about 20 min. and slightly throughout the day. . . . Bird beaks are dirty, and he jammed it way up into my nostril— I was afraid of infection or sinus injury.

> I was feeding a medicated cantaloupe to a tortoise and my hand got too close to the animal's mouth and the turtle bit my finger.

> I was feeding the Jamaica boa with tongs and the snake missed and bit my wrist.

> I was wearing bright orange rain gear and held a metal trash can lid up over my head. While talking to the bird pair, I picked up one egg from the ground and the Kookaburra flew under the lid, landed on my head, pecked me on my head and flew away.

One of our longtime elephant keepers at the San Diego Zoo, who several unenlightened coworkers sometimes made sport of, possessed more natural rapport with pachyderms than anyone else in the zoo. Some thought that he was a little slow, but I always believed that he was just unusually sincere and humble. Bob was an old-time elephant handler in traveling circuses for years before coming to the zoo. A big, quiet, gentle soul, he had several faded carnie tattoos on his massive, hairy arms. His calloused hands seemed the size of baseball mitts, and he wore black rubber boots to navigate the day's puddles of elephant urine and hose water. His habit was to talk to you with his eyes wandering in and out of eye contact, all in a slow, modest manner. Bob seemed to live more for elephants than anything else in his life. Several employees remarked that regular passengers on his city bus route kept their distance from him on his evening ride home in order to avoid the strong essence of *eau de éléphante* that followed him around like a little gray cloud.

Bob told me a story about a performing circus elephant that he had cared for at their winter quarters in Florida. As he reminisced about his old circus days, I could nearly smell the roasted peanuts and hear a calliope playing as he lapsed into a flashback of his life and times with the big top elephants. The look in his eyes grew distant as he began to describe what had happened to his pachyderm friend.

In the winter quarters, the public was allowed to visit for an admission fee and see the animals up close. A young boy who had strayed from his parents crossed a rope barrier and made his way over to one of the cow elephants, which was chained by a leg in a holding area. No one actually saw what happened next. People came running to where the boy's thoroughly trampled body was discovered. Emergency personnel and a large contingent of sheriff deputies soon descended upon the scene, with blaring sirens and flashing red lights. They worked furiously on the boy, although he was obviously dead. As they finally loaded his remains into an ambulance, a troubled discussion was under way between the deputies and the circus manager about the hopeless state of the victim and the uncertain fate of the big-eared perpetrator.

Tears came to Bob's eyes as he spoke fondly of his affection for his elephant friend, who he had fed, watered, bathed and talked to daily for years. Struggling not to choke up, he continued. "Later, they were talking about what they oughta do with her. The word had spread and more police arrived." He paused. "The police talked for awhile in a huddle with the circus manager. I couldn't hear what they were saying, but it wasn't long before they made a decision. When they came back to carry out their plan they opened up the trunks of their patrol cars and brought out the rifles. They had brought in a bulldozer and carved out a big pit. Because she trusted me to handle her, they had me walk her into the pit and fasten her leg chain to a steel post that they had driven into the ground."

I could tell by his breathing that these memories were wracked with pain and guilt. With his voice barely audible, he explained how he lost count of the number of bullets that it took before his old friend breathed no more. A bulldozer covered up the remains and it was all over. Bob fell silent and sat down on a straw bale, while his mind seemed to slip off completely to circus memories. It was impossibly sad. Then he finally got up, and said, "Doc, if you don't mind, my elephants are hungry and I have to go feed them now before I catch my bus to go home." Bob picked up a bucket of apples and carrots and shuffled off to greet his big gray friends.

Years later, during the writing of this book, I watched the 1952 circus movie *The Greatest Show on Earth* for the first time. Much of the movie, which starred Charlton Heston, Betty Hutton, and Jimmy Stewart, was filmed at the Ringling Brothers winter quarters in Sarasota, Florida, using circus workers as extras. I was stunned to see a short scene near the beginning of the film in which our keeper Bob, much younger, was gently bathing an elephant cow with a hose and a scrub brush as the circus manager, played by Heston, recommended giving her a dose of gin for a stomach ailment. Bob never mentioned that he had ever been in the movie, but I have a haunting feeling that I now know why.

Elephants have met similar fates throughout their history in captivity. In 1825, Chuny the elephant, the central attraction of Cross's Menagerie in London, became unmanageable. As he attempted to break out of his fortress-like cage, a civilian firing squad was hastily assembled and killed him by using a small canon and 152 balls of ammunition. Male elephants are notorious for the difficulties they eventually pose in captivity.

The daily animal care routine in the zoo involves the completion of a keeper report after the first check of the animals each morning. Each zoo keeper is in charge of a "string," a distinct group of animals and exhibits. The head keepers then gather these reports and confer with the veterinarian and curator to determine which animals need to be looked at and evaluated. Any out-of-the-ordinary findings, such as births, breeding, deaths, lameness, diarrhea, lack of appetite, or facilities problems, are expected to be recorded on the report. When possible, animals are mentioned by name.

The attempted escape of Chuny the elephant at Cross's menagerie, London, 1825

Keeper reports can be short or long, poignant or humorous. These are some actual samples from the San Diego Zoo:

> Keeper Report, Monkey Yard—The Douc Langur Monkeys have diarrhea again. They are eating it like shrimp dip.

> Keeper Report, Great Apes—Commissary: This is the third day in a row that we have not received bananas. What's the problem? Did the banana factory burn down?

> Keeper Report, Great Apes—Linda the Pygmy Chimp will only let Kakowet breed her if he gives her all of his apples and bananas first. We need to increase the fruit order again.

> Keeper Report, Bear Canyon—If the plumber doesn't get down here soon to unplug these drains, the bear and I are going to surf over and get his tools ourselves.

Keeper Report, Giraffe String—"Checkers" in heat—"Topper" in "Checkers."

Some keepers are more astute than others in detecting health problems. I always hoped that keepers would err on the side of overreporting concerns rather than ignoring them. In the beginning of my work at the zoo it seemed that some keepers would avoid bringing up certain problems, for fear that the veterinarian would want to drag a cherished specimen off to the hospital for "risky" diagnostic prodding and poking. Before the advent of improved anesthetic procedures, there was a much higher likelihood of injury or death for animals in routine procedures. It took time to build up confidence in the capabilities of the new veterinary medicine in zoos. Once we had the drugs and a near-perfect anesthesia batting record, however, we were the ones who had to tone down the new zeal of the curators and keepers for drug immobilizations.

The San Diego Zoo hospital had its own animal holding areas and its own elite group of animal keepers. This crew was among the most experienced in the zoo and had developed a wide range of skills required to medicate, crate, net, handle, and restrain the full scope of animals in the zoo. Hospital keepers had to be more creative than average, and masters at outwitting animals that would otherwise avoid eating food with medications in it. Handpicked for their skills and ingenuity, hospital keepers were expected to make their own handling nets, housing devices, and creative solutions for managing a wide variety of zoo patients. On several occasions this creative license caused some alarm in the hospital wards.

Murray, our most senior hospital keeper, prided himself on his ingenuity, and rightfully so. He would go to extraordinary lengths to solve animal housing and handling problems. One day, however, his initiative got the best of him when he went to move a Siberian tiger between cages on opposite sides of the outdoor hospital compound. Murray was very fond of this nearly grown female tiger, who vocalized to him through the bars every morning as he scratched her neck and fed her chunks of horsemeat. Murray was in love with this cat. As I was walking back to the hospital compound, from the adjacent research building, I glanced through a window and was jolted by the sight of Murray and the tiger *outside* of the cage in the central compound. This enclosed area was entirely roofed with chain link fabric and was, in effect, a safety cage large enough to hold a dump truck; it was entered directly from the zoo grounds through an electronically controlled sliding gate. Large carnivore cages capable of holding big cats and bears lined both sides of the compound. To avoid souring his pet tiger's sweet demeanor, he had decided to move her, gently, fraternally, by placing a trail of meatballs on the ground from her present cage to the destination cage some fifty feet away. "Things were going just as planned," as he later described, except that several of us bystanders simultaneously thought that a big cat escape was in progress. We were within a second of activating our zoowide emergency alarm on the radios. Just as I shouted to Murray to learn what he was doing, the tiger stepped into her new cage and he slid the door shut behind her. As far as I know, that was the first and last time the meatball transfer method was ever used at the hospital.

If the hospital keepers had any disputes with the keepers and curators in the main zoo, it was probably most aggravated by the use of the hospital for housing surplus animals. Our keepers had to run an animal hospital and hotel where the guests seldom made reservations and completely ignored the checkout time. Because of breeding successes, incompatibility issues between individual animals, or occasional managerial largess in finding homes for surplus animals with other zoos, the hospital was a place that animals could be warehoused until other disposition options were found. As a result, these long-term boarders, often big predators, had to be moved around from time to time as different cages were needed for new hospital cases.

A male lion named Sanetti turned out to be one of the easiest to move out of hospital storage. He was part of a population boom that happened in our zoo lion pride, thanks to the reliable virility of the dominant male, Chopper. Because of the limited housing available for big cats in the zoo, Sanetti lived in a hospital cage as a surplus animal, while the curators unsuccessfully sought a home for him. To cope with this overabundance of lions, I had begun by spaying a three-hundred-pound female lion, which involves surgically removing the ovaries and uterus. Thereafter, I immediately vowed never to repeat that laborious piece of surgery if I could avoid it. As I found myself up to my elbows in the lioness's abdomen, sorting out the abdominal fat from the ovaries and uterus, I came upon a better idea—sterilizing the male lions by perfecting a surgical vasectomy technique.

The San Diego Zoo animal hospital is located on the edge of the grounds adjacent to the Old Globe Shakespeare Theater. An elaborate but hastily built outdoor stage had been constructed to keep the theater operating after a fire that had totally destroyed the main theater area. Unbeknownst to the stage director, a male lion, who had a sixteen-pound bowling ball as a toy, lived only forty yards away. With their new production of *A Midsummer Night's Dream* in full swing on opening night, Sanetti roared and thrashed his ball against the steel cage bars for several hours. Miraculously, unlike all other surplus boarders, after just one phone call from the general manager of the Old Globe, the curators instantly found a new home for the lion. He was gone in record time, expedited, we learned later, by pressure from a Shakespeare-loving zoo trustee.

It is only human nature to take certain liberties with our access to animals during lapses of good judgment, though with certain zoo animals this can be unforgiving. I recall one such moment of my own involving a young Chinese leopard that was newly arrived from a Canadian zoo for routine hospital quarantine. This gorgeous creature had been hand-raised until fairly recently, and upon arrival from the airport he was very homesick. A perfect specimen with a thick, glossy, spotted coat, he was a marvelous animal, weighing in at ninety pounds. He pleaded for attention and companionship through the cage bars. It was hard to keep your hands off him, and I warned several staff members to be aware that he was a full-grown predator.

Alone late one afternoon, a week after his arrival, I walked past his cage in the main hospital compound. He stood up against the bars and licked my hand, purred, and begged to be petted. I couldn't resist. On impulse I unlocked the cage door, stepped inside, closed it behind me, and sat down on his resting bench. Obviously surprised, but delighted to see me, he sprang into my lap. As soon as I felt the impact of his weight, I realized that this was a huge mistake; he was definitely not a lap cat. I put my arms around him and gently attempted to slide him off of me while he purred and licked my face with his sandpaper tongue. His glistening canine teeth, now rubbing against my cheek, had evolved through the ages to dissect antelope and deer instantly. He wanted to play, but I was overwhelmed by the instinct to run.

The more focused I became on pushing him off my lap, the more determined he became to hold onto me. The leopard and I were not playing by the same rules—he was the cat, and I was his mouse. As I stood up, he slid down my front, wrapping both of his front paws about my ankles and panting up at me with his mouth open wide. His pupils dilated, and a look of primeval, predatory enthusiasm filled his eyes. Feeling like a trussed duck, I waddled over to the barred sliding door, dragging my leopard anchor. I cannot recall a single other instance in my life when concealing my true emotions was so vital. Before he could contemplate his next move, I scraped him off on the sliding door as I pulled myself through the opening and snapped the lock on behind me. The warm smell and feel of leopard saliva covered my cheek. I doubt that he actually knew what he was going to do next. Suddenly I felt some strange connection to that San Diego zookeeper whose lifeblood drained from him in the leopard exhibit, alone, in one careless, private moment. All of my future walks past the leopard enclosures kindled a dark and kindred feeling inside of me.

"Buzzi" Buzikowski, the assistant head bird keeper, was one of the most endearing of the career animal people I met at the San Diego Zoo. Standing slightly over five feet tall, he always had a devilish smile under his trim little moustache and a twinkle in his eye. Buzzi spent many of his working days worrying about his boss, Kenton "K.C." Lint, the curator of birds, who often placed any failings of the management of the bird collection on his doorstep. An old-school curator, the talented but eccentric K.C. relished reminding you, as he gestured with his smelly pipe, that he had "over forty years of experience with birds." He saw fairly little purpose for veterinarians in the zoo, with the possible exception of the pathologist—after all, at least he left his living birds alone. Resisting most veterinary encroachments, K.C. was annoyed to find out that even a near-comatose parrot had been taken to the zoo hospital without his consent.

Buzzi, on the other hand, was warm and affable, always upbeat. But his face flushed and he became agitated with a case of nerves whenever K.C. had him called on the zoo radio. He knew that he was due to be singled out for another scolding, and then the color would drain from his cheery face. Occasionally he would come to me, in confidence, and whisper in a conspiratorial tone, "Doc, I'm not supposed to tell you this—but there's a sick bird being hidden from the vets in the back of the Jungle Trail cages. Would you have a look at him? But don't tell K.C. that I told you!" In appreciation for his civic spirit, these cases were handled discreetly to keep him from K.C.'s wrath. Regardless of the personal risk, he had a conscience that required suicidal honesty.

Later on, at the zoo director's request, I traveled on an extended trip to Australia and New Guinea with the feared K.C. Lint to obtain koalas for the zoo. We became good friends while touring wildlife reserves and zoos across Australia and New Guinea, and together we negotiated arrangements for the donation of koalas for the San Diego Zoo as a bicentennial gift from Australia to the United States. K.C. finally concluded that vets, or perhaps at least this one, weren't all bad after all. Afterward, he trusted me to treat most, but not all, of his precious birds.

Buzzi, however, still remained the bird department's resident scapegoat. His zoo career was the personification of Murphy's Law, filled with innocent serial mishaps that got him into hot water, no matter how far he was removed from fault. When the annual Mexican Cinco de Mayo holiday school crowd from Tijuana terrorized K.C.'s nesting swans and their eggs came up missing, Buzzi was reprimanded for not having the foresight to erect a barrier in front of their nest. When Buzzi was attacked by a male ostrich that jumped across a wheelbarrow in an attempt to maim him, K.C. chastised Buzzi for scaring the ostrich. On several unfortunate occasions Buzzi was the last person seen holding one of the collection's treasured parrots before it suddenly dropped dead, when in reality he had picked the poor birds up off the ground when they were too weak to hold onto their perches.

It was fairly common for people to call the zoo to donate pet parrots that they could no longer keep, and it was usually Buzzi who met the donor to receive the bird and bring it to the hospital for quarantine prior to exhibition in the zoo. Since it was impossible to accept every donation, Buzzi had been admonished by K.C. to screen the donations carefully. One day, following its hospital quarantine, a recently donated green and yellow Amazon parrot went on public display in a cage along a busy sidewalk near the Bird Yard. Shortly thereafter, Buzzi received a terse radio summons from K.C. to get over to the cage and take the new bird off exhibit *immediately.* Dropping what he was doing, he went straight to the bird yard, boxed up the parrot, and brought him to the hospital. I saw him arriving with the Amazon in the back of his little zoo scooter and said, "I thought you just put that bird on exhibit. Why are you bringing it back?" Buzzi flushed, "I don't know, but the old man was really ticked off about something the bird said to a lady visitor and wanted it off of the grounds pronto." Just then, the bird stirred in his carrying cage and shrieked, "Screw you! Screw you!" Buzzi's face contorted into an "Ooh, noo!" as he shook his head and reluctantly refrained from wringing the bird's neck.

The morning after a zoo employees' party we received the sad news that Buzzi had died unexpectedly in his sleep of a heart attack. It was a dismal occasion on the day of his funeral, and I stood with several friends and his pallbearers outside of the church after the funeral mass, preparing to leave for the cemetery burial. We were fondly reminiscing and smiling about the trials and tribulations of Buzzi's life and times at the zoo, when, as only Buzzi could have it, the hearse's battery failed and it couldn't be started. Sensing that something had gone wrong, more of his old friends gathered in a crowd around the hearse. The funeral procession was delayed while we awaited a tow truck to provide a jumpstart. Adding some morbid humor to Buzzi's final earthly foul-up, someone suggested that we have them try to jumpstart Buzzi as well. We all laughed with Buzzi for the last time, and even K.C. smiled, barely concealing a tear in his eye.

5. ZOO BABIES

Promoting Motherhood

The keepers are the core of the zoo's conscience, and animals must rely on them to be physically and mentally healthy. In addition to ministering to animals' essential needs and idiosyncrasies, keepers are also the ombudsmen and advocates of their daily existences from cradle to grave. This nurturing process may begin in some cases with baby animals that may be born to animal couples with poor parenting skills (such as starving, beating, eating, ignoring, or mopping the floor with their offspring). In addition to monitoring animals for maternal neglect, the most common problems for zoo babies, which can be mitigated by watchful keepers, include hypothermia, hypoglycemia, and trauma.

Many newborns who fail to nurse from their mothers, especially hoofed species, are deprived of antibodies that pass to the baby in the first milk, which is called "colostrum." In the absence of these protective molecules, babies are much more vulnerable to infections with common bacteria and viruses in their environments. Other animals, such as carnivores, rely largely upon the transmission of protective maternal antibodies through the placenta, as well as in the mother's first milk. In humans, and other primates, these immune globulins are passed almost exclusively in utero, allowing them to start out life with some fundamental resistances to infections.

Zookeepers are accustomed to providing special accommodations for zoo babies, based on the maternal style of a particular species. One prickly porcupine baby in the San Diego Zoo became content to nurse from a bottle suspended on the wall of its incubator with minimum maternal contact. Baby primates, however, enjoy being doted upon and toted everywhere in a little papoose sack by an attendant.

Young ostriches, emus, and rheas, all flightless birds, may be good research models for attention deficit disorder, because their intellectual capabilities, based on their attention spans, are limited. A cynic might even cite their flightless state as further proof of my thesis. I say this with no malice, but these birds are pretty dim, even by avian standards. It has been said, by a few keepers, that ratites (the collective term for the large flightless birds) act as if every day is their first; and that if they encounter the same person thirty days in a row, they believe that have met thirty different people. When their babies are newly hatched, they imitate the parent birds in nearly everything that they do, which can only compound their problems in captivity. To make matters worse, in the absence of parents they imitate each other. Shortly after hatching, ratites quickly begin to trundle about, swallowing and pecking at nearly every strange object they encounter, including one another. This also may encompass fatal objects such as sticks, rocks, nails, and lost coins. One entire hand-reared group of rhea hatchlings in San Diego fell victim to gastrointestinal impactions from consuming artificial plastic grass, pecking and swallowing the green plastic strands until they developed fatal obstructions. No matter how cute these little guys are, one can't help but question their limited intellects.

Many animals are housed in variously modified cribs and incubators, and baby marsupials, such as kangaroos and wallabies, which require hand-rearing, are further cloistered in cozy little cloth pouches. Since marsupials are practically embryonic at birth (koalas are about the size of a kidney bean when born), pouch babies have to be well on the way in development before they can be successfully nursed by hand. Because they are constantly with their mothers and can nurse at liberty, their milk is comparatively dilute and low in fat. Other animals that leave their babies in dens and return at intervals to nurse them, such as wild dogs and cats, have more concentrated milk that is higher in fat content. Those who spend time in cold and wet environments, such as the walruses, seals, and whales, have even higher octane fatty milk for sustaining their babies.

Decisions about a suitable formula and feeding frequency are based on both experience and a growing body of literature on the composition of the milk of wild animals. While all milks contain the same principal constituents (water, protein, fat, sugar, and ash), they can vary enormously in the relative proportions of each, and in their enzymes. Some species, such as zebras, rhinos, and elephants, have milk that is higher in complex carbohydrates and lower in fat. Generally, the higher the fat content the lower the carbohydrate content, and vice versa. Those with the highest fat content are some of the marine species. Hand-rearing formulas for seals and walruses use whipping cream as the base ingredient. These wide variations of milk composition are the result of many factors, including suckling frequency, amount per feeding, and the energy demands of the environment they must cope with in nature.

Zoo personnel manage this nutritional diversity by dividing animals into groups according to milk types: equids (zebras, wild horses, and rhinos), primates (great apes and monkeys), cloven-hoofed animals (antelope, deer, giraffe, camels, wild cattle), carnivores (tigers, lions, leopards, jaguars, hyenas, wolves), and marine mammals (seals, sea lions, walruses). The largest and most remarkable infant ever reared in captivity was a California gray whale named JJ, who was found floundering in the surf near Marina del Rey, California, and cared for at San Diego's Sea World. He was fed a special formula through a feeding hose that required hundreds of gallons of dairy cream weekly, blended into a slurry with various marine-life proteins. Before his return to the wild he was trained to forage on the pool bottom to simulate more natural feeding behavior, and was consuming 900 pounds of fish, squid and krill daily. During his stay in captivity, JJ grew to more than seventeen thousand pounds and reached a length of thirty-three feet. His radio transmitter fell silent two days after JJ was released into the ocean, and he has not been spotted since.

Whenever possible, physical field checks of newborns are done in zoo exhibit areas. Keepers are often trained to obtain baseline information such as weight, sex, body temperature, and vital signs during this most critical period. Because of their propensity for cannibalizing their new offspring or abandoning them, leopards and polar bears are ordinarily left undisturbed and monitored by microphones or video cameras. Other common keeper procedures include the disinfection of the umbilical cord and the identification of newborn animals by tagging, ear notching, and

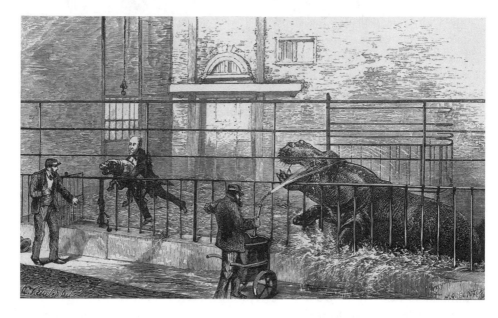

"Stealing" a baby hippo at the London Zoo

tattooing. Microchips are used in some zoos to provide certain, though not visible, identification.

Carrying out these procedures is not always feasible or without risk—not if a mother antelope or rhino catches you playing around with her baby. Nearly every zoo veterinarian and keeper has had to flee from an angry mother when she realized that her newborn was being fondled by a stranger. In the event that maternal care is not going well, foster-care decisions have to be made by the keepers, curators, and veterinarians about removing the baby from its mother and hand-rearing it. Every effort is usually made to encourage the success of mother rearing, given the adverse social and nutritional consequences of separation. Anticipating pregnancies and births allows for preparations to be made in advance.

In some cases, it is possible for keepers to supplement the feeding of a baby or take other measures to assure that it can remain with its mother. Our female okapi, Lisette, was a good mother, but she had one vice that was compromising her offspring. A relative of the giraffe, the okapi is a large, rare hoofed species that lives in the secluded

Okapi

forests of the Congo, where okapis hide their newborn babies in the forest and return at intervals to nurse them. Striking to behold, with dark brown body coloration and white, zebralike racing stripes on their hindquarters and legs, okapis are browsers, using their long blue-gray tongues to grasp and manipulate their leafy forage. Their tongues are so long that they can lick their own eyebrows and ears.

Lisette was an attentive mother, and the birth of her baby went well for several days until she began to overgroom his rear end with her tongue to the point of making it sore. Unless this behavior was stopped, the okapi baby would be taken to the Children's Zoo. By all means, we preferred him to be mother-reared on exhibit and tried to alter her behavior by applying bitter-tasting solutions to the baby's rear, but Lisette was undeterred. Next, we limited her contact with her baby to intermittent nursing sessions, but she was still obsessed about licking her baby's bottom. Finally, staff veterinarian Jim Oosterhuis devised a little custom vinyl jacket with Velcro closures that the keeper placed on the baby each time he was with his mom to nurse. Both Lisette and the baby tolerated the new apparel, the sore bottom healed, and mother and baby succeeded in remaining together.

Everyone eventually graduates from somewhere or something, and zoo animals are no exception. Though they may not receive paper diplomas like us humans, they move from one stage of life to another, often with as much drama and fanfare as accompanies human benchmarks in their social and educational development. With many species, the decision to hand-raise a baby is a painful one in a zoo, but this is particularly so with the great apes and monkeys. These highly intelligent beings acquire critical socialization skills by being among their own from birth, and they lack skills if denied the necessary role models. Like humans, their development from infancy to adulthood is cultivated and colored by their experiences, as well as their innate capacities to develop into unique individuals. They, too, can become misfits or neglectful parents if they are deprived of the psychological enrichment of life's critical passages.

To avoid these problems, some innovative efforts have been made in zoos to educate and reeducate such orphans and to teach abusive and neglectful mothers to care for their babies. There is nothing more troubling than watching an inexperienced ape mother scrubbing the floor with her newborn infant as it squeals in terror. Remedial education holds promise for some of these creatures.

When I first arrived at the San Diego Zoo, several orangutan and pygmy chimpanzee babies were being hand-reared, either because their mothers failed to hand-rear them or because they had acquired respiratory infections that made it necessary to care for them in the Children's Zoo nursery. A baby Bornean orangutan named Ken-Allen became the most boisterous of them all. Ken was eventually evicted from the infant nursery when he became too active, but he was still too small to return to the main zoo. Mischievous and demanding, he was transferred to a miniature ape exhibit nearby, where he could climb and tumble without knocking around the other babies.

Ken was going through a particularly spoiled and independent part of his development and would play with and evade the attendants like a frisky little kid. After he started to bite a few people to get his way, the day finally came for his repatriation to the big zoo. By then, Ken had become an overconfident little brat. This would all to change when he was in the care of the "real" ape keeper and away from the overindulgence of the nursery attendants

Ken went from being a big shot in the Children's Zoo to a punk kid in the big zoo. The other orangutans decided to teach him some life lessons. After a few days, Ken's only earthly possession, his security blanket, was in tatters. He struggled in tug-of-war matches with members of his new clan who wanted to share the blanket, and he ended up with only a small hanky-sized remnant that he would balance on his head or hold in his mouth lest he lose it. Fortunately for him, one of the female orangutans befriended him, and thereafter he sought her protection when others decided to give him head-to-toe physical inspections by pulling at him like a wishbone. Eventually, as Ken grew bolder and more confident, he found his new environment stimulating and the interactions with the other orangs a game. He gave the adult male, Big Bob, a wide distance, wary of the power and prestige that this huge individual enjoyed within the group.

Within a few months Ken was beginning to feel secure and accepted. Like some children, he was lulled into a false sense of independence as he grew, which eventually led to an overbearing confidence that caused him to discount the experience and capabilities of his elders. Big Bob, the group patriarch, mostly tolerated and ignored Ken at first, but as Ken became more annoying, he made the mistake of taking Bob's forbearance as a sign of weakness or capitulation.

As most adult male adult orangutans typically do, Bob spent much of his daily efforts in apparent meditation. His massive body and commanding presence were not designed for playful antics any more, or for juvenile trivia. Failing to engage him in play, Ken decided instead to make a fool of Bob. Capitalizing on his own youthful agility and energy. Ken taunted and tormented him. When Bob was deep in thought, resting on the large telephone-pole climbing structure, Ken would shinny up from behind and pull Bob's flowing dreadlocks. At first Bob tolerated this adolescent play and simply ignored Ken. When his efforts at stirring Bob from his repose failed, Ken would climb underneath and pull on Bob's toes. Still being ignored, Ken escalated the interaction by running along the horizontal beam on the climbing structure, slapping Bob on the leg or head as he dashed past. Becoming more agitated with each growing insult, Bob whirled around and flashed his lips at this little pest. It was clear that Bob was no match for Ken's speed and dexterity, and Ken knew it.

Ken became pleased with his newfound status as aggressor, while the other orangutans watched in apparent awe at his suicidal behavior. He had become a juvenile delinquent. The tables turned abruptly, however, when Bob finally decided to teach his diminutive tormenter a lesson. On a day following one of Ken's outbursts of insubordination, he made the mistake of walking past Bob, who apparently feigned slumber. Without warning and with lightning speed, Bob seized Ken by the ankle and gripped him tight. Surprised, and not knowing if terminal vengeance was coming, Ken screamed as if he had been caught in a steel trap. He beseeched the other orangutans to intervene on his behalf, but no one budged. For an entire day Ken went everywhere that Bob went, shackled like a prisoner in an apelike version of Woody Allen's chain-gang movie *Take the Money and Run*. Up and down the climbing structure, over to the water drinkers, and down against the glass windows, Ken was dragged along like Bob's terrified little doll. Big Bob didn't release his vicelike grip on Ken's ankle until it was time for the group to return to their sleeping bedrooms for their evening meal. The next day, and for many days to come, there was no more hair pulling, no more slapping, and no more taunting. Ken wouldn't get within twenty feet of Big Bob.

In time, as Bob's health failed, Ken replaced him as the group patriarch. Dental disease and an ensuing chronic sinus infection eventually were Bob's undoing. It all started one day when the keeper called to report that he was falling over every time he tried to stand up. The immediate culprit was an inner ear inflammation caused by a sinus infection, which had arisen from an abscessed tooth. After a vigorous course of antibiotics and root canal surgery at the zoo hospital, he bounced back rapidly, but a chronic sinus problem dogged him for months. Despite all of our medical and surgical efforts to cure Bob of his problem, he eventually succumbed. Unbeknownst to us all, he also had chronic heart disease, and he died in my arms despite resuscitation efforts.

Several of us stood teary-eyed as I phoned the zoo director and curator to break the sad news. Ken went on to become the next leader of the orangutans. When a new naturalistic exhibit was constructed, Ken continued to demonstrate his adventuresome skills. He was the only one in the group who managed to find the essential finger- and toeholds on the exhibit walls and escaped to temporary freedom three times before the zoo designers found and eliminated the architectural oversights.

One of the notable successes in retraining a mother took place with Dolly the gorilla. She was captured as a nine-month-old infant in Africa and brought to the San Diego Zoo, and then moved to the zoo's sister facility, the San Diego Wild Animal Park. She had missed the experiences of growing up among gorillas in her early childhood and related more to people than her own kind. When Dolly was ten years old she gave birth to her first baby, but, when the newborn tried to cling to her, she rejected his advances. After six hours of hopeful observation, the baby was removed to the park nursery for his own protection.

Steven Joines, a local graduate student in primate behavior and part-time keeper, collaborated with other keepers and organized innovative efforts for Dolly's reeducation for the next birth. It would be accurate to call this a course in Gorilla Behavior 101. Starting with confidence-building contact behind the scenes, he devoted considerable time to developing personal rapport with Dolly, and then began to introduce her gradually to novel stimuli, including a small pillow. He then transformed the pillow into a sturdy, cream-colored, denim object filled with foam and drew a face on one side. Dolly accepted these baby prototypes readily, and she was encouraged to treat her new object gently. She was taught to hold her pillow as if it were a baby, and she responded to requests that she rotate her pillow baby so that its face was properly oriented toward her own body. Because of her retraining, however, when she was encouraged to "be nice to the baby," she cooperated, and went on to rear it successfully, breaking the cycle of maternal ignorance and neglect.

Bern, Switzerland's old bear pit, c. 1900

6. EXHIBIT MAKING

Creating Zoo Ecosystems

O n a gray, overcast morning I stood by the out-of-the-way exhibit at the appointed time. A notice posted on the entry marquee announced the schedule for the world's shortest animal exhibition, and I was sure not to be late. It was a fairly simple-looking affair as exhibits go in Australian fauna parks—a gravel-bottomed glass aquarium measuring, perhaps, five feet wide, fifteen feet long, and six feet high, sitting under a shady wood canopy. If you were to spend the entire day watching for the grand entrance of the platypus you would be lucky to have it in view for a full twenty minutes, if at all. It might not be active that day and might instead remain secluded in its den. Fortunately, they are usually ravenous little creatures, consuming enormous quantities of worms, crayfish, shrimp, and other aquafauna.

Then, like clockwork, the keeper appeared with a cupful of earthworms and slid open a panel. He plopped them into the water in a wriggling mass that steadily sank bottomward, trailing a slimy cloud of debris. Suddenly, an impish, dark creature with a face like a duck, webbed feet, and a narrow tail swooshed into the water from its hiding chamber. Systematically, it attacked and gobbled down the entire clod of worms. And, just as quickly, after a brief exploration of its tank, the platypus was gone. The exhibition was finished.

Few zoos have exhibited the platypus. For years it seemed nearly impossible to keep them alive in captivity. This creature is a bona fide zoological oddity, and, along with its Australian echidna relatives, is the world's only egg-laying mammal—a mammal being defined as a warm-blooded, haired animal species whose female gives milk. The platypus has a toothless duck beak, with which it forages for invertebrates in its native stream habitat. The eggs have a surprisingly short incubation period of less than two weeks.

The Bronx Zoo's first attempts with platypuses failed to keep them alive for even two months in captivity. The early specimens cost the zoo $25,000 apiece in today's dollars. With their ability to consume half their body weight daily in worms, grubs, and shrimp, the platypus, pound per pound, was one of the most expensive species to keep in the zoo. In captivity, platypuses often died promptly from malnutrition or pneumonia until an Australian naturalist, David Fleay, came along. Fleay was the first to accurately chronicle the behavior of this species, and in 1943 he also was the first to breed and hatch it in captivity—a feat which has seldom been repeated since. Fleay was engaged by the New York Zoological Park to assist in its next attempt. It managed to keep platypus alive for some years, but still without reproductive success.

Platypuses are supposed to be completely protected in Australia, but they have a penchant for becoming entangled in man's plastic litter, nets, traps, fishhooks, and discarded fishing lines. Their capture and export to zoos has been banned for years. The keys to platypus husbandry include the prevention of hypothermia, stress, malnutrition, and infections. This is no small feat, however, but it is critically aided by proper housing arrangements. Fleay constructed their captive nesting areas in such a way that required the platypuses to climb through a narrow wooden chute that was lined with rubber squeegee blades. As they pressed along the snug passageway to return from water to the den, the moisture was effectively scraped from their hair coat, allowing them to dry off readily in the comfort of their nesting compartments. Captive platypus spend over 90 percent of their time in the seclusion of their dens. The wild platypus figured this squeegee thing out long ago, and they favor tight streamside burrows for their hideaways.

Barred exhibits at the New York Zoological Park, c. 1900

The earliest animal collections were private royal menageries that excluded the general public. Public animal displays in cities offered the confined viewing of captive wild animals in makeshift cages or walled pits, where they were difficult to care for, sometimes dangerous, and often victims of the curious eyes and taunts of the general public. The early perceptions of wild animals often placed them in the context of dangerous wild beasts. Their medical care was practically nonexistent, and it is no wonder that some of the earliest concerns for animal welfare in Europe focused on the plight of these pathetic creatures. Even earlier, in Europe's darker days, animals were

Zoological incarceration-style bear exhibit

put on trial occasionally for injuries they caused to humans! The first public zoos tended merely to the basics, providing visitors with the rudimentary opportunity, however unnatural, to see live wildlife curiosities for the first time. Only the most affluent adventurer could view animals in their wilderness habitats. They were displayed as caged specimens, taxonomically arranged, focusing on comparative anatomy and evolution. Little information about their ecology and behavior was provided to visitors; indeed, much of this was poorly known at the time.

In the zoo world, "cage" is a dirty word. Zoo animals are no longer allowed to live in cages, as it projects a feeling of sterile, cold, insensitive living conditions. It is also a reminder of what zoos are no longer supposed to be. Instead, terms like "captive environment," "zoo habitat," and other more politically cozy designations are being substituted for the "C" word. When all is said and done, however, a "cage" or a "habitat" represents the physical world that limits an animal's resources. A poorly designed or managed "captive ecosystem" is no better than a lousy cage. Zoo animals are entirely reliant upon their keepers for comfort, ambient temperature control, sanitation, food resources, social prospects, and, ultimately, their longevity. In nearly every respect, exhibiting animals in captivity is analogous to a journey on a spaceship, where the quality and dependability of the life support systems determine the well-being of the passengers.

Zoo exhibits have changed dramatically since their beginnings, and, like impressionist paintings, their public purpose in today's zoo is to create an illusion for the viewer. They are human versions and perspectives of the natural world and thereby have an innate bias toward the human orientation. From an animal's standpoint, however, exhibits take on much more pragmatic meanings. An exhibit determines the artificial limits of an animal's territory, and it should be judged by both the quality and quantity of space it provides, including the usable vertical and horizontal dimensions.

The next big revolution in zoos attempted to eliminate the viewing of the animals from pit railings and through unsightly bars and wires. The privately owned Hagenbeck Tierpark in Hamburg, Germany, constructed in the early twentieth century, became best known for the use of open, moat-enclosed exhibits, for which Carl Hagenbeck was even granted a patent in 1896. Of course, moats are no strangers to European castles and fortresses, though their intentions were usually to exclude intruders rather than confine the inhabitants. By their nature, moats err on the side of security rather than safety. The exhibit moats are usually dry rather than water-filled, although numerous "monkey islands" and other exhibits have been built in zoos with water barriers, sometimes to the peril of the animals. Some American zoo directors were put off by Hagenbeck's pseudo-geologic exhibit rockwork and his penchant for mixing animals together, which was contrary to the traditional zoo paradigm. The best examples of natural geologic exhibit backdrops in America were executed by projects at the Denver and St. Louis zoos in the early 1900s, when actual plaster castings of natural cliff faces were used to form the concrete zoo structures.

Moats and fences are constructed to confine animals in proportion to their capabilities for escape. Hedges, plantings, and rocks were used to conceal the moats and support facilities from the visitors. Though more complicated in seasonal climates, some of the larger zoos began to make a gradual shift to open, diorama-style animal displays that had been popularized in natural history museums. Uncluttered by traditional fortress-like visual obstructions, at least during good weather, bears, tigers, lions, and hoofed animals were observed from walkways that meandered past their airy compounds. This provided the exhilarating illusion that virtually nothing was separating the public from the beasts, and it often offered sightlines and overlapping

The Hagenbeck Tierpark's exhibit panorama

vistas that encompassed scenes of both predators and prey. A few zoos, such as the San Diego Zoo, beneficiaries of a subtropical climate, developed an early distinct flavor of their own because seasonal shifts to gymnasium-like indoor quarters were not a winter necessity.

As zoos experimented with moated displays, their grounds became a patchwork of old and renovated attempts at zoo design. Despite the desire to modernize exhibits, they often failed to provide convincing environments, borrowing more from contemporary architecture than from nature. Experimentation by architects and zoo planners has gradually honed the concept of naturalistic exhibits, beginning most notably in Seattle's Woodland Park Zoo in the 1970s. In collaboration with David Hancocks and zoo veterinarian Dr. Jim Foster, Jones & Jones Architects developed innovative African savanna and gorilla exhibits as part of a long-range plan to redevelop that zoo. Jones & Jones has become the dominant architecture firm internationally in zoo master planning and design, promoting the melding of animal, people, and service spaces into indistinguishable juxtapositions where boundaries are indiscernible, and organic materials and landscaping obliterate the structural elements that would disclose the illusion of naturalness. Several zoos have undertaken the construction of naturalistic exhibits without the essential outside expertise, only to learn in the end that this process is considerably more complex in the details than perceived. Because these projects are deceptively simple on the surface, shortcuts have spawned some embarrassing failures.

Many techniques are rigidly employed to accomplish these images and depart sharply from the older display conventions in zoos. Gone is the foreboding architecture of formal buildings that displayed human wealth and power, often taking the shape of castles and temples—segregating animals taxonomically into carnivore houses, monkey houses, and pachyderm palaces. Contemporary zoo architects sometimes refer to these older structures as "incarceration architecture." Their replacements are zoogeographic assemblies of animals that derive from the same continents or major ecosystems, blended in a manner that attempts to communicate ecological relationships. An essential departure from older exhibits is the viewing perspective—except for aquatic environments, nearly all terrestrial displays orient the observer to looking across or up at the animals, rather than down upon them. These perspectives are illustrated in the exhibits shown in the following photographs. Unlike the unrehearsed performances of old zoos, the new zoos are created in the form of a "zoological theater," where the moods, backgrounds, and actors have been carefully orchestrated to control visitors' senses from the time they enter the front gate. To complete their economic as well as their aesthetic and scientific missions, the constant challenge becomes the awkward transitions to visitor amenities such as food service, gift shops, and restrooms, which compete with the auras that the exhibits strive to foster.

First and foremost, an animal exhibit has to confine its inhabitants reliably. In the case of dangerous carnivores, the safety of the public is the paramount consideration. If it works out that the zoo veterinarian can capture the animal by chemically darting it, that's a bonus. But security guards in zoos are authorized to protect the public's safety first, and they give little latitude to a dangerous animal. In the 1930s, on the Fourth of July—the busiest attendance day of the year—a bear escaped from an exhibit that was being remodeled at the San Diego Zoo. As Mrs. Belle Benchley, the zoo director, and Dr. Wegeforth, the president of the zoological society, dined in the zoo café, an armed security guard shot the bear to death as it approached a large crowd of

Atlanta Zoo mock rock tiger exhibit

people nearby. During the escape of a zoo tiger in Poland, not only did policemen shoot the tiger, but they also accidentally shot and killed the zoo veterinarian who was attempting to sedate it with a tranquilizer gun. In another Polish incident an escaped circus tiger attacked and killed a veterinarian who was attempting to shoot it with a tranquilizer dart. Curiously, tigers are involved in dangerous zoo animal escapes and personnel injuries far out of proportion to their numbers in captivity.

When a new naturalistic orangutan exhibit was finally built in San Diego with authentic-looking rock cliff faces, our troublesome, now grown-up, orangutan Ken Allen escaped three times. We were considering changing his name to Houdini before workmen finally succeeded in eliminating the essential finger- and toeholds he used to climb out. On the first occasion he was found on the viewing deck sitting near a clueless tourist who thought this new ape exhibit, with the tame, trained animals, was the best he had seen in any zoo. The zoo spokespersons proficiently turned these embarrassing liberations into a series of lighthearted stories about the escapades of a loveable ape. In another zoo, however, the escape of a chimpanzee ended without a whimsical public-relations spin. The chimp left the zoo grounds and climbed a telephone pole in a nearby neighborhood. When the zoo veterinarian darted her with a tranquilizer, she fell, grabbed a power line, and was electrocuted.

Zoos must have plans to deal with the escape of large and dangerous animals. Some zoos classify animal escapes as "Code Green" situations, where the event in progress threatens the safety of visitors and personnel. And escape they do, in zoos around the world—chimpanzees, elephants, gorillas, leopards, lions, polar bears, rhinos, tigers, and other less intimidating creatures have managed to jump barriers, break down gates, or be liberated by one human misstep or another. A surprising number result in no major injuries, but the possibilities for disaster are sobering. In Tokyo's Ueno Zoo, a semiannual drill is conducted to simulate a polar bear escape to prepare for the possibility of earthquake damage to zoo exhibits. An employee in a cartoon bear costume runs around the zoo pretending to attack visitors while the staff practices their procedures to contain and recapture the bear, ultimately "tranquilizing" it and carrying it off in a blanket.

To account for the misbehavior of the public, some precautions are necessary to keep people from maliciously interfering with animals or readily entering exhibit spaces, although this has become increasingly difficult with the contemporary style of open spaces that lack walls and bars. As a veterinary student, I participated in a postmortem examination of Barney, a large male hippopotamus that had died acutely at the Detroit Zoo. He had been brought to the Michigan State University veterinary diagnostic laboratory, where we found him to be in overall good weight and condition. A thorough examination inside, however, revealed a rubber ball lodged in his small intestine, causing a fatal obstruction that resulted in peritonitis, shock, and death. Gaping hippos have been historical targets of mischievous zoo visitors.

Through their actions, zoo intruders have found their way into carnivore exhibits. One deranged person scaled the lion exhibit wall in a California zoo one night, leaving behind only scant remains when the keepers cleaned the exhibit the following day. At the National Zoo a paranoid schizophrenic climbed a fence and swam a moat to reach a pride of lions that devoured her. A number of suicides in zoos have occurred by people jumping into tiger and lion exhibits, and over the years some incidents have occurred when inebriated visitors—during and after hours—managed to come into fatal proximity to dangerous animals.

The following 1999 incident was the consequence of an alleged practical joke by "friends":

Man thrown into lion's den

Police in South Africa say a man was mauled by a lion in Pretoria Zoo after three men threw him over a fence and into the animal's den. Workers threw stones to distract the lion's attention and zoo staff sedated it, enabling rescuers to save the injured man. He suffered wounds to his arms, legs and chest and was said to be in a stable condition in hospital—though police say he was still too disorientated to make a statement.

Others have been due simply to flawed judgment:

Tiger kills youth in safari park

Eighteen-year-old Mohammed Khaja was mauled to death by a tiger at the Nehru Zoological Park here on Tuesday afternoon when he fell into the Tiger Safari park trying to catch a kite after clambering a 20 ft. wall and a steel mesh atop it. This is the second such incident in the safari park. Five years ago, a boy entered into it in search of a ball after having a bet with his friends that he would fetch it.

Captivity does not always spare zoo animals from local predators. Before zoos were enclosed with perimeter security fences, intrusions by stray dogs were fairly common. More nimble raccoons and foxes still take an occasional toll on captive avifauna in zoos. When the San Diego Wild Animal Park first opened in the Southern California back country, mountain lions shared in the cornucopia of exotic antelopes. To deter the still abundant coyotes, the perimeter fences of the large enclosures were further secured with "predator wiring"—fashioned by attaching metal fabric to the outside bottom of the fence and burying it horizontally to deter digging along the perimeter.

Finally, local wildlife occasionally find themselves accidental captives in zoological gardens. In the Steiner Zoo and Animal Orphanage in Monrovia, Liberia, a large python was found in the zoo's poultry pen one morning. Slithering between the cage wires at night, it consumed several of the avian inhabitants. When it attempted to depart with its belly full of fowl, it was trapped—its enhanced girth could no longer pass between wires and it became a zoo exhibit.

Occasionally, behind-the-scenes visitors, even celebrities, become involved in injuries in their desire to get up close and personal with zoo animals. When actress

Sharon Stone, of *Basic Instinct* movie fame, came to the Los Angeles Zoo with her husband Phil Bronstein, they received a VIP tour of the Komodo dragon lizard exhibit to visit and pet one of the "tamer" specimens. Here is part of the keeper's official accident report describing what happened next:

> I entered the exhibit first to touch the animal and talk to it. "Komo" was gentle and calm, so I invited one guest (the man "Phil") to come in. As he was stepping in, I noticed he was wearing white shoes and white socks. I asked Phil to step out of the exhibit because I knew "Komo" was excited by white objects (they look like the rats he eats).
>
> Phil asked me if he could take his shoes and socks off and go in barefoot. I said okay because I had never known the animal to be aggressive or excited by human skin. . . . Phil knelt next to the animal while I knelt on the other side to watch and possibly pick up "Komo" so Phil could be in the photo. Special guest Sharon Stone took a photo and was about to take another. At this time, "Komo," without warning, bit Phil on his left foot and held on. I grabbed "Komo" by his neck and yelled at him. He let go after an estimated one or two seconds. After a delay of 10 to 15 seconds Phil stepped out of the exhibit.
>
> The victim "Phil" was on his back on the floor and Sharon had already tied one of his white socks around the wound and this stopped the bleeding. Sharon had Phil's leg raised and he seemed to be breathing fast. I told him he was going to be fine . . . we got ice and cold packs and a towel and newspapers for Phil to rest his head on.
>
> I suggested washing the wound with surgical scrub—Sharon and victim Phil refused this first aid. By this time Security had arrived to help comfort Phil and he seemed calm. Sharon was concerned that the bite was venomous, so I quickly assured her and Phil that the animal was non-venomous.

Phil, and the keeper, apparently failed to foresee that offering a bare foot to a meat-eating dragon might appeal to its basic instincts.

Nearly all zoos today have experimented with moated exhibits, going back to Carl Hagenbeck's fundamental concept of barrier-free viewing. In the case of dangerous animals, the physical dimensions of the enclosures must be competently determined. More than one zoo has been surprised when, under extraordinary fear or stress, some animals that have been confined safely within their moated exhibits (bears, tigers, lions) managed to escape when alarmed. We have all heard parallel accounts

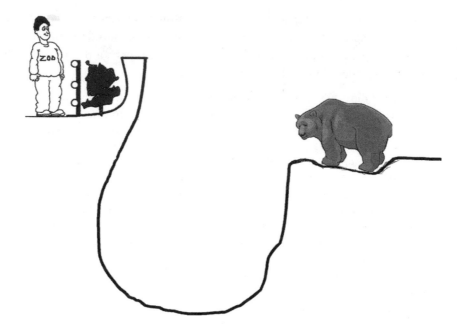

Zoo carnivore moat profile

of athletic feats during stress, such as little old ladies moving overturned automobiles to free a loved one. When sufficiently alarmed, some zoo animals have jumped moats and scaled walls that had held them captive for years.

The elevation on the public side of the exhibit moat is usually higher than on the carnivore side in order to make any attempt at jumping the moat span more difficult. Other techniques for foiling attempts to scale the public side of the moat wall include terracing the exhibit platform downward toward the public, and curving the moat face inward at the bottom on the public side. Large carnivores are usually confined at night off the exhibit area into smaller, more secure holding areas. One evening in San Diego, when a windstorm felled several trees in the zoo, night security guards went busily around inspecting animal enclosures for damage and found a huge eucalyptus tree limb straddling one of the bear exhibit moats. Fearing the worst, the security officer grabbed his flashlight and scanned the exhibit for the bear that had access to the outside area. Just as he approached the limb, he met the bear face-to-face on its way

St. Louis Zoo bear exhibit dry moat, c. 1920

out. He gave the bear a whack on the head with his light. The bear fell backward into the moat, where it spent the rest of the night under an armed guard until the arrival of the tree removal crew at dawn.

Hoofed animals are particularly prone to encounters with exhibit barriers and, when alarmed, are often oblivious to physical obstacles in their paths. Chain link fences and sprayed-concrete and cement-block walls have caused serious and fatal injuries when panicked antelope, deer, and zebra take flight straight into them. Newly arrived animals, unaccustomed to their new roommates and exhibit surroundings, are particularly at risk from panic injuries, and they must be handled carefully and quietly until they adjust. Any strange sound or object may set them off and put them to flight. Improved systems for moving and sedating animals in zoo hospital settings now often utilize padded walls and floors, subdued lighting and suppressed acoustics in order to reduce the stress and excitement induced by handling procedures.

St. Louis Zoo bear exhibit water moat, c. 1920

Temporary sight barriers, such as cloth or plastic fencing, are often installed in exhibits to make physical boundaries more obvious to newly introduced animals. I escorted the shipment of a white rhinoceros to the Los Angeles Zoo, where the staff had arranged for a construction crane to lift the huge transport crate over the wall and into the exhibit. As the door was opened with a rope, the rhino backed out of the crate, and snorted with alarm when she noticed a large gray object in front of her. In keeping with her species, which is notorious for both spontaneity and lack of visual acuity, the rhino charged and hit a large boulder at full speed, breaking her horn off flush with her face.

The fences and moats that are employed to contain hoofed animals in zoos are frequently psychological as much as physical barriers. The size and dimensions of these exhibits are often based on a perception of what is called an animal's "flight distance." Typically, this is the minimum amount of space that the animal allows between itself and a novel situation. In the wild, this is the distance at which it ordinarily runs from,

Himayalan tahr "turn-back" fence

or attacks, an intruder. Captive flight distances are much shorter than in wild animals since most animals become adapted to the presence of humans, other animals, and zoo vehicles. If confined to a small area behind the exhibit in what zoo people call "catch pens," however, animals can explode in fear if spooked, causing serious injury to themselves. Some species, such as the wild goats, are so agile that they can easily run around a small room or pen, bounding from wall to wall without touching the floor. These animals must be confined in fenced areas (solid or metal fabric) with "turn-backs," which are slanted appendages at the top of a fence that angle inward, making it more difficult for a nimble hoofed animal to scale.

Regardless of their benefits, the larger, more naturalistic animal exhibits should always be judged both from the public and the animal points of view. Despite the spacious appearance of an exhibit, is that space actually available and valuable to the animals? Even though the front of an exhibit may be aesthetically pleasing, do the

Pronghorn exhibit profile, San Antonio Zoo

support facilities out of the public view provide improved resources for the inhabitants? In other words, how much is illusion and how much is real substance? Animals live only part of their existences on the stage set for the zoo public. Is it a Hollywood movie set with mere wooden props holding up the building fronts like a fake Western town, or are there real general stores, saloons, and quality hotels behind those exhibit facades? The current status of every zoo, and the environments they offer their inhabitants, should be candidly judged by the actual conditions they provide, not by idealized visions of what they might become.

It is revealing to observe the behavior of zoo patrons as they browse through exhibits, totally bypassing some enclosures as if they were drab vacant lots. After a simple glance at one of these failures, visitors ordinarily pass it by, often not bothering to determine if something is alive inside. An Australian zoo I once visited had a prominent, blunt sign in front of one of their exhibit tragedies that simply declared, "This Ugly To Be Demolished Soon." Shortly after arriving in San Diego, I walked behind a group of zoo visitors and decided to have a closer look at one of the exhibits they had

Cougar exhibit profile, San Antonio Zoo

shunned. Inside a chain-link clad enclosure, about the size of a U-Haul van, was a beautiful, small, solitary cat, asleep on a concrete shelf with its back to the public, surrounded by moldy looking rock and a cement floor. Not a single plant or soft surface was present, and the attempt at a pool was a stark looking concrete box into which water dribbled from a small rusty pipe. The animal, bored and alone, had nothing to do. The enclosure had all the charm of a prison. Nearly every zoo still has these sorts of remainders on their grounds that are gradually being replaced. Every successful animal exhibit must overcome the oppressive sensation of confinement, and this one failed on all accounts. Any takeaway message about the biology or conservation of an animal species falls flat on its face when the predominant impression of an exhibit is one of incarceration.

Zoo visitors occasionally take the time and effort to express their likes and dislikes to zoo management, as these individuals did in these actual patron reports after they visited a major western zoo:

Patron Report

Problem: On Friday the 14th of January my family and I came to the zoo. One of the reasons in particular that I decided to come to your zoo was because in your web site that I accessed Dingoes was mentioned as one of the animals you have. You see, I was participating in a scavenger hunt and one of the items that I needed was a picture of a Dingo. Well, when I got there and inquired where the Dingo was, I was informed that the Dingo was no longer there. I was very disappointed to say the least. We drove all the way from Las Vegas to get this picture. If I would have known the Dingoes were not there, I would have selected another zoo. —John C.

Suggestion to correct or improve the situation: For my inconvenience I am requesting a full refund. A copy of the receipt is attached.

Patron Report

Problem: For the last three visits here (different hours) the animals are always sleeping. It greatly disturbs me.

Suggestion to correct or improve the situation: Check to make sure the animals are not sick. Do something to make them more active. —Shallon R.

Patron Report

Problem: All I see is butt all day. Animals sick looking like they are about to die. That's the problem. I want my eight dollars and twenty-five cents back.

Suggestion to correct or improve the situation: Clean up the animals. Less pay. More animals. Feed them three times a day. —Veronica B.

Patron Report

Problem: The Chilean flamingoes smell worse every time I come. I almost vomited today.

Suggestion to correct or improve the situation: Clean the exhibit more often? —Clara M.

Patron Report

Problem: While observing the gorillas, a black one threw a pebble or small stone in my direction and it broke the left lens of my photo tint prescription glasses with rhinestones all around both sides of the frame. The break is from top to bottom. I need my glasses to see.

Suggestion to correct or improve the situation: Very urgent—I don't have a spare pair of glasses. —Gayle P.

Patron Report

Problem: Gorilla threw his waste, landing in my baby stroller resulting in having to throw out the stroller.

Suggestion to correct or improve the situation: Post a warning to the possibilities of what may occur. —Michael S.

An entrepreneur friend once told me a little story when the subject of animal exhibits came up in a discussion. He was in the business of exporting various types of top-quality cooking utensils to premium markets overseas, and he had several major customers in Japan. On one occasion he was visited by two Japanese buyers who toured his showroom looking for new items to import. Out of all of the expensive cookware and dining accessories that they perused, they finally focused on a small, inexpensive white microwave-safe rice bowl and immediately placed a large order for this item alone. They were so ecstatic about their purchase that nothing else in the inventory interested them. On a trip to Japan several months later this same businessman paid a reciprocal visit to his Japanese buyers and discovered what had become of the bowls. In their elegant showroom in Tokyo their newly featured product was prominently displayed on a handsome hardwood table that was covered with an ornate, hand-woven tapestry. In the center of the table was an exquisitely lacquered, hinged rosewood box lined with red satin and velvet. Nestled within this box, with grace and simple beauty, was a solitary white microwave-safe rice bowl. In Japanese culture, the presentation of a gift is often more important than the object itself. A \$3 rice bowl had been transformed into a \$250 treasure. This same lesson could be applied to every animal exhibit in a zoo. I haven't visited any Japanese zoos, however, to see if they have followed their own cultural predilections with captive wildlife.

Zoo animal collections have often been rated by the numbers of species they hold. Large ones are frequently referred to as "postage stamp" animal collections in the zoo trade, where the numbers and kinds of animals possessed, rather than the quality of their existences, was the way of keeping score. Zoos with fish collections squeezed every minnow into their statistics in order to compete in this inflated numbers marathon. Then insects became popular and skewed the numbers game completely. Eventually, however, the emphasis has shifted more to the quality and aesthetics of the visitor experience, which is greatly influenced by the perceptions of how natural and content the animals appear to be. The consciousness of the public has changed. Many people no longer settle for sideshow types of displays, although most still demand to be entertained. The arklike collections have given way to more specialization and to thematic animal assemblies, where breeding success and naturalism trump sheer numbers.

It is a given in most zoos that at least six animal types are mandatory in order to appease the public's most fundamental expectations—apes and monkeys, big cats and carnivores, elephants and rhinos, giraffes, pretty birds, and fearsome reptiles. Zoo public-relations staffs lobby for new attractions that they can zestfully promote, such as San Diego's "SuperCroc" exhibit or Brookfield Zoo's Ituri Forest exhibit. With enough creativity, however, even diminutive, near-blind animals like the Pittsburgh Zoo's naked mole rats, which weigh in at only two ounces, can be whimsical attendance magnets. With a clever marketing campaign, they attracted a loyal media and visitor following, generating renewed visitor zoo attendance and T-shirt and souvenir sales. Several zoos, realizing the appeal of such microfauna, now have Internet-based "Rat Cams" to cultivate the public's ongoing curiosity about these offbeat exhibits.

The best and most interesting zoo exhibits usually contain family groups of animals. This requires reproductive success to sustain, more husbandry expertise than static pairs and an ongoing capacity to find homes for the surplus offspring. Several major schools of thought prevail on how zoos should exhibit animals. In the more dynamic and aggressive style, exhibits are mini-representations of the classic ecosystems or habitats of the earth, such as rainforests, deserts, or savannas. In fact, the main thing that separates this school from the others is money. A "naturalistic" (not to be confused with "natural") exhibit must convey an "impression" of authenticity to the visitor. It must look real and transcend the mundane. The far greater challenge, however, is to make that artificial exhibit truly meaningful to its animal inhabitants; this takes more considerable insight, money, and time to plan and implement. The present generation of exhibit planners in zoos must continue to address seriously and define exhibit success by rigorous self-assessment of their projects. Unfortunately, there are few objective criteria yet available by which to rate the effectiveness of an exhibit from the animals' point of view. Perhaps tomorrow's zoo biologists will develop useful models for making these assessments. Already there are researchers compiling detailed inventories of animal species' behavioral characteristics called ethograms. One approach of these assessments will be to correlate the diversity of captive vs. wild repertoires as measures of behavioral fidelity in captivity.

Accurate information is entirely lacking on what percentage of the average exhibit project budget is devoted to strictly animal vs. strictly people needs. I would venture a guess that the costs of people amenities, such as aesthetics and viewing logistics, easily outweigh the functionality costs attributable to animals' needs alone. One of the costs of an exhibit that I propose should be obligatory for all exhibitors of endangered species is a sort of conservation tax. Perhaps 5 percent of the construction budget should go into a conservation research fund to benefit that species in the wild. Bring this notion up at a zoo staff meeting, however, as I have, and some people may stare at you as if you just emerged from a Martian spacecraft. For a $5 million gorilla exhibit, that would be $250,000 for the conservation of wild gorillas—enough to fund the startup of a new national park in some parts of Africa.

The newer naturalistic exhibits are far more expensive propositions than yesterday's animal displays, but they still tend to emphasize popular, charismatic species. Their construction often involves corporate sponsors and support from community bond issues and revenue taxes. Simulating nature well in a zoo or rehabilitated wild habitat is costly, which is why the economics of protecting natural ecosystems is so self-evident. Animals have far less trouble reproducing than in surviving habitat loss and human disturbances. Captive propagation, as a primary conservation strategy, should be reserved for the emergency cases.

Today's megazoo exhibits often take the form of major redevelopment projects and are usually multistaged, as parts of master plans to reinvent a zoo as a whole. Rather than striking the viewer as two-dimensional monoliths, these eco-replicas are layered presentations, meant to be viewed and sensed from multiple viewpoints, in a sort of ecological striptease that reveals its subjects gradually—more like discovering animals in the wild. Microviews of animals are replacing the crowded railings of spectators, requiring the visitor to become, instead, an observer, working at it a little for the reward of glimpsing an animal. Viewing rights are being supplanted by viewing privileges. Lush meandering paths are replacing exhibit plazas. The emphasis of these exhibits is on customizing the animal encounter so that it resembles a personal foray into natural habitat, as opposed to yesteryear's parade past an array of bleak cement boxes. Just don't go for the experience on a busy day! My general advice about visiting a popular zoo—be there when the gates first open on a weekday morning.

Realistic rock surfaces made of colored concretes are carefully cast using textured templates, incorporating authentic looking, air-brushed mineral stains, incrustations of lichens, and, yes, simulated, state-of-the-art bird droppings. Relying on the botanical contributions to contribute to a sense of authenticity, there is a heavy emphasis on horticultural plantings. The popular architectural designation for this approach is "landscape immersion." The overall objective is to provide the visitor with a sensation of being within the exhibit environment, without perceptions of barriers, or even being in a zoo at all. Compared to the original Hagenbeck-style exhibit, where the visitor was placed on the outside looking in, immersion exhibits attempt to engulf the visitor within the exhibit itself. Today's Hagenbeck Tierpark has been surpassed by newer exhibit paradigms in scores of modern zoos, surrendering its status as the old benchmark for zoological exhibition.

The technology of replicating natural surfaces has advanced tremendously in recent decades with several notable contractors in the United States. Artificial trees, stumps, and bark lend realism and durability to the close-up details. The Arizona-Sonora Desert Museum and its building consultants set some of the contemporary rockwork standards that other zoos have sought to emulate. Much of the older fake rockwork attempts in zoos now look like garish backdrops at cheap amusement parks or lunar landscapes. Today's tumbling waterfalls, shady passageways, boggy mists, buzzing insect acoustics, and clearwater ponds add realism to exhibits, capturing stimulating sensations of sound, motion, and solitude. All are intended to add new dimensions to the visitors' "adventure" and lead them with anticipation to a tantalizing proximity to animals, who bask in the exhibit spotlights. Too often still, however, more space is allocated to the visitors than the visited, and the design is strongly influenced by managements' compulsions to have animals on exhibit for the public at all times, offering fewer opportunities for seclusion or privacy.

The underlying challenge of naturalistic exhibit-making is in creating a finely finished experience that is enticing to viewers, enriching for animals, and functional from an operational standpoint. Today's visitors don't want to go to a zoo that *feels* like a zoo. Most of the core housing and animal management infrastructures are buried in bunkers behind and beneath the exhibit facades, away from the sight and minds of the visitors—the zoo they never see. Requiring large amounts of capital, these are ambitious undertakings involving commitments to future planning. This approach has become the norm in evolving major zoological gardens such as in Atlanta, Basel, Denver, New Orleans, Orlando, New York, San Diego, Seattle, and St. Louis. One of my favorites is the Northern Trail exhibit at Seattle's Woodland Park Zoo. The striking result of the new exhibits, from a visitor's standpoint, is the shift in their perspectives and, hopefully, their perceptions of animals. Patience, reverence, and respect are better cultivated through these exhibit experiences, in contrast to the more carnival values of traditional cement jungles.

Teaching visitors about nature in their own backyards is being undertaken in zoos in order to connect with the zoo-going public on local *and* global environmental issues. Whereas zoos have been prone to elevate and emphasize so-called charismatic mega-vertebrates (large, popular species such as gorillas, elephants and giant pandas), some are turning homeward to showcase their own local wildlife, and lesser species, in order to instruct the public in biology and conservation. The urbanization of America has disconnected many people from direct experiences with both wildlife and domestic livestock. For some, this change has been a homecoming. Common swampland exhibits and temperate climate pond and woodland habitats are examples of the local emphasis in some zoo exhibits. This familiarity is used as a bridge between the visitor and everyday lessons in ecology. In the end, the greater goal should be to create more informed and enlightened citizens, who will, it is hoped, have the conscience and motivation to educate themselves about, and support, appropriate environmental measures in the form of relevant legislation, research, and public policy. These types of thoughtful and inspirational naturalistic exhibits, when done well, can utilize common species, as well described by Dr. William Conway, the long-time director of the New York Bronx Zoo, whose favorite example was a common bullfrog exhibit. While a well-orchestrated animal exhibit of the lowliest creatures can work miracles of understanding for animal and environmental conservation issues, a poor one can quickly deflate the magic of even the world's most charismatic and endangered fauna.

Several images stick in my mind as measures of how far zoos have come since I started as a zoo veterinarian. The big male gorilla I saw during my veterinary school days visit to the Lincoln Park Zoo in Chicago occupied a bare cage whose only internal fixtures were a resting bench and a platform scale. This occasionally permitted the

Educated chimpanzees dining at the London Zoo, c. 1900

public to verify how much he weighed, a play upon our pop-culture fascination with mega-apes such as King Kong and Godzilla. At about that same time, the Cincinnati Zoo still had trained chimpanzees that entertained visitors by riding little motorcycles around in a circle. For years, the St. Louis bears also rode motorcycles, while the chimpanzees dressed up as members of a swing band, wielding trombones and drumsticks. Meanwhile, in San Diego, a monkey was exhibited without a cage, wearing a waist tether that permitted him to travel between trees parallel to a visitors' moving sidewalk by means of a ring attached to a long wire. Even earlier, numerous zoos featured young apes and monkeys in people clothes in tea parties, where they demonstrated their abilities to drink milk from a glass, eat with a spoon from a bowl, and perform other examples of humanoid table etiquette.

Offbeat animal attractions still survive yesterday's showmanship efforts, such as the display of atypically white or albino specimens. Snowflake, the Barcelona Zoo go-

Early tortoise ride at the New York Zoological Park

rilla that died in 2003, was perhaps the most notable albino animal. But albino snakes, alligators, koalas, kangaroos, and other pink-eyed, white specimens are often displayed in zoos, as well as the occasional two-headed snake, such as the late Dudley Duplex and the late Thelma and Louise, the San Diego Zoo's bicephalic king and corn snakes. Experts on these oddities describe some of the challenges that arise from this condition, such as conflict over which direction to travel, which head decides that it is time to eat, or, even more troubling, which head will swallow the prey. Sev-

Mike the chimpanzee walks a tightrope at the St. Louis Zoo

Rollerskating chimpanzees at the Detroit Zoo in the 1940s

eral instances have been observed where one head has attacked the other head. In defense of these creatures, and their supposed rightful place in zoos, Gordon Burghardt, a herpetologist at the University of Tennessee, asserts, "These animals shouldn't be looked at as freaks. They're organisms with motivations and individuality just like any other. They provide us with an opportunity to study cooperation [or perhaps the lack of it] and the processes of controlling the same body with two nervous systems. Studying them might provide some insight into the survival issues faced by Siamese twins." Perhaps I hadn't given due consideration to this less than compelling medical angle, but, justifications aside, such creatures do consistently provoke acute visual and mental perturbation in zoo visitors.

Most zoo animal collections are now being organized biogeographically, rather than by animal species groups, a system that used to have all the cats, monkeys, great apes, parrots, and other like creatures lumped into separate areas of the zoo. Animals in biogeographic exhibits are from common ecological settings. These exhibits are often made up of mixed species to convey a more cohesive impression of an African or South American rainforest or savanna. Some attempts at mixed species groupings have had mixed results, and add a new level of complexity to providing veterinary care. A group of Diana monkeys in one zoo had been integrated with gorillas and seemed to be getting along just fine for months without incident. One day, as the zoo director stood in front of the viewing glass speaking with visitors, a gorilla suddenly seized one of the monkeys, and, as horrified guests looked on, the gorilla decapitated it and ate the remains. Other zoos have found that zebras and Mongolian wild horses can be very predatory upon baby antelopes in mixed exhibits and have had to segregate them.

Without question, the most interesting animal exhibits display family groups, whether it is primates or meerkats, those small, weasel-like creatures from Africa (Timon is the meerkat featured in Disney's *Lion King*). They stand on their hind legs like little Grinches. The activity and social repertoires of intact social groups of animals provide the enrichment that animates an exhibit in the most intricate ways. Zoos need more meerkat and naked mole rat types of exhibits. The public always seems to connect the most, intellectually and emotionally, with the primates. The evolutionary relationship of monkeys and the great apes to people provides a sense of kinship that humans find irresistible.

Designing meaningful exhibits in zoos is phenomenally complex and difficult. Using a metaphor, one might regard this visually by picturing a large tree. The leaves and branches of the tree represent the more visible portion of an exhibit, whereas the roots underground are the invisible, but critical, infrastructure that supports and nourishes everything above. These rooted elements of the project are critical to the flow of personnel, food, and services to the exhibit.

The two major aspects of the design of successful animal exhibits are aesthetics and functionality. Special care is required to assure that neither is unduly compromised. Rather than claim that one is more important than the other, it is most constructive when both aesthetics and functionality are wedded. Building a new animal habitat is an expensive and complex undertaking, one bound to be executed with a sense of trepidation. After all, no one wants to be affiliated with a $5 million flop—whether it is a movie or a zoo exhibit. Unlike a dud movie that can straggle on in video stores generating some residual revenues, an exhibit bomb stands as a monument to the failed vision of its creators.

To lessen these risks somewhat, a significant portion of each project needs to be devoted to the "programming" and "design" phases in order to prevent elephants from tipping into moats and apes from scaling the walls. The animals themselves are the silent stakeholders who must rely upon people to provide suitable environments. Their agendas must be articulated by humans, who, for better or worse, add their own interpretations to their needs. The key players in this process are:

1. The animals. One of the proposed inhabitants should be appointed to the design group and be referred to deferentially by the other team members throughout the whole process. Team members can take turns being a spokesperson and advocate for this silent member.

2. Keepers, who generally report to the curators and are charged with caring for the animals in the exhibit that is being designed.

3. Curators, who manage the animal collection and have primary responsibilities for breeding and exhibit programs.

4. Veterinarians, whose job is to prevent and control disease, as well as to treat illness and support the management of animals for curators, keepers and applied research.

5. Physical services departments, which supply the plumbers, maintenance workers and groundskeepers to keep the exhibit physically fit and running.

6. The zoo director, who represents the board of trustees or city government, fiscal managers, marketing, and public relations staff.

A key element that binds this team together is a capable and experienced architect.

Their individual points of interaction with the exhibited animals influence the priorities of each of these groups. Because nearly everything eventually affects animal health, the veterinarian has an especially important role in bridging the gaps between these interests. The zoo director wants an exhibit that is appealing to the public and that will bolster the public's patronage of the zoo. Gate revenues, and the things that drive them, set exhibit priorities in most zoos. Exhibits have to draw the public into the zoo, and, it is hoped, create opportunities for secondary income thorough the sales of food, merchandise, memberships, and donations. Whereas colleges often secure the patronage of alumni by building their basketball and football teams (sometimes to the point of prostituting themselves), zoos attract benefactors and visitors by creating new and appealing exhibits and programs.

Zoo curators are also driven by multiple masters in the exercise of designing exhibits. A new exhibit must improve substantially upon the outmoded facilities being replaced. Curatorial priorities include a long list of past facility shortcomings to avoid, coupled with a vision for new visitor experiences. Many people now go to zoos seeking meaningful outings, not merely to gawk at the animals. Since curators are in charge of animal exhibition, it is critical for them to avoid any catastrophic aesthetic disappointments. Team-oriented design methods have blunted their risk. Curators' priorities must also take into account the practical duties of the keeper staff, as well as the logistics of providing an environment conducive to safety, breeding, pregnancy, and the raising of young. Research capabilities would also be a plus in any new animal exhibit; this most often takes the form of behavioral observations, but may also require the collection of urine for endocrine studies to manage captive reproduction and ready apprehension for related procedures.

Keepers must be fully integrated into this team of designers, since it is they who will expend, daily, the time and energy to mitigate any shortcomings. The operation and maintenance costs of an exhibit over its lifespan can be astronomical if it is carelessly designed or constructed. Once brick and mortar are set, it will be years before a replacement facility will be seen. Drains clogged with food and animal feces and uncleanable surfaces will be their recurring nightmares if these details are botched. More than one exhibit has been built where two-inch diameter floor drains ended up having to attempt to accommodate four-inch animal droppings, food, and bedding debris.

Exhibit design is a pernicious concern of the veterinarians. Conditioned by past animal illnesses ranging from fight injuries and diarrhea to maternal neglect of infants, veterinarians usually have opinions on most aspects of new exhibits. Since much of a veterinarian's daily activity is based on what is going wrong, rather than what is going right, veterinarians may sometimes be viewed as nitpickers on project teams. Lighting, heating, cooling, shade, sanitation, toxic plants, safety, catching, handling, crating, observing, isolating, and zoonoses (diseases that people can catch from animals) all ramble through their veterinary thoughts in endless permutations. How can all of these variables be kept in play and still avoid having a new exhibit that ends up looking like San Quentin Prison?

Plain and simple attention to detail resolves the majority of the veterinary issues about new exhibits. After a proper analysis of a project's direction, good design is always in the details. Poor basic choices for layout, cage mechanics, floor and wall surfaces, lighting fixture placement, and plumbing specifications are all avoidable design traps into which, unfortunately, too many projects have stepped. The sad part is that an animal exhibit need not necessarily cost more to function correctly the first time. Any truly innovative project, however, will involve risk-taking, and with that will come some failures. Two of the priciest mistakes in the development of exhibits are oversights and subsequent changes, which require expensive changes by the project engineers, architects, and contractors. Also significant in the costs of early failures in the plan, however, are the time burdens placed upon the client team members, who are called upon, often at short notice, to devote additional efforts to overcoming programming and design oversights.

If I ran a zoo, I might be tempted to find the very best exhibits in the world and duplicate or improve them rather than starting from scratch—especially if the exhibits were a long distance away from my zoo. An entire zoo could be built by modeling the best of what works in other zoos around the world, so long as climatic and thematic considerations prevailed in these judgments. However, exhibits and whole zoos should take on their unique character because of the necessity to fit them into the local physical, climatic, and cultural topography.

Construction cost overruns can start immediately after the "conceptual" phase of a new exhibit, and again when oversights are made in the "programming" phase. The task of programming is to develop the working plan (program) of what the exhibit must accomplish, the interrelationships of its subparts, and the whos and hows of accomplishing them. Only when all elements of the plan have been determined in tabular fashion can any first attempt be made to rough out the physical aspects of the project. There is a perpetual temptation to narrow the focus of exhibit or facility design by prematurely creating a visual image. This happens because visual images are needed to inspire donors and other supporters to raise needed money. Above all else,

an exhibit must fulfill the mission of its residents, the animals, and this is then married to the aesthetic aspect of the overall project. Sounds complicated, doesn't it? Programming is a dynamic process of meeting with all key parties in the exhibit project and rooting out their expectations, priorities, and knowledge. The best methods of accomplishing this involves determining the main goals of each group, understanding their underlying needs and concerns, and preserving the details of their visions in the end product. Another vital step is to place each group's information into the project as a whole when negotiating (often bartering) construction compromises or deleting things from the plan. Some mistakes occur when changes are made by one party to the design without the input of the others, who might easily foresee the negative ramifications.

As with all major construction projects, there can be "mission creep" resulting from including an excess number of secondary features at the expense of the primary project objectives and budget. Slipping in unbudgeted expenditures, such as souvenir and snack stands, escalators, and the like, can subtract from the fundamental product unless the budget is supplemented. In the long run, a poorly planned project will cost far more to operate and maintain.

Another common mistake is for the project team to disassemble once the working drawing phases are finished, leaving things to fate, luck, and the skill and goodwill of the contractor to bring the project to life. Even Dr. Frankenstein tended to his monster after the initial electrification event, yet zoo projects often are inadequately shepherded by their creators, as the following list of shortcomings illustrates.

1. The door mechanisms throughout a new chimp exhibit were so weak that there were three breakouts in first three days of inhabitation. The animals ransacked the service area, broke plumbing fixtures, set off fire alarms, and caused a flood.

2. An orangutan found enough handholds on an artificial cliff face that he climbed out hand-over-hand. He was found sitting with a visitor on the public viewing platform. He repeated the feat several times in a row before modified rockwork finally thwarted his new climbing career.

3. An exhibit of subtropical animals was sited on a north-facing slope with poor sun exposure, making the outdoor exhibit cold and uninhabitable until the sun was directly overhead.

4. The orangutans in a newly opened exhibit unearthed concrete waste that had not been removed by landscapers prior to placing grass sod. Using the concrete chunks like hammers, they destroyed thousands of dollars worth of bulletproof viewing glass during the first week of inhabiting the new enclosure.

5. As an economy measure, several large sand and gravel filters were eliminated from a new hippo pool with underwater viewing, resulting in a maximum visibility of about twelve inches. Hippos, like babies in swimming pools, almost always do their business in the water.

Underwater hippo viewing is not a brand new idea, though it is relatively recent in zoos—the Sedgwick County Zoo in Kansas probably had the first. Toledo, San Diego, and several other zoos now have them as well. But in Kenya, East Africa, at Mzima Springs (Mzima means "well" or "good" in Swahili), tourists have been able to see underwater hippos in crystal-clear visibility conditions for decades. These springs, arising from lava flows in the Chyulu Hills region, are the headwater source for the coastal city of Mombassa, Kenya, miles away. The springs create an enormous water flow that keeps the water clarity extraordinarily transparent. This is the location where the world's best underwater hippo and crocodile photos have been taken. In nearly any ordinary hippo habitat the normal muddy, silted water would eliminate underwater views altogether, but at Mzima hippos perform underwater ballets that can be seen through a glass window in a submerged tank that is entered down a set of narrow steps. More recently, this hippo haven has been featured in several *National Geographic* television specials.

It is not uncommon for new exhibit residents to demolish many of the new plantings, and it requires some ingenuity to protect vegetation to some degree. When a new primate exhibit opened in the Atlanta Zoo and the animals began to destroy valuable trees, zoo director Dr. Terry Maple's response to the horticultural staff was "plant cheaper trees."

Experience has shown that animals respect certain physical boundaries and that this can be exploited in exhibit design. The giraffe is a peculiar animal that is unafraid of heights, but fears just the opposite—small depressions in the ground. Unlike other hoofed animals, which climb and jump across uneven terrain, top-heavy giraffes are reluctant to walk or step down into depressions. Giraffe exhibits can be built with minimal surrounding moat barriers, as shallow as three to four feet deep. They are so concerned about misplacing their feet on irregular terrain that one female giraffe at the San Diego Zoo refused to exit the back holding area to enter the exhibit at times of day when a pole cast a suspicious shadow across the path. It acted, for all purposes, like a solid fence. Some of the less creative animal enclosures have employed electricity, dangerous obstacles, or sharp implements to encourage animals to stay within the boundaries of their exhibits. Such prickly surfaces, such as those to confine elephants, risk puncturing their feet and are reminiscent of the old spiked railings used around urban buildings to deter public loitering.

Animal exhibits often need unique assets to function well. For example, special areas may be required to introduce new animals successfully to one another, or to separate or recombine groups in the event of breeding seasons, pregnancies, illnesses, and infant rearing. When you consider how much must be contemplated in creating new, complex animal environments in the zoo, it's a wonder that they get built at all. No matter how much care is taken, ways will always be found later to improve on the final product.

As more animal behaviorists consult and work in zoos, their talents lend critical skills to exhibit design teams. Predicting how animals will live in a new environment is an educated guess, and behaviorists strive to reduce the guess factor. The behavior of each species is taken into account in each successful animal exhibit. Although conditioning in captivity can modify the needs of individual animals, spatial behaviors are genetic characteristics of a species. For example, animals tend to separate themselves apart from members of their own species, as demonstrated by how close birds sit near one another while perching on branches or telephone wires. We all have experienced a human who has invaded our own "personal space" and can relate to the discomfort that it can bring. Animals have certain minimum distances that they prefer to keep between themselves, companions, and intruders before they react negatively or flee. These types of distances will determine the success or failure of an animal exhibit, since too close proximity to the public or cagemates will be distressing. The lack of adequate interpersonal space between animals may induce aggression and stress, and is a principal cause of fighting and injury in zoo animals. Veterinarians experience these spatial constraints when they approach an animal to observe its condition, and they learn to respect these behaviors in order to obtain information on the animal's condition without undue intrusion.

The general public is unaware of how important species behavioral patterns affect animals' prospects in exhibits. Some species are highly social, while others are loners. In the wild, some animals of the same species seldom interact except when females come into seasonal estrus and mating takes place. Such is the case with giant pandas in captivity, where males and females often ignore or even attack one another because forced proximity is not the norm in nature. Just as some species are quite solitary and have reproductive strategies that overcome this separateness in the wild, others are highly gregarious and thrive best when they are able to live in colonies. A variety of aquatic bird species, such as penguins and flamingos, are good examples of this. Exhibit design, along with consideration of the social groupings of animals, has critical impacts on both compatibility and reproduction.

A common dynamic of herd animals, such as the antelope species, is the development of bachelor male groups. In the struggle to maintain social order and hierarchical relationships, many young males depart (not always gracefully) from family clans when they begin to transcend into sexual maturity. In confined settings the lack of space for this social segregation often leads to injuries from aggression if contesting parties are left to their own devices. These bachelor males hang together in separate groups as they are ejected from the main herd by the dominant male. Over time they may attempt to reenter the herd and to take on a place of leadership if they are able to dominate the ruling male. In a zoo exhibit where this social dynamic is in play, it is important to have sufficient room for these graduating males to find adequate room to escape the aggressive actions of the alpha male. Failing to ensure this space is available can cause fighting and injuries. In many cases it is necessary to remove these surplus males from the exhibit to prevent aggression and stress in the entire group.

The classic animal signs of inadequate exhibit environments in zoos are behavior aberrations. Historically, the more common ones seen in zoos are stereotypic locomotion such as pacing, weaving, overgrooming, and walking in repetitive patterns. Solitary animals in mixed exhibits may even become sexually fixated on animals of the wrong species—like the squirrel-raccoon odd couple I once saw in an East Coast zoo. Primates often do somersaults or bound endlessly from one object to another in their enclosures. Bears may walk to and fro with exaggerated head-swinging movements, or they may practice an embarrassing level of self-gratification. Just as a well-orchestrated animal exhibit of the lowliest creature can work miracles in understanding animal conservation issues, so can a poor exhibit undo the magic of the world's most charismatic species.

Fortunately, animal enrichment is a flourishing discipline in zoos and many zoos are employing people as "enrichment specialists." Some of the contemporary work in this area was initiated by Dr. Hal Markowitz at the Portland Zoo in the 1970s, with the stated objective of giving captive animals "more control over their own lives." Some found his techniques "unnatural," tending to focus on interactions with humans rather than encouraging social intercourse within their own species. One project, for example, had mandrill monkeys playing computer games with zoo visitors. Markowitz's reply to this criticism was, "We owe it to them to make the best possible life for them. . . . There was a feeling that what we did was unnatural . . . but everything about the existence of captive animals is unnatural." Unconventional types of behavioral stimulation, Markowitz seemed to suggest, are often better than none at all.

The primary job of enrichment staff is to provide zoo animals with a wide variety of activities, ranging from toys, trampolines, swinging ropes, novel diets, and food puzzles, such as pushing a peanut reward through a maze. In many ways this job resembles that of the recreation director on a cruise ship, devising creative ways to occupy the leisure time of the ship's passengers. Some animals respond to unenriched confinement by reclusive or aggressive reactions to the presence of humans or roommates. With some species, where visual cues play a critical role in social etiquette, visual barriers can be vital to providing relief from the constant forced interaction with their more dominant group members. Enrichment may involve food, foraging activities, novel objects, and opportunities to exercise or engage in nest-building activities (a common daily ritual among great apes in nature). For many species, one of the best forms of enrichment is the chance to engage in social activities with compatible individuals of their own species. On the other hand, putting in the wrong animal can be as terrifying as acquiring *Silence of the Lambs'* Hannibal Lecter or *Misery's* Annie as your new roommate. As one down-to-earth keeper bluntly put it when discussing the aggressive tendencies of one of the solitary male primates, "All he needs is a woman!"

Animals can be taught many behaviors that can facilitate their health care, including cooperating to allow ultrasound imaging, blood collection, semen collection, and artificial insemination. The typical training methods utilize operant conditioning procedures, whereby patient, systematic, positive reinforcement techniques are employed to modify animals' responses to aversive stimuli (such as proximity, novel situations, and social groups). A diabetic drill was managed for years at the San Diego Zoo by positive training that permitted the regular testing of her blood sugar levels, as well as her insulin administration. Cooperative behaviors permit zoo animals to participate in their own health management, and they can reduce the need for physical handling and sedative procedures.

The best-known zoo animal behaviorist was the late Dr. Heini Hediger, who was also the director of the Leipzig Zoo in Germany. Hediger wrote several books and numerous papers on the behavior of zoo animals, His findings became an early basis for considering the psychological, as well as the physical, welfare of animals in captivity. Students of animal behavior and zoo employees in general can gain much from his perspectives about keeping animals healthy in zoos, for the stresses that captive animals experience often turns into physical disease if not ameliorated. Two of his most notable publications, *Wild Animals in Captivity* (1950) and *The Psychology and Behavior of Animals in Circuses and Zoos* (1955), have been translated from German and reprinted for widespread use in behavioral science classes. Hediger was a strong proponent of zoo research that improved the understanding of factors that compromised the successful keeping of animals in captivity.

Several zoos are doing a fair amount of work on environmental enrichment in order to provide for exercise, mental stimulation, and a sense of well-being for zoo animals. Since boredom and inactivity are such prevalent issues facing any creature's confinement, too much emphasis cannot be placed on occupational therapy. This promotes conditions conducive to the exhibition of animals that interact more normally within their social groups and reproduce. No one imagines that nature can be truly replicated in the zoo, but attention to environmental enrichment can significantly improve animals' mental and physical well-being in ways that many zoos did not always strive to do. Animals need a variety of foods, bedding materials, play objects, and opportunities for displaying and exercising their innate physical capabilities, such as climbing, digging, running, and swimming.

Exhibit makers need to make displays that are appealing to the public in order to attract repeat visitations and new donors. There is a relentless search for exhibit activities that make animal-visitor interactions more politically correct—something a little less carnival than a pony, camel, or elephant ride. Since traditional education seems stiff to a significant number of visitors, the Indianapolis and Fort Worth zoos now opt to call it "edzootainment"—nonfattening education, or soft-sell learning without the term papers and final exams. I also like the term "edventure," used at the Roger Williams Park Zoo in Providence, Rhode Island. The following blurb from one zoo's web site appeals to the Camp Granada spirit in all of us: "Monster BUGS! Exhibit—The Monster BUGS exhibit continues to be one of the most popular attractions at the Zoo. This exhibit will stay through December and is presented by Arab Termite & Pest Control." Wanting to appear hip and fun-loving, there is "Big Al"—"The star of this summer's sea lion keeper chats is Big Al, the zoo's male California sea lion. At more than 1,000 pounds, this magnificent marine mammal is a huge, impressive and extremely interesting fellow whose antics are sure to delight zoo visitors. Although different sea lions will be featured at different times for keeper chats, we will be sure to have Big Al available for the 12:45 P.M. daily sea lion demonstration." For the more intellectually inclined there is "Giraffe Feeding—As the weather warms up, limited numbers of zoo visitors have the chance to hand feed giraffes with fruits and vegetables by going out on a specially-designed platform that is built into the giraffe exhibit." And for the unaware or nearsighted, there is "Elephant Awareness Week, June 26–July 4—Dedicated to the world's largest land animal, Elephant Awareness Week gives zoo visitors the opportunity to see these huge pachyderms exhibit a wide range of their natural behaviors."

Meanwhile, at the Artis Zoo in Amsterdam, Holland, programs to reach out to the public have broken new ground in order to relate to all niches of society. Special walking tours and lectures are available for the adult and gay and lesbian communities for the purpose of reassuring them that all lifestyles can be found in the animal kingdom. Among the featured exhibits are flamingoes, where it is pointed out that group orgies are the norm, a chimpanzee that keepers have concluded is lesbian, and a pair of allegedly gay monkeys. According to the zoo director, Dr. Maarten Frankenhuis, "The idea behind it is to show that homosexuality is a natural phenomenon. . . . We get mostly gay people and mothers with their sons after they've just come out." The tours are available by appointment only and cost the equivalent of $12.

Naming new zoo facilities and exhibits is more in the realm of the public relations and marketing people, and is ordinarily out of the scope of veterinary and even curatorial decision making. Names have to project favorable images and sound appealing, like new housing developments such as the stereotypical Rustic Oak Estates, Meadowbrook Pointe, and Emerald Hill Farms. It was always interesting to overhear these peculiar debates, but as long as the exhibit works for the animals, what they called it wasn't much of my concern.

As an exhibit project is developing, it's inevitable that some kind of name will finally be agreed upon, and such was the case with the costly monorail tour train ride that was built for San Diego's country zoo, the San Diego Wild Animal Park. This facility opened in 1972, the same year I arrived at the zoo, and after much debate the monorail was finally dubbed the Wgasa (pronounced Wah-Gah'-Sah) Bush Line Railroad, a name visioning a rustic safari train that traveled the game-rich savanna wilds of East Africa. Its naming had been problematic from its inception, and it was referred to by many different titles, eluding a consensus by the project's design team.

A member of that team, Charles Faust, was architect and chief designer for the Zoo and Wild Animal Park. A salty, talented, Air Force veteran who had flown B-16 bombers in World War II, Charlie was a splendid artist in his own right and drew beautiful sketches of wildlife on several East African safaris in the late 1960s in preparation for the conceptual design of the Wild Animal Park. His large, pictorial sand castings of San Diego history and wildlife still decorate the walls of prominent San Diego businesses and public places. Charlie's blunt, dry humor made him an enjoyable conversationalist, and I often stopped by his office near the zoo maintenance shop to chat over a cup of coffee. I always mused over his eclectic office decorations, which included jars of bird feathers, models of zoo exhibits, dangling replicas of military airplanes, and a cardboard mockup of the instrument panel of a Superfortress bomber once used for training wartime pilots.

Charlie made no bones about other zoo people and some of their ideas that irritated him; he never suffered fools gladly. Ordinarily the resident cynic and humorist in any group, he had become bored by the lack of agreement in the naming the park's new tour train. While everyone else seemed hung up on finding the perfect title, Charlie was more interested in making the design work. One day, in yet another train meeting, after continued nominal malaise, Charlie was observed doodling the initials WGASA on a drawing in front of him and someone asked, "What's that?" Charlie replied, "You folks can't agree on a name that makes you happy, so let's just give it a name that *sounds* African, and let it go at that—it doesn't make a damn bit of difference what it means." The group stared at Charlie, and at one another, until someone said, "What's that you've written on the plan?" Charlie turned his drawing around and replied, "WGASA—let's call it the WGASA Bush Line Railroad." Eyes lit up with relief and approval, and someone said, "Wow, that does sound *really* African, Charlie—I recommend that we go with the name." And finally it was done.

Later, a zoo trustee came to Charlie and asked, "By the way, Charlie, what does WGASA really mean?" He just smiled and replied, "Who Gives A S—Anyway?"

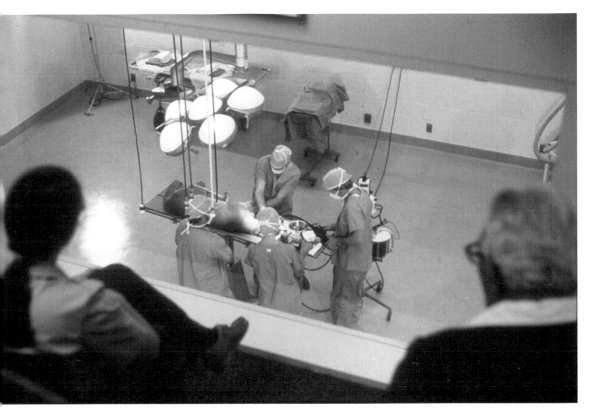

Surgical theater at the Jennings Center for Zoological Medicine, San Diego Zoo, 1977

John Ball Zoo chimpanzee exhibit

Busch Gardens' Great Ape Domain exhibit

**Please Do Not
Annoy, torment,
pester, plague,
molest, worry,
badger, harry,
persecute, irk,
bullyrag, vex,
disquiet, grate,
beset, bother,
tease, nettle,
tantalize or ruffle
the Animals.**

Northern Trail exhibit at the Woodland Park Zoo

Woodland Park Zoo gorilla exhibit

Woodland Park Zoo Bornean orangutan exhibit

Sumatran Tiger Forest at Zoo Atlanta

7. CREATURE COMFORT

The Power of Microenvironments

One of the most remarkable lessons about keeping animals in captivity is the enormous difference that tiny embellishments in living accommodations can make in their ability to thrive. Just as there was probably a statistically greater survival rate for prehistoric humans whose cave dwellings were oriented to the warming rays of the morning sun, so do seemingly minor improvements provide significant benefits for the comfort and prosperity of zoo animals.

In my home state of Michigan, we had some little tricks to getting a car started in subzero weather. One of the simplest ones was simply to place a hundred-watt light bulb under the hood of the car at night. This small heat source from a single bulb made a vast difference in the ease of starting a car on a frigid morning. The significance of this idea always stuck with me as I looked at zoo animals placed in the environments that we provided. Even subtle changes in wind, cold, heat, and solar exposure can have profound effects on how animals fare.

Good medicine—for people and animals alike—involves eliminating a multitude of small problems in order to bring cumulative benefits to a patient. Simple tweaks that can be made in animal husbandry improve the vitality and well-being of animals in many underappreciated ways. Animal environmental science, the engineering technology that promotes efficient livestock production, takes into account the physical and the psychological worlds that agricultural species encounter. The productivity of the livestock industry often depends on a combination of seemingly minor, but collectively significant, techniques for housing, handling, and feeding animals.

Investments in sound management practices have been shown, overwhelmingly, to improve the economy of livestock farming practices worldwide. For example, adjusting the dimensions of a pig farrowing (birthing) pen by a matter of a few inches can dramatically enhance the survival rate of baby pigs, keeping them from being accidentally crushed by their mothers. The traffic-flow pattern and consistency of procedures in milking parlors affect overall milk production in a dairy herd. Some cows have a significant drop in milk production if they are not in a particular order, in line with other familiar cows when they file in for milking. In some agricultural species, seemingly minor adjustments in light cycles and temperature make significant differences in weight gain, feed conversion efficiency, and fertility.

Unlike zoo animals, humans have a wide range of options to seek shade, shelter, heat, and other accommodations. We automatically buffer ourselves from much of the variation in our daily environments; if we are hot we remove clothing, if we are cold we add it, and so on. In Southern California there is a pervasive illusion that weather is universally mild. This notion is so ingrained into the culture that people often attempt to go without wearing jackets when the winter temperatures drop into the forties. Schoolchildren wear shorts and T-shirts to school in temperatures that would cause Iowa kids to put on long pants and sweaters. We have become so accustomed to having options to make ourselves comfortable that it is a stretch for most people to consider seriously how daily and seasonal variations place stress upon animals. And zoos are no exception.

When San Diego Wild Animal Park was first constructed, the accommodations for elephants amounted to a Stonehenge-like megalith built of sprayed concrete, having the appearance of several freestanding walls with a high roof balanced between them. This Flintstonian piece of architecture came about upon the instructions of Dr. Charles Schroeder, who played a visionary role in the development of the park, even to the point of pounding stakes in the ground where he intended many of its features to be erected. We took up the elephant housing at a zoo health meeting, since the shelter was inadequate in wintertime—for even in sunny Southern California, it can be windy and cold. Schroeder was a convincing advocate for the park and an enchanting conversationalist about zoo history. The Wild Animal Park was his pride and joy, and because we realized his sensitivities about the park's facilities and the emotional equity he had in its design, we did not deal lightly with the subject of cold elephants. True to form, as he sat down at the health meeting and noted that "Cold Elephants at WAP" was on the agenda, his face began to contort in anticipation. Accustomed to addressing first the agenda items that concerned him most, Schroeder sat painfully through the pathologist's report about the animal mortalities of note and then immediately moved the "elephant problem" to the top of the meeting. "Now what is this nonsense about cold elephants at the Wild Animal Park?" he groused, looking around for the culprit who had added it to the meeting agenda. (The veterinarians, again.) "Before we discuss this, I want to tell you all something about elephants that you might not know. When I was in British East Africa, I heard of elephants walking in the snow on Mt. Kilimanjaro! Imagine!" (Schroeder loved one-word sentences ending with dramatic pauses and exclamation points.) Raising his hands in frustration, he continued, "Now how on earth did someone come to the conclusion that we need to do what—build a barn to keep them warm? Do you know how much that would cost? And then you couldn't see the elephants well at all." The response was simple: the animals were shivering in the cold. I could hardly believe that a longtime veterinarian would question the necessity of keeping elephants warm, but then I realized that, for the moment, he was wearing his visionary hat, not his old veterinary coveralls. The park had been a huge financial drain on the zoo in the beginning, and here was one more money pit that he would have to find a way to shovel dollars into. The enthusiasm about the Zoological Society's new park had already begun to create a rift in the two keeper staffs—those in the new park taking the view that their mission was more natural and avant-garde than that of the "old zoo" in the city, and the old zoo's keepers feeling that the Wild Animal Park was sucking the zoo dry with its endless costs. First reactions aside, after the shock of a new project obligation passed, Schroeder conceded to shelter the elephants, and he found the money to do so. Before long, an elephant barn was on the planning boards, but now with a mini-arena to host the public to displays of elephant's physical abilities. In true Schroeder fashion, he made the added financial burden into a new park attraction.

One of the best ways to bring home this message about animal microenvironments is to actually put oneself in the animals' places. Spend the night where the bears sleep and see if you can get a good night's rest on a cement floor. I once suggested that to a keeper who resisted the use of straw bedding and to an administrator who resisted supplementary heat. Many people would be surprised at how intolerably cold and miserably uncomfortable it is to camp out on bare concrete without other heat sources, and how quickly a chill sets in as the sun moves away from an exhibit, leaving animals in involuntary shade. You or I would move a few yards into the sun if we were sitting in a city park, or we would slip on a sweater or jacket.

Each zoo has its own unique set of microclimates, and all animals fare appreciably better if given effective protection from the prevailing wind, particularly in combination with a substrate that conserves body heat and pads them from hard surfaces. The effects of these seemingly trivial matters of husbandry are always underestimated and underutilized, perhaps even more so in milder climates than places where there is a strong annual cycle that profoundly reminds humans of seasonal changes. Keepers sometimes referred to me, discreetly, as "Dr. Bedding" because of my nagging insistence that animals be provided with softer, warmer surfaces to rest on in their enclosures. I always took this as a compliment rather than as an insult. One of the simplest, most immediate, ways to provide warmth is to offer dry straw or wood shavings as an option to dirt or concrete. We gave the great apes burlap sacks to make nests with, and some proceeded to decorate themselves Sadie Hawkins–style by fashioning their own versions of burlap hats and shawls.

When safely installed, useful heat-producing devices include infrared heat lamps, gas radiant heaters, electrically heated rocks, and warm resting platforms. There is no mistaking how animals appreciate these small appliances, huddling on or near them during inclement weather. The older or younger the animal, the more beneficial supplemental heat is. The zoo's red kangaroos and wallabies, which lived on a slope with unfavorable sun and draft exposures, responded dramatically to the addition of heat lamps, bedding areas, and windbreaks. Before we made these simple improvements, many marsupials had chronic problems with weight loss and foot and tail infections, and they often lost their pouch babies because of the cascade of problems induced by the stress of cold and dampness. The numbers of ill and infirm animals dropped dramatically in some groups with just several simple heat-conserving changes to their husbandry.

For semiaquatic and aquatic species, water temperature affects behavior greatly, and some animals avoid water altogether when temperatures are allowed to drop too low. Hippos, in particular, dislike frigid water and spend more time languishing outside their pools, even though they prefer to be in water most of the day. Hippo births were also more successful when the babies got the extra help of just a few degrees rise in water temperature, since they are born directly in the water. They have to make the shocking transition from 100° F inside the mother's uterus to the chill of a water pool. They emerge like a basketball that has been released by a submarine and pop to the surface, dragging their umbilical cords like rope tethers. Pygmy hippos simply stay out of cold water altogether, and, unlike their larger relatives, give birth on land.

Social interactions between animals should be monitored continuously in exhibits, for not all animals appreciate company, and some become extremely aggressive when they encounter strange cagemates. Bringing new individuals into existing social groups is a common cause of trauma in zoos. Zoo veterinarians expend a disproportionate amount of time in the case of primates, which are particularly prone to social discord of this type. Carelessly planned and executed introductions to one another greatly increase the likelihood of serious injury. In order to avoid aggression and excess competition for resources, it is often necessary to provide for redundancy in cage furniture, resting places, feeding stations, and water supplies. Sight barriers that permit an animal to retreat from the stares of edgy companions can lower tensions and avoid antagonism and trauma. The adage "out of sight, out of mind" works in many introduction strategies.

Most newly arrived zoo animals undergo a period of quarantine in the zoo in a location separate from the exhibit area. During this two- to four-week period, physical examinations, medical observation, tuberculosis testing, blood studies, and parasite screening establish known baselines before the animals take up zoo residency. Social contact with their new group is seldom possible during this period. Primates are among the most sensitive species in this adaptation process. Since the new arrival is at a social disadvantage to the resident inhabitants, special care must be taken to introduce the new animals to established ones gradually. Placing the new arrival in visual, auditory, and olfactory range of its new companions while keeping it physically separated is typically the first step. This is followed by allowing the new animal a solo adventure into the new exhibit to explore and learn the novel territory. A third phase may permit limited physical contact of the newcomer with more benign members of the group, and then full contact with selected individuals in attempts to establish a mentor or buddy system. The final step is the integration of the entire group, often by adding the most volatile member last, when the newcomer is already functioning in the exhibit area. By contrast, "cold turkey" ("hard") kinds of introductions are done out of ignorance, impatience, or carelessness and frequently causes injuries or even deaths. The temporary removal of an individual for hospital treatment may disrupt social relationships enough to require a careful reintroduction protocol in some cases.

Sequential ("soft") introduction techniques provide the best prospects for success in most zoo animals. This often employs the psychology of "home court" advantage, similar to the strategy used by lion and tiger trainers in circuses. The trainer *always* enters the cage first, establishing a psychological territorial advantage over the lions and tigers, which are then funneled into the show cage for the performance. Similarly, depriving the established alpha monkey of such leverage in a zoo exhibit tends to reduce the impact of this first physical encounter with a newly introduced animal and allows more social latitude for the integration of the newcomer. On the fateful day of direct contact, other techniques, such as overprovisioning with foods or unfamiliar furnishings (for example, straw or hay bedding) can provide useful diversions and lessen the possibilities of conflict.

Despite extensive introductory efforts, a pair of giant pandas in the San Diego Zoo was never able to get along compatibly enough to breed, which led to the program for artificial insemination that succeeded in producing a baby in the year 1999. Some species do not tolerate the ongoing presence of more than one male without conflict. This is the way of life for the endangered California desert tortoise. Male tortoises relentlessly pursue one another and attempt to turn their opponents upside down. There is little hope of them ever living compatibly together. The two male desert tortoises I have in my care at home live proximate but entirely isolated existences, despite all of the well-wishing sentiments that we have in caring for them. They hibernate for months in adjacent boxes in our bedroom closet, only inches apart, but live entirely apart the rest of the year when awake.

Like people, animals get bored, which can lead to destructive and undesirable behaviors. The animals that exhibit this to the greatest degree are the primates. Most animals become bored because they are unemployed from the time that they arrive at the zoo. In the wild, most of their waking hours are spent in foraging, predator avoidance, and social engagement. In captivity, all the groceries are provided, usually in forms that require little investigation, preparation, or manipulation prior to consumption; zoo animals were eating fast-food meals long before most of their human counterparts were. Husbandry programs that make efforts to provide animals with occupational therapy are rewarded by the reduction in negative behaviors of boredom, and also create richer visitor experiences.

Because of boredom, animals may carry out many undesirable activities, such as stereotyped locomotion, overgrooming, stool-eating, self-stimulation, exhibit destruction, regurgitating and reingestion, fecal flinging, and aggression. Our baboon groups at the zoo experienced noticeably reduced social tension and boredom when items such as uncooked rice and millet seeds were scattered through their exhibit several times daily. They spent large amounts of time finding and gathering up these bits of food. Animals that might ordinarily pick on others seemed to have an occupational release by walking around and methodically gathering up tiny food morsels, one grain at a time.

Many zoos use puzzles or other devices that require animals to search for some of their foods and solve simple problems to acquire their daily rations. Chimpanzees have been conditioned to insert small sticks into artificial termite mounds to extract small sticky treats—often spaghetti sauce or oatmeal—similar to the termite-feeding behavior of chimps that has been documented in the wild. Some animals are challenged to discover concealed raisins, nuts, mealworms, and sundry nutritional tidbits, in the spirit of a daily Easter egg hunt. Animal groups are often fed multiple times daily in smaller allotments to reduce hoarding and improve the equitable distribution of foodstuffs.

Because of the close confinement of animals, sanitation can be a significant problem. However, some of the traditions concerning cleaning zoo exhibits have been questioned. The most common cleaning practices involve lots of soap, water, and bleach to remove soil left by feces and food. It is not known how this hypercleansing affects animals' natural behaviors related to scent-marking in their territory, or what social consequences result from this practice—a consideration for additional behavioral work in zoos.

Husbandry research with primates has revealed some innovative alternatives to cleaning traditions. One such approach involved housing primates with a technique called "deep-litter bedding"—a composting technique. No group of zoo animals experiences more cases of diarrhea than zoo monkeys, and their care for such problems has always consumed much veterinary effort. The typical list of "rule-outs"—the likely causes of the problem that must be systematically eliminated—involve diet, parasites, infection, and stress. (In fact, it seems that several of these factors often interact to give rise to the problems.) The floors were covered deeply with wood chips or straw, and when they became soiled a fresh layer was added to the top. Layer by layer the floor litter was built up. Only periodically was the entire decomposing substrate replaced. The results of utilizing this compost-bedding technique were convincing from both behavioral and disease standpoints. Normal husbandry practices employed the frequent hosing away of wastes, which produces floors that are wet and contaminated, as well as frequent animal contact with aerosolized feces. With the deep-litter approach, animals spent more time on the ground foraging for their food, and the incidence of gastrointestinal disease diminished significantly; they also experienced fewer cases of aggression, injury, and abnormal behavior. As the bedding accumulated and aged, it actually inhibited the growth of bacteria as urine was absorbed and decomposed along with the feces.

The constant addition of the litter substrate provided new opportunities to replicate normal feeding behaviors of monkeys by requiring greater exploratory efforts in acquiring food. In the wild, some primates are estimated to spend as much as 70 percent of their active times finding their food, during which significant social interaction takes place. For species that spend large periods of time ground in their natural environments, this sort of novel approach is the type of innovation that zoos need more of. The monkeys were no longer unemployed, but their keepers periodically had a big shoveling project to remove the accumulated litter, which is a laborious down side to the practice. The use of the deep-litter method has been limited by both practical concerns about the attractive nuisance that it provides for rodents and insects and aesthetic concerns for visitors. Judging by the state of my teenage son's room, though, I am convinced that primates of all kinds take naturally to deep litter, and I continue to be intrigued by this approach.

Health staff observing a gorilla at the San Diego Zoo

8. WHAT'S THIS THING?

Searching for the Normal

Only thirty years ago, there were no textbooks, no classes, and few training programs in zoo animal medicine. Every practitioner had to start from scratch to learn what was even normal. At one time or another in their career, each zoo veterinarian has probed, prodded, biopsied, or at least puzzled over structures that turned out to be normal for that species. For example, the first time that you observe spider monkeys climbing around in a tree you can't help but assume that the ones with the little dangling appendage on their rear ends (the size of a finger) are the males, although it turns out they are the females. The external genitalia of male spider monkeys, while respectable by monkey standards, is surprisingly more obvious than that of a four-hundred-pound gorilla, which can hardly be seen except when it is sedated.

When I first examined a male koala as a zoo intern, I noticed that he had a discharge coming from a swelling in the middle of his chest, and I suspected a draining tumor or cyst. This was the only male koala in the world outside Australia at the time, and the chests of the only two females looked normal by comparison. Fortunately, my concern was delayed long enough to find out from a biology book that male koalas have a scent gland in that location, which they use to mark trees in their territories. Happily, I avoided a surgical blunder by leaving his alone.

Zoo veterinarians routinely rely on changes in an animal's typical individual behavior as indicators of illness. In many cases, observation, rather than leaping to hands-on diagnostics, may be the best method of understanding a problem. Elephants, for example, ordinarily lie down to sleep for a period of time each night, even though it may last for only three to four hours. Ill elephants, however, have been known to remain standing for months at a time. Like horses and cows, rhinos and other large herbivorous species, such as elephants, can doze for short periods of time while standing up, but all of the large herbivores in zoos, including the giraffe, should lie down to sleep at night. Failure to follow such a routine is a cause to suspect illness.

Veterinarians are trained to recognize disease by classical clinical "signs." A good example of this principle is the use of so-called textbook pictures. Imagine yourself as the author of a medical book or article, or giving a lecture to veterinary students. You want to illustrate a particular disease, but, as we all know, photographs seldom do reliable justice to the subject. Therefore, more extreme, obvious cases are chosen that have progressed to the stage where even the near-blind could not miss the visual presentation. These cases often come from situations of neglect, where the owner or attendant ignored the problem far past its initial signs and let it become a textbook case. Most veterinarians are not consistently presented with the classical images of a disease; rather, we often see diseases in their formative stages. If you observe embryos throughout their development, it is remarkable how similar a human, pig, dog, and cat are in the earlier stages. It is only after many important developmental steps that they each begin to gradually emerge as recognizable species. Such is the case with diseases—they share many general characteristics, such as fever, lack of appetite, lethargy, and discomfort. They all have to start at some point and progress to a recognizable stage. The first challenge is for owners or keepers to recognize that something is abnormal to decipher the emerging problem at the earliest point possible.

Not all of the listed symptoms or signs described for a disease may be present. Textbooks enumerate the most common manifestations of a disease, but that seldom means that they all will express themselves in each case, even if left untreated. Not all animal hosts are created equal, each having their own unique characteristics, such as age, environment, genetic background, nutritional status, and immune competency. The effects of a disease are expressed through these backgrounds and ultimately determine their severity, significance, and clinical portrayal in an individual.

In fact, technically speaking, animals do not have "symptoms" at all, since this term is defined as the "subjective" observations of a human patient (pain, numbness, confusion, depression), rather than objective (observable or measurable) conditions, which are referred to as "signs," such as fever, skin rash, lameness, and swelling. Few things are more frustrating to the veterinary student or new practitioner than to be presented with sick animals whose signs of illness are vague and "incomplete." Most of those signs don't look like they do in the textbooks, but show more gradual and changing indications of disease. The overwhelming dilemma for a new clinician is that the list of possibilities of what *can* go wrong is huge, but lack of experience prevents one from tempering this list with the insights about what is *likely* to be going wrong in a particular case.

Learning the normal anatomy of the animals in the zoo is a formidable undertaking and can never be adequately accomplished. Every animal that died in the San Diego Zoo was examined by a pathologist, creating many hands-on learning opportunities. Gradually, as zoo veterinarians have pursued their own favored groups of animals, they have integrated a broad knowledge of anatomy, pathology, and clinical disease. There are now veterinary subspecialties in avian, reptile, amphibian, marine mammal, wildlife, and primate medicine.

In contrast to a zoo clinician, about the only fatal mistake that a zoo pathologist can make is doing a necropsy on a live animal, which has happened a few times in reptiles. Over the years, the San Diego Zoo reptile department brought several animals for postmortem examinations that were (it was later determined) still living. Declared dead by the keepers, they had been temporarily placed in holding coolers. Several snakes and tortoises, disconcertingly, later came back to life. One poisonous snake had been placed on the necropsy table by a pathologist to warm up for several hours prior to dissection, and it turned up missing when the pathologist returned to the necropsy room. He went around the hospital in search of the snake, suspecting a prank. When no one confessed, he returned to find the snake alive and coiled on the floor next to the leg of the necropsy table. It was returned alive to the exhibit collection. After that episode it was mandated that all poisonous snakes have their heads removed prior to necropsy. The clinical veterinarians, however, had no such luxuries of safety and always had to work on the poisonous snakes with their heads on. Perhaps this is another good reason to be a pathologist instead of a clinician.

Determining drug doses in zoo animals is an empirical task, since all drugs are potential poisons. If you read any drug pamphlet and the list of potential side effects (blindness, impotence, gastric ulcers, deafness, and so on) closely, you might begin to question whether the cure might inflict more damage than the disease itself. The challenge with all medications is to use them in a manner that maximizes their benefits while minimizing their toxicity. The use of new drugs in unfamiliar animals have caused many sleepless nights for zoo veterinarians. Pharmaceutical companies appreciate zoos because their veterinarians are inclined to experimental drugs and are usually willing to use them in trials on their patients. Zoo veterinarians are always on the lookout for newer, safer ways to medicate or sedate animals and try to acquire new drugs before they are available on the market.

Since so many types of animals have to be treated, misgauging drug choices and dosages is always a hazard, as their metabolism and toxicities are often poorly understood in many species. Few comprehensive safety and efficacy studies have been done on medicines in zoo animals, and veterinarians have to make judicious, but often experimental, use of nearly every drug in the formulary. In reptiles, for example, the metabolism of many drugs is extremely slow, allowing the injection of certain antibiotics only every three days—compared to two to three times daily, as might be necessary in a mammal.

Even the most cautious approaches to using medications in zoo animals can run amok. The rule of thumb with new drugs is to start conservatively—don't medicate the whole herd at once! One very capable zoo veterinary colleague rigidly observed this principle, and from his cautious experience he had found a common worming medication to be safe and effective when used on his valuable collection of Sumatran tigers. This same product had also been used widely in many zoo species and was generally regarded as low-risk. None of his tigers had ever experienced any side effects, and this wormer was used annually in his preventive program of vaccination and parasite control. One year, however, all hell broke loose when all of the medicated animals began to show acute signs of nausea and retching, followed by convulsions and collapse. The signs progressed to respiratory failure, and, in only eight hours, every one of his beautiful tigers was dead or dying. The zoo staff frantically attempted to determine why this catastrophe was taking place. One of a veterinarian's worst nightmares had become a reality.

Complete necropsies were done on all of the tigers, but nothing conclusive was found at first. The immediate suspicion was that the medication may have contained some contaminants that caused the deaths, but toxicology tests of the product proved it to be free of any extraneous chemicals. Bewildered, perplexed, and in shock, the medical staff undertook a painstaking review of the care of these animals, and the cause was finally revealed. Employees had been spraying the tiger enclosures for several months with an organophosphate insecticide, and this prolonged chemical exposure had lead to subclinical organophosphate poisoning in the entire tiger group. The result was to render important enzymes ineffective in their systems that were critical in metabolizing the dewormer, turning it into a lethal poison. Safe and effective in normal circumstances, an inadvertent chemical exposure put the entire group into a fatal spiral.

From infectious diseases and parasites to the ingestion of toxic substances and foreign bodies, the list of husbandry and environmentally induced problems is lengthy and evolving in zoos. In 1983, for example, to save on cost of materials after a rise in the price of copper, the US Treasury minted new pennies that contained 98 percent zinc and 2 percent copper by weight—earlier pennies were a 95 percent copper alloy. As a result, the numbers of cases of zinc poisoning in zoo animals rose noticeably, especially in marine animals that consumed coins tossed into pools by visitors. Exposed to the acidic gastric environment, zinc leached out and caused intoxication. Zinc poisoning in domestic dogs likewise increased for the same reasons.

In the 1970s, zoo medicine articles started to appear in abundance in journals and veterinary magazines, reflecting the efforts of a critical mass of veterinarians who were now collaborating internationally. Pathologists began to summarize their findings, labs compiled the comparative results of various blood tests, and clinicians wrote about anesthetic drugs that worked, surgeries that were successful, and problems they had seen and treated. Many basic veterinary techniques had to be developed, some as simple as determining where to draw adequate blood specimens from various species. We poked a lot of holes in zoo animals simply to find the best places to obtain our diagnostic specimens. The animals with domestic counterparts advanced most quickly, and zoo veterinarians have always been grateful for that familiarity.

Some of the blood samples that we examined raised interesting questions, such as why camels and llamas have red blood cells shaped like footballs and why an animal the size of an elephant has red blood cells that are smaller than those of humans. After you obtain a blood sample from an animal, the next challenge is to obtain significant diagnostic interpretations of the findings—there is the chance that some of the resulting lab values are not meaningful. Few blood chemistry tests and other analytic procedures have been specifically developed to measure disease in zoo species. For example, even in domestic dogs, the human test used to measure the enzyme amylase (which may reflect pancreatic disease) is interfered with by the presence of several saccharides (sugars) in dog blood, invalidating the analysis. Fats present in the blood of some species may obscure the technology of some tests, and normal serum pigments may also create false readings for tests that measure color changes in serum samples.

Physical exertion can markedly alter animals' white blood cell counts, and excess muscle activity prior to and during the sample collection may raise the quantities of certain enzymes in the sample and eliminate their diagnostic value. One zoo pathologist suggested that the only way to truly determine the "normal" blood values of a wild animal is to cause its instantaneous death while it is in a blissful state at a feeding trough, and then immediately withdraw a cardiac blood sample for assay. Morbid imagery aside, he illustrated the problem fairly well. Overexertion of animals during forced exercise or physical restraint, particularly in hoofed animals, can produce muscle damage known as "overstraining disease" or "capture myopathy." The damage to muscle (including heart muscle) can be severe enough to cause serious tissue injury, kidney failure, and fatalities. Parallel problems have been well known in overexerted race horses for centuries. Improved handling and chemical restraint techniques have significantly reduced injuries and made blood tests more useful by minimizing stress and exertion.

Body parts that we might ordinarily expect to be present in an animal are absent in some of our zoo patients. For example, not all animals have gall bladders. Among the species in which this organ is absent are horses, zebras, elephants, rhinos, dolphins, camels, tapirs, and rats (mice have only a miniscule one). Carnivores have managed to avoid losing theirs, perhaps due to its usefulness in processing dietary fats. The gall bladder–"deficient" animals lack much in common, at least superficially, and I cannot explain why they are on a different evolutionary compass course, although their must be some underlying metabolic motives in play. Humans eagerly dispose of the gall bladder when it causes digestive pain and discomfort. Unfortunately for bears, their gall bladders are used widely in Asia for medicinal purposes, making this seemingly optional organ more of a handicap than an asset.

Some traits are more evident than missing internal organs and a visitor to the zoo can observe the more obvious ones. Nearly all mammals have nasolacrymal ducts, the tear ducts that take the tear secretions from the eyes and direct them into the nasal passages. When humans' eyes water excessively (from allergies, colds, crying, and the like), it causes our nose to run. But, ordinarily, the tear secretions that keep our eyes from drying out are not noticed because of their small volume. In the absence or obstruction of tear ducts the tears would spill onto our cheeks. When you next go to the zoo, observe the eyes of elephants and seals and sea lions—none have nasolacrymal ducts. They can almost always be seen with a wet tear streak below each eye. In elephants, given the length of their trunks, long tear ducts would present "engineering" problems. With marine species, constant presence in and around water makes tear ducts unnecessary. Snakes have solved the problem by lacking tear glands entirely. Instead, they have a clear, dry spectacle covering the eye, which is shed periodically, along with the skin.

In defense of veterinarians, biologists in general are no smarter when it comes to deciphering anatomical variations. For some years it was thought that the beautiful eclectus parrot was two species. The males and females are totally different in their spectacular coloration—the males are a bright green and the females are a striking crimson color. This led field biologists to name them as two distinct species, until they finally came to the impossible conclusion that one species was all male and the other all female. In many parrot species, the external differences between males and females are more subtle and often inconspicuous altogether, and those species are referred to as lacking sexual dimorphism. In order to avoid ascertaining sex in parrots by a surgical endoscopic procedure to visualize internal testes or the ovary, the San Diego Zoo research department developed an innovative laboratory assay to measure the sex hormones that were excreted in their feces. Other tests are now available using a blood sample. Biologists also had it wrong again with a species of bat, *Ametrida centurio*; the females are so much larger than the males that each sex was classified as separate species for years.

Historically, because of the nature of the animal trade, there has always been an element of uncertainty about the exact geographic location of origin of specimens caught for sale to zoos. While species may look very much alike, significant genetic differences may be present between different populations of the same species. These differences, especially when they involve something as fundamental as chromosome structure, can result in incompatibilities that cause infertility and unviable offspring. The San Diego Zoo's spider monkeys were such a group until the zoo research director, Dr. Kurt Benirschke, decided to have a look at the chromosome profiles (karyotypes) within the zoo's primate colonies. While outwardly similar in appearance, the spider monkeys were a mix of individual animals of closely related, but distinct, subspecies, geographically separated in their home ranges in the wild long enough to diverge genetically. As a result of this type of work, it has become possible to sort animals by their genetic profiles and to resolve genetic incompatibilities in spider monkey breeding programs. Chromosome analysis has been performed in a number of zoo animal species, thereby avoiding similar problems in other zoos. Cheetahs, on the opposite extreme, are extraordinarily homogeneous when it comes to their genetic makeup. Studies carried out in East and South Africa by the Smithsonian's Dr. Mitch Bush and his colleagues have shown that the genetic differences between widely spaced populations of these cats are remarkably tiny. They are so similar, in fact, that skin can be taken from donor animals and easily grafted to animals more than a thousand miles away without any of the expected problems of rejection that would ordinarily be predicted to occur.

The objective of collaborative breeding programs is to maintain enough ancestral gene diversity to preserve the potential of animals in captivity to be representative of wild types and to avoid inbreeding, which may lead to infertility, lower birth weights, and increased neonatal mortality. Only carefully managed breeding initiatives have the potential to assure this objective over time, through the creation of studbooks (genealogy documentation) and planned matings according to statistically calculated indices of "inbreeding coefficients." In this manner, specific matings between individuals can be managed in order to avoid creating overrepresented lineages and overlooking the perpetuation of rare lineages in the captive population. Such evaluations can also provide objective information about the need to recruit additional founder animals from wild stocks.

Zoo breeding programs generally strive to avoid interspecies hybridization or atypical variations. Occasionally, a "tiglon" or "liger" (tiger × lion), "lepjag" (leopard × jaguar), "zorse" (zebra × horse) or "zonkey" (zebra × donkey) is produced by private breeders for curiosity's sake. The first portion of these names denotes the male and the second the female of these cross breedings. Sidewalk souvenir photographers in Tijuana, Mexico, create a zonkey by simply painting black stripes on a donkey. To appeal to the "believe it or not" sentiments of the visiting public, some zoos exhibit "white tigers," "white lions," albino animals, and even some bicephalic reptiles. The last two categories occur regularly in nature, but their survival is often short owing to their increased susceptibility to predation and other cumbersome issues. The purposely crossbred animals are throwbacks to man's banal curiosity with the genetic manipulation of life and serve no real scientific purpose in zoos.

Most zoos have a policy whereby every animal that dies on the zoo grounds will be subjected to a necropsy, helping us to understand what is normal for them and why they died. This information on disease is invaluable as a health management tool, as well as a great surgical anatomy preview. Contagious diseases, environmental intoxications, nutritional imbalances, parasitism, and numerous preventable conditions have been identified in deceased animals that can alter management practices to benefit the living. Important too, is the detection of diseases such as tuberculosis that may have a direct effect on employee and visitor health.

After the necropsy, some rarer animals are reserved for shipment to museum collections while others are reduced to ashes in the hospital crematorium. An animal incinerator was installed in the original San Diego Zoo hospital building, and Dr. Charles Schroeder, the zoo's veterinarian, nearly burned the hospital down when a lanolin-rich wild sheep exploded in flames, shooting a fiery plume out the top of the building. This led to the construction of a succession of freestanding crematoria that saw every imaginable species enter their heavy steel doors over the years. The later zoo crematories had their own episodes of incendiary indigestion. In one, a large dromedary camel was being burned in sections when the custodian pushed in a bushel-sized load of fat from the camel's hump. For the next twenty minutes a grease fire engulfed the firebox and got so hot that the fire department was put on alert. The coup de grace for our crematory, however, was a large seizure of hashish that we destroyed as a special favor to the federal Bureau of Narcotics and Dangerous Drugs. Seized in a drug bust on the Mexican border, the hashish arrived in several vanloads under the watchful eyes of drug agents, who meticulously inventoried each parcel as it was stacked into the fire chamber. The burners were lit and the inferno got underway, ejecting a huge cloud of cannabis smoke from the smokestack. Fueled by plant resins, the flames rendered the contents into ashes. Shortly after this incendiary bravado, an inspection of the firebrick liner revealed severe cracking, along with warping of the support steel, requiring an expensive overhaul. Future requests for cremating drug bust seizures were politely declined, and the greasy animals were sent to a rendering contractor.

Pathology work brings up a lot of "What's this thing?" questions. If I had it to do over again I might be a pathologist—if only for the reason that pathologists' mistakes are seldom fatal with animals, and they get the coveted last word.

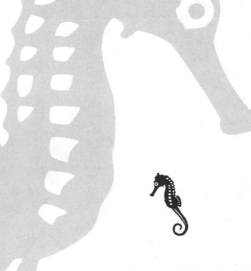

9. HOLDING THE TIGER

Zoos Say Yes to Drugs

The air was heavy with musky scent as we dragged the tiger through the steel-barred door and into the unlit animal bedroom behind the big cat grotto. Several keepers pressed closer to look when the tiger suddenly reared his head in a wild-eyed stupor. Dr. Sedgwick admonished the keepers blocking the entrance: "Just remember folks, if he tries to get on his feet, I won't be the last one out the door!" Everyone stumbled backward, ducking their heads in a hasty retreat through the narrow opening and into the sunlight. Two locks were snapped in place on the metal door as a third secured the chain-link safety cage. The tiger was left in peace to reorganize his brain cells, which had been temporarily derailed by a substance that went by the street names "Angel Dust," "Monkey Juice," "Rocket Fuel," and "PCP." The drug's proper chemical name was phencyclidine hydrochloride.

A breakthrough in zoo medicine, phencyclidine hydrochloride was eventually replaced by a shorter-acting compound called ketamine, now known widely by its con-

Dr. Charles Sedgwick sizes up leopard anesthesia candidate

temporary street name, "Special K." After observing hundreds of animals sedated with this drug, it is difficult to imagine the appeal that drives the illicit manufacturing and abuse that continue today. Starting in the 1960s, phencyclidine had become the new miracle drug for sedating nearly all nonhoofed mammals in zoos, from monkeys and gorillas to lions and grizzly bears. From a terminology standpoint, zoo animals can be "chemically immobilized," which means that they are restrained so they can be safely handled, or "anesthetized," which indicates that they are not experiencing pain while immobilized.

Zoo veterinarians are expected to forgo the basic preliminary processes of competent anesthesia that are mandatory in virtually every other type of medical practice—the comprehensive pre-anesthetic physical examination. In human and veterinary practice, the lack of this critical evaluation would be considered malpractice if there were complications. With zoo animals, however, it is simply part of the normal territory and places great reliance on prior observations to assess risk. An animal may have serious preexisting problems that are not evident, even to experienced eyes; yet zoo veterinarians lack the benefit of comprehensive screening for cardiac malfunction or compromising liver and kidney diseases—the very organs essential to detoxifying the drugs they must use on their patients.

It is a well-established rule that the veterinarian is ordinarily the first person to make contact with a dangerous zoo animal that has been drugged for handling. Everyone seems to agree that this incentive-based rule is a fair one, since the person giving the drugs should take responsibility for knowing how animals are supposed to react and risk their own neck first. And all of us who sedate zoo animals have had lingering thoughts that a malevolent bear or lion would fake its drugged state, await the touch of a zoo veterinarian, and savage him or her to a pulp.

The keeper culture in zoos around the so-called magnum animals (dangerous cats, bears, and pachyderms) is a little different from that for animals such as kangaroos and birds. While many keepers have a pocketknife handy to take care of miscellaneous husbandry tasks, the big carnivore keepers often liked to carry a more formidable piece of cutlery in a belt scabbard. If I were stuck in a cage with a bear or a tiger, however, a CO_2 fire extinguisher would probably be my choice of a defensive implement over a Bowie knife.

Working on dangerous animals has been a touchy problem for generations of zoo veterinarians. Without chemical restraint to provide safety for both the animal and the handlers, accomplishing anything physical, however simple, was a daunting undertaking. With hoofed animals, it was common to rope and tie the more manageable species for treatments, hoof trimming, and other medical and husbandry tasks. Most zoos began by building steel "squeeze cage" contraptions that made it possible to force fractious animals into shipping or transfer crates and to restrain them by compressing them against a wall for as much time as it took to administer an injection. Oral tranquilizers are often unreliable and unpalatable and may have poor safety margins for patients in the high doses necessary for useful effect. On some occasions, it was possible to give an intravenous injection to a large animal that was mechanically compressed in a cage, but often difficult with all of the struggling, excitement, and limited access to veins amid the splashing urine, flying hair, growling, snarling, and confusion.

Some of the early anesthetic procedures involved placing a rag soaked with ether or chloroform into a crate containing the patient. In the end, the combination of

Treating a sedated bear at the New York Zoological Park in 1906;
Dr. W. Reid Blair (*left*) and director Dr. William Hornaday

stress, along with the overheating and poorly suited drugs, caused an unacceptable number of injuries and deaths. Broken teeth, fractured legs, hyperthermia, and damaged muscles left another host of new problems to contend with. Neither were the risks to zoo personnel negligible in such close encounters, which had to be factored into all decisions to use manual restraint on larger creatures. Since the treatment could be more damaging than the original disease, attempts at physical interventions in larger animals were often avoided, except under the direst circumstances. I was fortunate to arrive in zoo practice when chemical restraint was well on the way to replacing the rodeo style of animal handling.

In his 1929 book *In the Zoo*, Dr. W. Reid Blair recounts several anesthetic procedures at the New York Zoological Park in the early 1900s: "In order to secure an ani-

Dr. Werner Heuschele trimming antelope's hooves at the San Diego Zoo, c. 1960

mal properly and successfully, nothing is so important as that the person in charge of controlling the animal should possess good judgment, associated with plenty of courage and confidence. He must retain a level head in spite of any unusual incident which may chance to take place. He must guard against getting excited or unduly alarmed and provoked in case everything does not transpire as expected or desired." These early anesthesia procedures involved generous quantities of inhaled chloroform and ether. The use of ether as an anesthetic was first described in the United States in the late 1840s, and, around the same time, chloroform anesthesia was first performed on humans in England. The public was slow to embrace general anesthesia with these two substances because of the occasional sudden death that occurred in humans due to the cardiac arrhythmias that they caused. In animals, the likelihood of anesthesia-related death was substantially increased as a consequence of the necessary use of physical restraint and the ensuing excitement and overstraining that ensued. To control pain, Blair often employed local anesthesia in his zoo cases by injections of cocaine and morphine. An eye cataract surgery on a partially grown Indian rhinoceros at the New York Zoological Park required eight ounces of chloroform and twelve ounces of ether, mixed together and applied through a large mask, while the rhino was tied and restrained on a floor covered with mattresses and straw. It took an hour before the rhino was sufficiently anesthetized to perform the surgery.

For many years, however, keepers, veterinarians, and curators stood by helplessly as many animals experienced injuries and diseases that were not treatable with existing technology. As with yesteryear's domestic horse, a major leg fracture in a large zoo animal, especially hoofed species, was often managed by euthanasia. Fortunately, with many problems, time is a great healer. An important element of practicing zoo animal medicine is simply knowing when to leave something alone, despite all of the well-intentioned enthusiasm and encouragement—actually, pressure—to try to fix it. Providing solitude, warmth, comfortable bedding and tempting foods often were the best prescriptions available. This still has great merit in the golden age of drugs in zoos.

Beyond everything else, zoo veterinary medicine operates on the "precautionary principle"—a sort of Hippocratic credo which translates to: "The good achieved should not be exceeded by the harm inflicted," or, in other words, if a proposed activity has significant consequences, and you don't know what you are doing, don't do it! After all, there are plenty of opportunities for catastrophe even when you know, or think you know, what you are doing.

Overdosing with drugs is a prevailing veterinary concern because so little is known about the metabolism of many chemicals in zoo animal species. Zoo veterinarians have always sought out deceased animals to learn more of their anatomy and metabolism, and to pick up clues as to how they are likely to respond to medications. For example, if you needed to know how much of a giant tortoise's body weight was made up of more metabolically active flesh, you simply waited for one to die and then dissected it into two piles and weighed them—muscles and other vascular tissues go in one pile, shell and bones into another.

Later, reptile medicine took a giant slither forward with the embarrassing discovery that injecting certain drugs into the hind limbs of tortoises was more dangerous than giving the same injection in the front limbs. This may seem nonsensical, but the blood circulation of some reptiles, such as tortoises, is different from that of mammals. The veins that drain the rear limbs make a preferential circulatory pass through the kidneys (the renal portal system), where high concentrations of some drugs can

Jenny the elephant at the London Zoo in 1874;
she suffered from a paralyzed trunk and arthritis and died in 1875

cause tissue damage. If the drugs are injected instead into the forelimbs, this chemical toxicity is spared. Of course, as luck would have it, veterinarians typically give hind leg injections to most animals, as they learn to do in their training—an unfortunate custom for some earlier tortoise patients.

Determining safe and effective drug doses in zoo animals is an empirical task, since *all* drugs are potential poisons to some degree. We administer drugs to both animals and people with the objective of maximizing the therapeutic benefits while minimizing the toxic side effects. The use of new drugs in unfamiliar animals has caused many anxious moments in zoo practices. Pharmaceutical companies, as I have said, universally like zoos because zoo veterinarians are keen to try new experimental drugs. Due to simple economics, there are virtually no drugs developed and marketed specifically for zoological species. In fact, many drugs used in normal pet animal practice have not been created specifically for dogs and cats either. Part of the passion for newly emerging pharmaceuticals derives from the relentless attempts by zoo veterinarians to find safer, more effective ways to sedate and treat their patients. The combination of improved injectable anesthetics and restraint agents with inhalation anesthetics—methoxyflurane, halothane, isoflurane, and sevoflurane (in the order of their introduction into medical practice)—made surgical interventions common and relatively safe for most animals. One of my patients was a Komodo dragon lizard that managed to fracture its arm; with the use of halothane inhalation anesthesia we were able to repair its fractured humerus with a metal bone plate and screws and achieve a total recovery. Hippos and giraffes, however, remain the top two anesthesia and restraint challenges in zoo practice today.

Chemical restraint and anesthesia of zoo animals are used for a wide variety of purposes. In addition to physical examinations, imaging studies, treatments, and surgeries, there are myriad other tasks that are facilitated, such as genetic testing, semen collection, and artificial insemination. Zoo veterinarians were to find out by trial and error that some drugs worked well in some species but were entirely contraindicated in others. For example, a synthetic opioid drug called etorphine (M99), while highly effective in a rhinoceros, has disconcerting effects on felines. I tried it only once in an African lion and observed the animal apparently experiencing hallucinations, fear, and disorientation as it lunged around its cage and tried to scramble up a bare wall in terror.

The dose range for different species of hoofed animals is significantly different between the San Diego Zoo and its sister facility, the San Diego Wild Animal Park, only thirty-five miles away. I attribute the reasons for these to the degree of confinement and differences in the physical condition (cardiovascular fitness and muscle mass) of animals that reside in larger areas where they received much more exercise. Compared to animals in the zoo, most of these animals also are accustomed to greater freedom of movement and personal space, which undoubtedly affect the level of arousal and excitement during the apprehension process. Similar parallels occur in free-ranging animals in the wild, which ordinarily require even higher doses for successful immobilization in the field.

The new age of chemical restraint in zoos was exciting, but sometimes disconcerting, involving daily experimentation with unfamiliar drugs in novel patients. The word about new drugs, both good and bad, traveled quickly among zoo veterinarians in widely separated institutions long before the first results were published in veterinary journals. If there was an oddball case to sedate, we often telephoned around to find a trusted colleague with the same or similar species in the collection to see if he or she had any useful experiences to share. On one such occasion I called Dr. Clint Gray, the head veterinarian at the National Zoo in Washington, about a pygmy hippopotamus in San Diego that had a dental problem. I needed to do an oral examination on him and possibly cut back his tusks to correct a malocclusion. Chemical immobilization procedures in the larger common hippo in zoos have had a dismal track record—about half of the hippos under sedation died of anesthetic complications, mostly from respiratory collapse from their inability to breathe properly under their massive weight when unconscious out of water. I could find no published drug doses for the pygmy hippo, its diminutive relative, which weighed in at about six hundred pounds. Dr. Gray, a former cattle and horse veterinarian (and life of the party at annual zoo veterinarian conventions), immediately offered me an exact dose of a sedative on the phone. Given his extensive experience, I felt greatly relieved. As soon as I hung up the phone I made plans for dental surgery the next day. The dentistry went well, and our little female hippo recovered fine from the anesthesia. Grateful for such capable advice, I called Clint back to thank him for sharing his drug doses with me. He said, "Great! I'm glad it worked out on your pygmy because, well, I've never actually had to sedate one of them before—and I always wondered if that drug would work on them. . . . And since it worked so well for you, I'll be sure to try it the next time I have to handle one of those critters. Thanks for the information, Phil."

The fundamental strategy of modern zoo medical practice is the prevention and early diagnosis of problems. In the late 1950s new drug-delivery equipment came on the scene and began to allow veterinarians to intervene diagnostically and surgically

Cap-Chur pistol and tranquilizer dart

with increasing degrees of success. The invention of the Cap-Chur dart gun system by a Georgian named "Red" Palmer made it possible to inject drugs remotely into animals with aluminum projectile darts. In the 1960s, the Marlin Perkins *Wild Kingdom* television series showed this equipment at work in numerous episodes involving the chemical restraint of wildlife. Unlike real life, however, the show conveniently left out the tedious and risky segments of film where animals run off, stumble, bash into trees, or experience other, sometimes fatal, complications. In Marlin's world, darted animals safely fell under a reliably sublethal chemical spell while hardly blinking an eye. Jim Fowler, his trusty assistant on the program, was always there to explain how marvelously well things were going.

These new darting systems were based on three formats: a Crossman CO_2 pistol, a CO_2- charged rifle, and a .28-gauge rifle powered by .22-caliber powder charges. An earlier crossbow model proved too brutal for general use. Their practical darting ranges are from ten to one hundred feet, and the hollow aluminum darts typically hold between three to ten milliliters of liquid drug. All immobilizing darts are capable of inflicting serious injury to animals—bruising muscles, breaking legs, puncturing ten-

Darting a patient at the bear grotto, San Diego Zoo

dons, and penetrating body cavities. The aluminum ones are much more hazardous than later, lightweight varieties. The Cap-Chur darts were made up of three segments: the body, the tail, and the needle. These latter two parts screw onto each end of the threaded aluminum tube. A rubber plunger within the body of the dart separates the liquid drug on the forward side from the small impact-activated powder charge that fits into the rear side of the plunger. When the dart strikes an animal, a spring-loaded internal weight strikes and ignites a powder charge, driving the plunger forward and expelling the contents through a large 14-gauge needle. To reduce the tendency of the dart to bounce off of an animal, metal collars or barbs adorning the needle shaft catch in the skin, retaining the dart long enough for injection of the drug. In its earlier applications, its intended markets were for "non-lethal chemical restraint of criminal suspects," for medicating domestic livestock and in urban animal control work. It was tested on so-called volunteer prisoners in the beginning, who probably sought to perform good deeds in exchange for future consideration at parole time. However, it

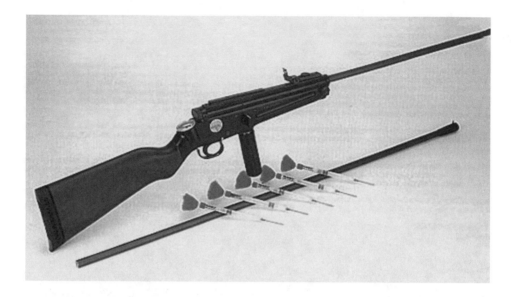

Telinject rifle and darts

found its most versatile market among zoo and wildlife veterinarians, who used it for delivering both immobilizing drugs and antibiotics. While it never caught on in law enforcement, they have been put into wide use by municipal animal control agencies and wildlife biologists. Several other, more recent, systems, most notably the "Telinject" brand of dart rifles and pistols, are now available. These are superior, lighter plastic or nylon darts, which are significantly less traumatic and more accurate. The immobilizing drugs used in these darts must be readily absorbed by intramuscular injection, which eliminates many sedative drugs in human and veterinary medicine to begin with. The margins of safety for some chemicals were narrow between an immobilizing dose and a lethal dose, especially with nicotine alkaloids ("Cap-Chur-Sol") and muscle-immobilizing drugs. The green Cap-Chur-Sol label appropriately displayed—in bold print—a large skull and crossbones and the word "poison."

The drug curare was originally obtained from the leaves of the tropical plant, *Chondrodendron tomentosums,* by indigenous South American native hunters, who applied it to hunting darts projected through long blowpipes. It causes neuromuscular paralysis, but not relief from pain; alone, is inappropriate for surgery. A drug that similarly causes muscle paralysis without analgesia, called succinyl choline, was used by equine practitioners for years in the absence of other, safer drugs for castrating horses in the field. Overdoses of both of these compounds can cause severe temperature regulation disturbances, paralysis of the respiratory muscles, and asphyxiation, unless artificial ventilation is employed. Their unpredictability, especially when given intramuscularly, resulted in highly variable and risky procedures in zoo animals.

Many animals, particularly free-ranging wildlife, died of complications from earlier capture drugs in the field because the compounds lacked reasonable safety margins and were often administered by personnel who were untrained in emergency treatment measures required to resuscitate animals. Neuromuscular paralyzing drugs quickly fell out of favor as soon as the first glimmers came from newer pharmaceuticals. In the 1960s the growing availability of a new class of drugs called dissociative anesthetics (cyclohexamines) opened a new vista for safely restraining cats, bears, apes, monkeys, and a host of other zoo animals. These have been subject to widespread human drug abuse and require close oversight to prevent diversion for "recreational" purposes.

Other delivery systems for remotely administering drugs to exotic animals include a variety of commercial and homemade blowpipes. Used for centuries by South American forest peoples for capturing monkeys, birds, and other small game with drug-laden dart projectiles, the blowpipe has proven to be an effective device at shorter range, delivering liquid drugs through lightweight nylon and plastic darts with a minimum of noise and traumatic impact. The ideal anesthetic/immobilizing agent would have certain key properties—none have them all. Some drugs are meant simply to provide physical control of an animal so that it may be handled safely and without injury to itself. Others have analgesic (pain-relieving) properties essential to performing surgery. The ideal immobilizing drug is (1) rapid-acting; (2) suitable for intramuscular injection; (3) effective in volumes usable in a projectile dart; (4) safe over a broad dose range; (5) chemically stable without refrigeration and when mixed with other drugs; (6) not highly toxic to humans with accidental exposure; (7) reversible with a specific antagonist (antidote); (8) analgesic in surgical procedures. No existing drugs qualify for all of these criteria. In many cases, inhalation anesthetics are used as a supplementary adjunct to injectables for longer procedures involving surgery.

When the animal tranquilizing agent xylazine came on the market, zoo veterinarians immediately set about the task of sizing up its potential applications with their patients. This drug was rumored to be a good sedative in horses. We used it for the first time to sedate and surgically repair an umbilical hernia in an antelope, and we found ourselves spending the next eighteen hours combating hypothermia and depression in that patient. It also turned out to be a poor analgesic in most animals, which limited its use to that of a tranquilizer, for which it is quite effective in elephants and several other species. At that time no reversing chemical was available to counter its effects. Before long, after it was more widely available as a veterinary drug, I received a desperate phone call from a wild animal dealer whose local equine veterinarian had given this drug to two valuable oryx antelope in order to collect blood samples for some mandatory government blood tests. It had been nearly twenty-four hours since both oryxes had been drugged, and they were still flat out on the ground like limp dishrags. Other than supportive care, I was unable to offer any suggestions to revive these animals, and it would be some years before drugs were available to counteract this drug when overdosed. The veterinarian, who worked mostly with horses, gave the equine dose of this drug to the oryxes. It turns out cattle and antelope are ten times more sensitive to it than horses, and the animals never did get up. It was depressing to learn of this huge dosing error with this drug, and I empathized with both the owner and the veterinarian in their hopeless plight. Several drugs are now available to reverse the sedative effects of xylazine.

Before we used xylazine on elephants at the zoo, we waited for other veterinarians to go first before we jumped into a procedure of our own. Often, a conversation with a colleague would go something like this: "Have you used that drug on any big animals yet? "No, have you?" "No, not yet." "Well, give me a call when you have an idea how it works." It was often a waiting game to see who went first. Xylazine turned out be excellent for producing standing sedation in elephants. Because of a difference in species sensitivity, a full-grown elephant can be sedated (standing) with less than the amount required for the average horse.

One day I received a panic call from the Ringling Brothers Circus about one of its Asian elephants, which had had an accident in a performance in Phoenix, Arizona. A large cow elephant named Iki had gradually developed a large, cantaloupe-sized tumor, which hung from the abdomen in front of her rear legs. The circus manager was concerned because she had snagged this dangling mass in another elephant's armpit during that day's performance during a gymnastic maneuver, tearing it slightly at the base of its attachment. Worried by a pulsating artery they felt in the tumor,

Ringling's Axel Gautier and the author with Iki's tumor in 1978;
years later Axel was killed by a circus elephant

they envisioned a gory scene in which it might be ripped loose in front of thousands of spectators. The tumor had to be removed, and I was asked to examine her during the circus's next stop, the San Diego Sports Arena.

After examining Iki's appendage, we set a surgical time for the following day. Word had gotten out among the circus cast that Iki's surgery was going to take place, and a procession of jugglers, trapeze artists, midgets, and clowns strolled by the back lot, offering their skeptical best wishes. The night before the surgery, I began to worry about how to control the bleeding, and I fashioned a tourniquet clamp out of a split section of a broom handle and two stainless steel radiator hose clamps. I sterilized the lot and packed up the other surgical instruments for my project.

Restrained fore and aft by leg ropes, Iki swayed precariously while her trainer, Axel Gautier, reassured her. After an intravenous injection of a tranquilizer into an ear vein she began to show its effects. Her gentle swaying ebbed and the probing motions of her trunk subsided. When she was fully affected, her trunk dangled like a limp hose, giving the appearance that it had grown substantially longer. Iki was off in peanut land. She seemed to glide in and out of a sleeplike trance, shifting her weight from one leg to another. I had the insecure sensation of working under a large dump truck with a wobbly support jack, expecting that she might flop down without any warning. After a generous injection of local anesthetic into the surgical site, and with the tourniquet in place above the tumor, I went to work separating her from the mass and tied off the veins and arteries. Soon, the eight-pound tumor, which turned out to be a benign growth, was free from Iki and was being passed between the trainers like a newborn baby. A cheer of approval came from the small crowd of onlookers, but the final sighs of relief came only after the tourniquet was released and a hemorrhagic catastrophe failed to materialize. In a matter of minutes following an injection of the sedative antidote, Iki was back to her old self and eating peanuts from her trainer's hand as reward for her cooperation. Our sideshow was over, and the unusual little audience drifted away to prepare for the afternoon's matinee show.

If I thought circuses were strange enough in the United States, I shouldn't have been surprised that they take on additional twists in Mexico. The Tijuana Humane Society asked for help in examining several circus animals that had been brought to its attention in our sister border city. When I arrived on their lot, I felt a clear air of hostility from the general manager of the circus, who grudgingly walked me to the side of the big top where the menagerie animals were displayed. Circuses like Ringling Brothers, Barnum and Bailey Circus, had animal menageries as part of their traveling shows and exhibited such "oddities" as giraffes, hippos, and even gorillas. I had been asked to come down to look at a tiger with a toothache, but first the Humane Society representative led me directly to a half-grown rhinoceros that was tethered by a hind leg chain. Exhausted and underweight, this sad creature stood passively as the sideshow patrons filed by; most were viewing a live rhinoceros for the first time in their lives. A cadaverous odor came from the infection in the rhino's leg where a chain was fastened. It disappeared completely into the flesh. The chain had been placed there at a younger age, and the leg was now growing into this unyielding tourniquet.

The Humane Society officer translated my conversation with the manager—not word-for-word, however, as they were obviously having a tense disagreement about being compelled to tend to the leg problem. He finally agreed to have the chain removed, a task that required general sedation. I discussed my plan to sedate the rhino, and the manager winced at the suggestion as if he were being forced to sign the animal's death warrant. Because of the creature's deteriorating condition, I used a low sedative dose of the narcotic immobilizing drug called etorphine. The chain was painstakingly sawed free as the rhino lay on its side and, and a new soft cotton rope was placed on the opposite leg. The manager looked around as if deciding where to dig the hole for the rhino, while several children daringly crept up to touch the recumbent beast. Laid out flat on his side, to them it had the appearance of drawing its last breath. When I injected the antidote intravenously, I didn't tell everyone what I expected would happen next, but patted the rhino on its horn. Then, as if a miracle was happening, it rolled its eyes, lifted its head, and stumbled onto its feet. The children scattered, and the manager grinned in bewilderment as though he had witnessed a resurrection. Speechless, he rushed off to the main tent, and in a few minutes he was back, insisting that I join him and the owner as his guest by the main arena.

There in the center ring was the pride and joy of their show—the tiger with the toothache. Now treating me like a VIP instead of the grim reaper, the circus owner introduced himself in clear English, smiled gratefully, and thanked me repeatedly for not killing his rhino. As the spotlights focused and the music came up in a fanfare, a large horse, outfitted with blinders and a stout leather back pad cantered around the ring with a tiger on its back. The tiger jumped through flaming hoops and back onto the horse in perfect cadence. The audience cheered—it was an awesome spectacle. I asked the owner, "How do you get the tiger to do such a stunt?" He responded, "Well, doctor, it is not the tiger that's the problem, but the horse. . . . You see, this is the third one we've gone through this year." "And what about the tiger's toothache?" I inquired. "I'd recommend a root canal on the broken tooth." "Oh, Doctor," he sighed, "we would be pleased if you could look at that next year—one miracle is all my heart can take just now."

Several very potent synthetic narcotics proved useful for sedating most of the hoofed animals in zoos; first and most notable was etorphine, which is reported to be thousands of times more potent as morphine. Etorphine was first synthesized in the early 1960s by Edinburgh professor Kenneth Bentley while he was searching for a new nonsteroidal anti-inflammatory drug. This drug virtually revolutionized the practice of zoo medicine with elephants, rhinos, and most hoofed animals. One drop of it can be fatal to a human, however, and great caution is required in handling it, including eye protection and rubber gloves. The *Washington Times* reported that etorphine or fentanyl, another potent synthetic narcotic used in zoo work, was likely to be the drug that Russian police commandos placed in the ventilation ducts in the opera house hostage crisis in Moscow in 2002, which resulted in scores of fatalities. Its potency was further noted when it caused several fatalities in Africa after people ate the flesh of animals that had been drugged with it. A British equine veterinarian who used this drug on a horse died when he accidentally stuck himself with a wet needle contaminated with etorphine that he had just used to inject a horse. The fallout from this death was its removal from the British veterinary market as a drug too dangerous for general practice. Less than a teaspoon can render a rhinoceros immobile, yet the injection of the antidote, called "M50–50" (diprenorphine), brings it back to consciousness within a matter of minutes. Never before had such a dramatic form of animal restraint and reversal been possible with zoo animals. Its potency placed it in the highest security level of controlled substances in the United States and strictly limited its sale to zoo and wildlife veterinarians. Carfentanyl, another synthetic narcotic, and several even more potent, reversible drugs, have been added to the drug armamentarium of zoo veterinarians since the advent of M99.

In response to a request from a Mexican veterinary friend, I made another odd house call, this time to the old Tijuana bullring to examine a fighting bull in need of first aid. This *toro bravo*, or *indulto*, as spared fighting bulls are called, had been saved from the typical coup de grace of this sad "sport"—a sword inserted between the shoulder blades and into the heart—because he had exhibited superior traits of "honesty" and "bravery," qualities the bullfighting industry strives to preserve in breeding stock. This can only be known from the actual arena performance of a bull against a matador, and amounts to the sparing of fewer than one in a hundred fighting bulls. Neither the matador nor the spectators play any official role in deciding the fate of the bull, but crowds often let their sentiments be known about the bull and the fighter. It is entirely up to the judge to decide on the performance of each. The bullfighters are divided into professionals (matadors) and novices; the pros face bulls that are over four years old, while the amateurs get the younger ones. Depending on their performance with a bull, a fighter may be awarded nothing, one ear, two ears, or two ears and a tail. For the bull it is an all-or-nothing proposition with few survivors.

The culture of bullfighting has some of the same shady elements as professional boxing, and it seems that all blood sports attract unsavory characters. Long after the demise of Roman gladiators, bullfighting is one of the few human vs. animal mortal-

Loading a white rhinoceros at the San Diego Wild Animal Park in 1974. Following the animal's immobilization with M99, a crate is positioned in front of the animal. A reversal drug (M50-50) is then given, and the animal is directed into the crate with a heavy rope tether.

combat events that has managed to survive man's slowly evolving enlightenment. Ironically, true to our human system of pecking orders in sports, bullfight aficionados probably would look down upon the Afghan sport of buzkashi ("goat-grabbing") as primitive—this a cross between polo and rugby, played on horseback by two teams that use the decapitated carcass of goat as a "ball." Unlike bullfighting, cockfighting, and dogfighting, at least the goat is dead before the game begins.

The hot, dusty bullring in Tijuana felt desolate when we arrived after the crowd had departed for the day. The only lingering signs of animal life were two black bovine tails that dangled from a corral fence and several feral cats that skittered away at our approach. Charcoal embers still warmed a small hibachi behind the spectator stands, where token remains of the losers had been roasted after the entertainment was over. The rest of the day's sacrifices had long since been dragged off to local butcher shops.

As we made our way to the bull corrals, our eyes met a surprisingly small, muscle-bound, jet-black bull, who was still fighting mad. My Mexican colleague referred to him as a half ton of angry *carne asada.* Pound per pound, he looked tougher than any zoo animal I had yet encountered. He had ample reasons for his rage, inasmuch as his entire upper neck and shoulder region had been brutalized by the picadors, the padded horsemen who incessantly prod the bull with spike-tipped poles. Swinging from the top of his neck was a cluster of *banderillas,* metal-barbed sticks adorned with colorful crepe paper streamers, which are jabbed into the bull's neck and shoulders by the matador as the animal sweeps past the cape. The damage to the bull begins just as he is released into the arena when a short, barbed shaft the size of an ice pick and decorated with the colors of the bull's home ranch, is plunged to the hilt into his shoulder with the apparent object of vexing him.

During a bullfight, "cowardly" bulls, as distinct from those considered *bravo,* retreat from the picadors and often try to run or climb the arena walls to escape. This *indulto,* however, pawed up a cloud of dust with a front hoof and charged across the corral toward us, determined to seek revenge on the next living thing that dared to come near him. If glares could kill, we would have been dead, and the wooden corral now seemed pathetically flimsy. My heart rate jumped as the cloud of dust from his sudden halt blinded us as he swept past.

The single human in attendance, a toothless gaucho, led us to a better vantage point at one side of the pen for a shot with the dart rifle. We drugged the raging bull with a well-placed dart in the rump, and he went down within fifteen minutes. After removing the harpoons from his neck, and about ten pounds of macerated muscle, we partially closed the gaping wounds and primed the bull with generous doses of penicillin and fly repellent; this animal was sure to heal with little intervention from man. Within just a few minutes of giving him an intravenous injection of the drug antidote, he was back up, glaring and stamping his feet, and two days later he was on an airplane to reproductive retirement in Monterrey, Mexico.

I have never attended a bullfight, but soon after this experience I saw one broadcast from a Tijuana television station. The spectacle was one of the most troubling episodes I could ever expect to witness, causing me to regret having been even remotely connected to the perpetuation of this pathetic version of entertainment. Just as the Roman gladiator spectacles came to an end, bullfighting will not last forever, but, like the bulls, it will die a slow death in both Spain and Mexico, where this tradition is sustained by machismo-ridden subcultures that are loath to neuter their dogs.

There are no true miracle restraint drugs, in the sense of safety, for animals or for people. As modern chemical restraint has become more routine in zoos, there has been a sense of complacency that has developed about its proper use. It is inappropriate to use chemical restraint as a substitute for developing safe animal-handling facilities and techniques. Veterinarians are sometimes overly relied upon to compensate for short-falls in the proper design of animals pens and buildings. Perhaps our success has bred some excess. The practice of anesthesia is a little like flying an airplane: it looks safe and easy as long as the weather is good and there are no mechanical surprises, but it's hell on a bad day when the black clouds roll in. As with aviation, you need to be prepared to cancel your flight plans if a storm suddenly changes the conditions.

Today we can do dental surgery on an elephant, repair a broken leg on a Mongolian wild horse, perform ultrasound on a rhinoceros's ovaries, or artificially inseminate a panda—a far cry from the times when anesthesia was so risky that it was considered a last-ditch option.

He never even said he was sick.

10. FINDING THE SICK IN THE ZOO

Seeking Out Disease and Discomfort

Wild animals experience a full range of risks from disease and injury, although there is a lingering notion that they are excused from most health problems because of their natural lifestyles. In fact, the seriously ill drop rapidly into nature's recycle bin and are seldom observed by humans. Early medical practitioners of all schools had to master the powers of observation to determine the causes of illness. Lacking today's diagnostic equipment and laboratory resources, observation was the most powerful tool they had, and its importance is still vastly underestimated in all aspects of clinical practice. Other senses were also used—even taste for detecting sweetness in a patient's urine to diagnose sugar diabetes.

The physical examination of a patient traditionally begins as a hands-off exercise, observing first from a distance. Assessing the patient's condition before it gets disturbed or excited is essential, whether it is a horse, a rhino, or a parrot, because clinical signs often quickly conceal themselves when an animal's suspicions are aroused.

In nature, the observer and judge is often a predator. Lameness mysteriously disappears and depression may be stoked with adrenalin, obscuring precious clues. The heightened awareness in a sick animal may be mistaken for normal vigilance. In our human experiences with doctors, the simple act of putting on a paper exam gown and removing our shoes and socks in the doctor's office can make us puzzle about exactly where that pain was just ten minutes ago. When animals realize they are being watched, their antipredator radar switches on and camouflages many indicators that may be important clues to a problem. It may be necessary to revisit a patient several times and under different circumstances to obtain an unbiased impression of how an animal is acting. In the case of creatures that are particularly sensitive to strangers, entire reliance may have to be placed on the information of the animal keeper or video surveillance. An astute keeper is often the best judge of subtle changes that indicate illness—minute variations from the norm, such as diminished socialization, eye contact, mobility, appetite, or responsiveness.

Most of the diseases of zoo animals are diseases caused by captivity, although many people expect exotic plagues from faraway places to be the norm. Several reviews of animal pathology cases involving thousands of zoo animal mortalities refute this notion and affirm that most diseases of zoo animals are relatively mundane. The annual medical report for the San Diego Zoo hospital in 1934 concluded: "The majority of our fatalities are preventable . . . [and] can be directly traced to poor sanitation and improper food handling." Some thirty years ago, Chicago's Brookfield Zoo veterinarian Dr. Joel Wallach determined that about 30–40 percent of zoo deaths were from diseases caused by bacteria, parasites, and viruses, and that the remaining 60–70 percent could be attributed to poor animal management and husbandry. The actual numbers are probably even worse, however, since infections often have their origins in stresses of various forms, which magnify the effects and opportunities for infectious and parasitic agents.

Parasitism is widespread among nearly all forms of the world's animal life, ranging from pesky skin infestations to microscopic malarial organisms that infect blood cells, and a mind-boggling variety of worms that migrate through body tissues, destroying cells and siphoning off protein and other nutrients from their hosts. A good parasite, like a good houseguest, is one that does not seriously trouble its host, at least not consistently. In other words, on a population basis, while the damage to the host does not ordinarily affect its survival as a species, it may occasionally have mortal consequences for individuals. This moderation is not because of benevolence on the part of parasites, but simply an evolutionary game in which the parasites that survive to reproduce tend not to destroy their primary domiciles, their animal hosts.

The impact of parasitism within the confinement of the zoo depends on the organisms' life cycles, as well as factors relating to sanitation. Most tapeworms, for example, require an intermediate host, such as an arthropod insect, to complete their life cycles; in the absence of arthropods in the zoo, the tapeworms' cycle is short-circuited. I once received a call from an agitated curator who learned through the grapevine that I intended to release a bear from quarantine that was still testing positive for tapeworms. He was annoyed, fearing that this problem would become transmitted to the other bears that inhabited nearby enclosures. When I explained the parasite's life cycle in detail and how transmission was not possible due to the lack of intermediate hosts, he realized that eating a bucket of tapeworms could not transmit the parasites.

Parasites with more complex life cycles or with available co-conspirators can thrive in zoos under the proper conditions—the lungworm of sheep and goats is a good example. Snails, which are abundant in Southern California, are ideal intermediate hosts for the lungworm, *Mulleria,* which can cause chronic verminous pneumonia in its victims. Control of this parasite in exotic zoo goats has been achieved with specially medicated feeds and the control of its abundant intermediate hosts, common snails, with nontoxic, bubblegum-like sprays that glue the snails' mouth parts shut when they feed on the treated vegetation, again short-circuiting the parasite's life cycle.

Parasites with direct life cycles require no third-party transaction for transmission, or even a transition stage in the environment prior to reinfestation. These have a propensity to produce heavy parasite burdens in confined animals because the eggs passed into the environment can cause reinfestation with adult worms in the absence of an intermediate host organism. Regular worming programs may be important in confined animals to prevent parasite damage to hosts tissues and the loss of nutrients that result. Small parrots in the zoo are particularly prone to roundworm infections of this type from *Ascaridia* and require regular monitoring, deworming, and husbandry measures that reduce fecal contamination of their feed. (Don't put their feed pans under their perches!)

In one major zoo, a tragic parasite problem occurred when gorillas and South American bush dogs alternately shared a grassy exercise area. Unbeknownst to the

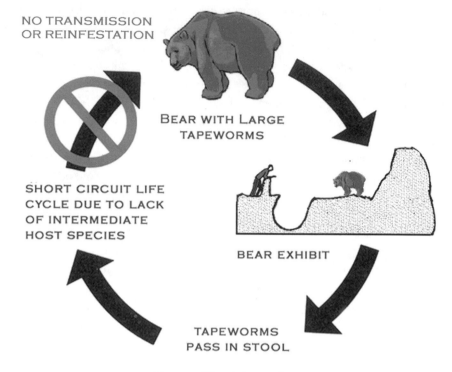

NO TRANSMISSION
OR REINFESTATION

BEAR WITH LARGE
TAPEWORMS

SHORT CIRCUIT LIFE
CYCLE DUE TO LACK
OF INTERMEDIATE
HOST SPECIES

BEAR EXHIBIT

TAPEWORMS
PASS IN STOOL

Tapeworm life cycle in a zoo bear

medical staff, these carnivores were infested with a type of tapeworm that produces destructive parasitic cysts in the major internal organs of some species. The gorillas became contaminated with the infective tapeworm forms by playing on the bush dog–soiled grass, and they developed massive parasite cysts in their livers and abdominal cavities. Unfortunately, no effective treatment was available, and an entire group of valuable breeding animals perished from the infestations.

Wild animals frequently recover from a wide variety of infections and injuries during their lifetimes, although any serious injury can make an individual much more vulnerable to death from predation. Some insightful studies have been done by the examination the skeletons of wildlife that have been collected for museums in various parts of the world, revealing a wide range of dental and skeletal diseases that animals must have experienced for extended periods of time. Primates in one study had arthritis and healed fractures of arms, legs, fingers, and toes. Of all the primates examined, the group with an astonishingly high rate of healed fractures of arms was the gibbons, which are highly arboreal in habit, swinging dramatically between tree branches. Fortunately for early zoo veterinarians, many animals healed from their injuries despite their lack of medical treatment. Dental disease, such as tooth abscesses and fractures, has also been found to occur in many primate species, but more particularly in wild apes, especially older individuals. Not surprisingly, comparisons with zoo apes revealed that dental decay is much more common in captive animals than in their wild counterparts, suggesting shortcomings in diet, behavior, or environment.

As animals age in the wild, the loss of dental competency limits their lifespan. Wild Weddell seals, for example, live under large ice packs in the Antarctic and survive far from open water by maintaining open breathing holes through the ice, gnawing them clear with their teeth. A study on the longevity of this species revealed that aging Weddell seals whose teeth had worn down could no longer perform this task, so the durability of their teeth ultimately determined how long they lived before they suffocated under the ice.

Wild elephants also have their life spans limited by their teeth, which give out after around sixty-five years, should they survive other life challenges. As with human statistics, most animal longevity records far exceed the average lifespan; the maximum recorded for a captive elephant is around seventy years. Over an elephant's lifespan it has six sets of molar-like teeth (premolars and molars), which erupt, one by one, in single file, from the rear of the jaw and migrate forward in a line as they wear over the years. No more than two molar-like teeth are ordinarily present in each dental quadrant at any given time, and they appear somewhat like glued together stacks of poker chips lying on their sides. Gradually, they break apart in flakes at the front of the jaws and are shed in fragments, as if they were dropping off the end of a conveyor belt. When the last molar is expended and food can no longer be chewed, elephants rapidly start to lose body condition from malnutrition. In captivity, aging elephants can be fed special diets if chewing food becomes a limiting factor.

In general, animals in captivity live significantly longer than their wild counterparts. The reasons include the absence of several major mortality denominators, such as predation and food supply, not to mention the availability of veterinary care.

There is a millionfold difference in the weight of a pygmy shrew (2–3 grams) vs. a 5,000 kilogram elephant. The energy costs of being small are huge, particularly when we view the problem in terms of "metabolic body size," which correlates metabolism to body surface area rather than weight. Smaller animals have larger surface areas in relationship to weight than do larger ones, causing more rapid energy losses by the radiation of body heat. Other factors, however, including behavior, climate, food gathering costs, and the energy costs of locomotion, factor into the energy economy of a free-living animal. In the zoo, small animals have narrowed options for energy conservation and less ability to select high energy foods. The negative consequences of small body size make them particularly vulnerable in confinement, while larger animals generally allow greater margins for error in captivity. Shrews can live twice as long in captivity as in nature with competent husbandry, although in the wild they rarely live longer than a year. Imagine the pressure that this puts on a species to complete its entire existence on earth in less than 365 days. By then they have been parents and grandparents, racing through life like hairy little comets (their normal body temperature is a toasty 105° F). Short childhoods and gestations, serial mates and pregnancies, and early senescence—before a human can even have a memorable thought, a shrew is history.

Several years ago a *New York Times* article concluded that "as animals get bigger, from the tiny shrew to huge blue whale, pulse rates slow down and life spans stretch out longer, conspiring so that the number of heartbeats during a stay on Earth tends to be roughly the same—around a billion." If this is truly the case, we should all do everything possible to use our (and our zoo animals') heartbeats in an economical fashion and avoid unnecessary stresses that raise heart rate, especially those that provide little pleasure. More philosophically, comedian George Carlin once observed: "Life is not measured by the number of breaths we take, but by the moments that take our breath away." If we are going to splurge and consume this limited resource, perhaps it might better be spent downhill skiing, surfing, riding a motorcycle, or doing conservation research in a war zone instead of worrying about trivial things in life over which we have little control. We all probably know people who live their entire lives by this philosophy. My dog figured this out a long time ago.

Philosophers like George Carlin consider longevity in relative terms where qualitative rather than quantitative measures are employed. Whenever a person dies prematurely, there is usually a particularly acute sense of loss, and a feeling that the deceased was cheated out of his or her fair share of life's temporal entitlements. Those left behind often rationalize this circumstance by pointing out the "quality" of the decedent's life. This probably helps the survivors to cope with the injustice and the inexplicability of their own mortal existences. Life, like zoo medical practice, seems meant to be experienced looking forward and understood looking backward, which is why most medical textbooks tend to be constructed by analyzing our failed experiences with the dead and dying.

Livestock businesses, professional sports, and many corporate enterprises define longevity in terms of productivity. Nature, however, operates exclusively within the productivity model of longevity—scientists usually call it "natural selection." Agriculturalists have made a quantitative science of productivity in the poultry, livestock, and milk industries. With dairy cows, it is referred to as the "Duration of Productive Life" or "DPL"—the ability of a cow to remain in a herd based on her capacity to produce profitable quantities of milk. The public expectations of zoos, however, differ radically from agricultural and nature models: zoos are now often expected to provide for their animals from cradle to grave without regard to DPL. In many zoos, the productive life of an animal has been defined by how long it is suitable for public exhibition or breeding. Where do all of the surplus babies go? What becomes of the tiger that no longer fits into the group, or is not presentable for exhibition? In response to part of this problem—unplanned parenthood—the Contraception Advisory Group, comprising zoo curators, veterinarians, and reproductive physiologists, was formed in 1989. In 1999, the American Zoo and Aquarium Association established the Contraception Center at the St. Louis Zoo, where the CAG is now based. It currently provides advice on thirty different birth control methods, in addition to the oldest and most reliable method of all—abstention.

Zoo veterinarians probably have the ultimate form of house call practices. This yesteryear style of medicine provided chances to see patients undisturbed in their home environments. Farmers and horse owners have long benefited from this ambulatory sort of veterinary practice, although it is now gaining ground in small animal veterinary medicine as well. In some respects, the old-fashioned human house call was on the cutting edge, but now it has been replaced by impersonal managed care systems. Human medical practices (and veterinary practices too) seem to have forgotten the value of making good, clean, firsthand observations, but instead require their patients to run the gauntlet of the waiting room and the nurse long before making that first eye contact with their physician. By the time you reach the doctor's office and the blood pressure cuff goes on your arm, what are they measuring—your vital signs, or the stress of traffic and the doctor's office? When, and if, they check your blood pressure at both the beginning and the end of your office visit, the second measurement is almost invariably lower. Doctors call this scenario "white coat hypertension." Medical offices, human and animal, don't always bring out the best in either the doctor or the patient. There is an inherent confusion that springs from ringing phones, multitasking, and concerns about insurance copayments.

Our domestic dogs and cats take bumpy rides in the family car before being presented for veterinary treatment. The mere act of bringing out the pet carrier at home is enough to send some pets into hiding under the nearest piece of furniture. Some pets go with enthusiasm for a ride in the car but panic at the sight or smell of the animal clinic. In an ideal world, human patients should be seen as they live daily on their own turf and without the side effects of traveling through miles of hectic traffic, scrambling in from the parking garage and whooshing up six floors in an elevator to a place that smells like a doctor's office. Zoo doctors still make house calls.

Field biologists who research and observe animal behavior continually strive to devise methods of keeping their presence from affecting their observations of animals. An observer is seldom invisible or totally unobtrusive, and some of the study methods have to be a bit contrived. One always has to question the effect of an observer's physical presence on the behavior of the observed—including that of the late Diane Fossey, sprawled in a patch of nettles with her *Gorillas in the Mist,* and of Jane Goodall, camped out in Gombe Stream Reserve in her *Life with the Chimpanzees.*

Dr. Goodall—who, like Fossey, seems to prefer socializing with animals than with her fellow humans—pioneered her techniques in chimps by allowing them to habituate to her presence. Slowly and patiently, she made contact with the chimps in the forest, hoping that they would begin to accept her as they would a harmless bird on a branch. One day she allowed herself to touch a chimp, and the rest is history that you can read about in *National Geographic.* Like a news reporter covering breaking events in volatile parts of the world, the effects of the participant-observer on real events is always a lingering question. Goodall's work took enormous commitment and patience, and she probably thinks of herself, in many ways, as more akin to chimps than to humans, a conclusion her students would not dispute.

Some years ago, I was invited to a small meeting with Dr. Goodall at the National Geographic Society headquarters in Washington to discuss a proposed plan for a

West African chimpanzee reserve where retired research subjects could live out the rest of their lives in semicaptivity. Because she is an enormous icon in the animal world, people treat Dr. Goodall with great courtesy and reverence. When, in the course of our discussions about chimpanzees, I innocently referred to them as "animals," her face flushed, and she admonished me: "They are chimpanzees, *not* animals! I prefer to refer to them as 'chimp beings,' just like we call people 'human beings.'" I then realized just how passionately she identified with them, and while verbally groping to acknowledge her sincerity, I inadvertently used the "A" word again. My African friend sitting next to me radiated a horrified look as if I had accidentally dropped a soiled handkerchief into Dr. Jane's soup bowl and implored, in a whisper, "She doesn't like it when you call them *animals!*"

I don't think that Dr. Goodall is naive enough to believe that the presence of people does not interfere in some manner with the behavior of her chimpanzees, and, after all, many astonishing things have been learned from her studies that forever changed the way that the world views chimpanzees. Presuming to be to be an unobtrusive observer would be a bit of an exaggeration, however, since she did offer bananas as bribes to gain their ongoing trust and cooperation. Jane became a sort of banana goddess who brought fruit to their forest—fruit, in fact, that wasn't even African, but had originated in South America. Behaviorists call this study method "provisioning," a sort of icebreaking and sustaining technique for narrowing the human/animal distance. Some have quietly criticized the advantage that she took of the chimps' weakness for bananas and privately call her Gombe study site in Tanzania her "Banana Republic." This Third World reference is somewhat deserved, inasmuch as competition for the bananas apparently became abusive and undemocratic at times. Some chimps even traded bananas for sexual favors, while others simply hoarded them. Rarely did the "chimp beings" exhibit more high-minded communal benevolence when it came to their food. In the end, it is difficult to know what effect this method had on their normal behavior. If nothing else, their actions bolster Dr. Jane's contentions that chimpanzees are, indeed, very much like people—complete with such unpleasant characteristics as greed.

Wild animals must be competent at disguising their diseases. Don't humans conceal their weaknesses from bullies for similar reasons? It is an essential skill for survival. Imagine, for example, a sick bird perched on a branch. The odds of being the target of a hawk or cat increase appreciably if it displays external signs of illness. After all, predators, by occupation, must be masters at detecting vulnerability. Animals at the familiar African waterhole are usually aware that predators are surveying the herd for a victim. In fact, there seems to be a tacit understanding—a sort of gentlemen's agreement—that someone among them will be tonight's supper for the lions, leopards, and hyenas. To me, this is reminiscent, in our society, of the presence of traffic cops apprehending speeders on a highway. The speeders know they are speeding and that the police are around. The patrol officers know that they are going to give out some speeding citations (they may even have an established quota). There is a safety-in-numbers mindset among the speeders, who hope and expect that it will be someone else, not they, who gets the ticket today—and usually it is. Animals also seem to go about their lives with the notion that they, too, will not be the ones on the menu. The placement of eyes on hoofed animals is no accident. Located more laterally on the head, their field of vision—in some cases more than three hundred degrees—is much greater than for most other species, in order to detect the presence of approaching predators.

Concealing illness has been conditioned as a survival mechanism through many millennia, and it is a hurdle that zoo veterinarians are always looking for ways around. Undetected animal observations are the purest, most valuable ones of all, and, like Dr. Jane, I also often bribed the great apes with small tokens behind the scenes to curry their trust and cooperation.

Our human medical counterparts who relate most to zoo veterinarians are newborn specialists and pediatricians. Like zoo veterinarians, they labor under many of the same constraints because their patients cannot talk to them. With relatively few exceptions, however, their patients don't attack and bite, although I recently saw a recruitment ad for a recreation therapist at a mental hospital in which the job description noted under the conditions of employment that "incumbents may be exposed to residents who may be abusive or combative." At least human patients, mental and otherwise, have family members to fill in some of the information gaps. I wonder how physicians would feel if they had to practice exclusively on illiterate mimes. After all, isn't that the case in a zoo?

The presence and interactions of veterinarians and animal keepers have marked effects on the behavior of the zoo animal patient, and they must be constantly placed in context. Making useful patient observations takes planning and coordination with the animal keepers. One of the worst things a keeper can do is to alter the daily routine before the veterinarian arrives to view a sick animal; the presence of a veterinarian will do that soon enough anyway. Animals are quickly alarmed by changes in the familiar. In their eagerness to help, some keepers will change that routine by not feeding animals or by segregating the patient from others. In some cases it is only because of the trust that animals may have in their keepers that a veterinarian is able to get close enough for meaningful observations at all. The keeper/animal bond may also be vital in encouraging individual animals to consume medications that are essential to their recovery. When anything out of the ordinary happens, many captive animals automatically go into a state of apprehension, simply because familiar activities have ceased.

Stress, like oxygen, has its pros and cons. We can't live without it, but too much at the wrong time and place is damaging (it's called oxidation). Stress is one of the most fundamental biological mechanisms that animals and people have to cope with life challenges. It was scientifically described in 1950 by Dr. Hans Selye, a famous Austrian physiologist in his 1956 book *Stress of Life,* which initiated a focus for the medical profession on a broad new area of physiological research. In the preface, Selye writes, "No one can live without experiencing some degree of stress all the time. You may think that only serious disease or intensive physical or mental injury can cause stress. This is false. Crossing a busy intersection, exposure to a draft, or even sheer joy are enough to activate the body's stress-mechanism to some extent. Stress is not even necessarily bad for you; it is also the spice of life, for any emotion, any activity causes stress."

This field of research had centered on defining the hormonal and chemical events related to various forms of stress. Selye dubbed this remarkable system of alarm and coping mechanisms the "General Adaptation Syndrome" (also called GAS for short). This complex of biological events has also been called the "fight or flight" mechanism, since, in its more dramatic form, it takes place when an animal or person has either to run from an attacker or stand and fight. The accumulation of stress, both good and bad, can lead to physical disorders to the point of producing "distress." The negative effects of stress have been widely examined in both people and animals. Recently it was reported that actors who were the recipients of Academy Awards outlive their less honored peers by an average of four years, and those receiving multiple Oscars lived an average of seven years longer. Is less stress from achieving long sought-after recognition and the ensuing sense of inner serenity translated into beneficial physiological events that can extend longevity? Possibly so, if this is any measure.

Since Selye's original work, thousands of articles have been published on the subject of stress. Pleasure itself is simply a form of stress, technically speaking. People attempt to modify their behavior and lifestyles to reduce unwanted stress (we all seek the pleasurable kind) through transcendental meditation, Tai Chi, biofeedback, vitamin supplements, special diets, colon-cleansing enemas, sabbaticals, vacations, and Covey day planners. Those same dynamics that allow us to adapt to everyday variations in our environments can also lead to our demise when they are excessive. When we remodel zoo exhibits, alter diets, or add new cagemates, we seldom know for certain whether we are increasing or decreasing distress in animals.

Selye was able to identify important physical and chemical changes that are life-sparing adaptations. These same mechanisms are essential, for zoo animals and people alike, to survive in an ever-changing world. Without these coping mechanisms, it is doubtful that we could survive for long at all. It goes something like this: An organism is subjected to a stressor—it could be a sound, a sight, an emotion, an infection, or a menacing threat. In response to this challenge, neurological and chemical circuits become activated. The initial event is called the "alarm reaction," wherein the body's defense mechanisms are marshaled to meet the challenge of the stimulus. This is followed by the "stage of resistance" in which adaptive mechanisms are brought into full, sustained force. Last, if the stressor does not relent, the third stage takes effect, the so-called stage of exhaustion, resulting in either disease or death.

It is difficult to overstate the importance of Selye's work to zoo animal medicine. The concept is not limited to things that scare animals, but also encompasses environmental stresses, such as cold, heat, sound, or improper diet. The success of a species in perfecting the flexibility of its "fight or flight" capabilities is a major factor in survival and evolution. Those animals that are most adaptable are more likely to reproduce and continue their evolutionary pathway. The others go the way of the dinosaurs into the fossil archives.

Once the GAS is activated, more subtle signs of disease are masked in zoo patients, and we are left with the physical part of the medical exam. Or we can persevere and return at a later time when they have achieved a more normal state. In everyday kinds of stress cycles the body gears up for fight or flight, to one degree or another, and returns to normal when the stressor goes away. Over time, when GAS is in full swing, immune mechanisms become suppressed, increasing susceptibility to infectious and metabolic diseases. In other words, too much stress is bad and can eventually kill you. But people seem to have known this long before Selye documented it. During this GAS process, the body's intrinsic steroids are released from the brain and the adrenal glands to serve valuable purposes in carrying our bodies through an acute crisis. We all understand from popular medical news reporting that chronic stress causes ulcers, heart disease, stroke, and death; all are indicators that we have failed to cope fully with our life stressors in the context of our genetic makeup and environment. Some animals seem to cope poorly with captivity because of the limitations of their behavioral and adaptive capacities. Many more fail, however, because we have fallen short of understanding and providing for their unique physical and behavioral requirements. This is the overall preventive objective of an animal health program in zoos—the reduction of unwanted stressors.

Some animal species seem much less malleable in captivity than others, and zoo veterinarians keep little mental lists such as "Animal Species Not Suited for Captivity." However, our prejudices can change quickly when someone finally figures out what it takes to keep a particular species consistently happy and alive. The list titled "Zoo Animals That Hardly Ever Get Sick" is one of my shortest, but favorite, ones. I would put hippos first on my list, followed by a few other species, but this would probably vary from zoo to zoo. Rhinos, camels, and crocodiles would also probably be highly ranked.

Koalas moved off of my "not-suited" list after we finally figured out how to care for them properly, and they are a good case study for the management of a novel species in captivity. A cute, but historically challenging, species to maintain in captivity, they illustrate many points about the nuances of animals' adaptive capabilities for captive living. The techniques for keeping koalas alive and well were pioneered in several Australian fauna parks, but particularly at Lone Pine Koala Sanctuary in Brisbane. People find koalas to be very charming, perhaps somewhat undeservingly so, given their penchant for sleep and general inactivity; and in many ways they depart from the traditional model of choosing exhibit animals. First, they are largely nocturnal (boring to many people, since zoos often exhibit nocturnal animals in daylight exhibits), and most often they present as a furry lump on a branch, offering visitors a view of their hunched-over backsides. Nonetheless, the teddy-bear mystique and cultural affinity people have for them have put koalas in the class of highly desirable, charismatic exhibit species.

A second koala management anomaly is their highly specialized diet. Most zoos do not have the food supply to support these obligate eucalyptus-leaf eaters. Fortunately for koalas, their diseases are relatively few, since their nursing care options in illness are more limited than average. Koalas don't appreciate handling, unless conditioned from an early age, and this contact should start as soon as they leave the pouch. Unconditioned koalas run, climb, bite, scratch, and become stressed. Unlike squirrels, monkeys, and other arboreal mammals, koalas can be readily chased down from a tree if you succeed in putting a pole over their heads with a small banner on it. I once accompanied a koala field research trip with Australian researchers and saw this demonstrated. On the ground, however, wild koalas can run like rabbits when motivated.

Most koalas did not survive life aboard ships during attempts to take them to zoos outside Australia. But all that has changed with advances in husbandry knowledge and rapid transportation options. If you ever observe a koala drinking water, it most likely has a terminal illness and its hours of remaining life are numbered—after all, koala is an Aborigine word that means "doesn't drink." They obtain virtually all of their water from their leafy diet, and they soon dehydrate if they stop eating. The only koala that I've ever seen consume water from a bowl was one that I gave steroids in its last few days of life in a last-ditch effort to encourage him to eat.

The practical solution to keeping captive koalas is their semidomestication. They have an extraordinary capacity for taming if conditioned from the time they emerge from the mother's pouch, even to the point of tolerating a dog as a mode of transportation. Koalas should be weighed regularly to detect nutritional problems. They also should be examined with experienced hands along their shoulder blades, to identify the loss of muscle mass, which indicates declining health. When trained, koalas will sit on your hand or with their bum at the crook of your elbow, their two hands resting comfortably in yours. They seem to fare best when housed primarily in sheltered cubicles, where their food intake and microenvironment can be closely monitored.

Once these husbandry measures were implemented in a new koala facility at the San Diego Zoo in the 1970s, the koala population boomed. To assure a bountiful supply of eucalyptus species, their favorite varieties can be readily grown in small plantations in suitable climates. The San Diego Zoo now provides koalas on loan to zoos in snowy latitudes and sends freshly cut eucalyptus boughs via Fed Ex airfreight. Koala medicine is mostly preventive and based on detailed husbandry procedures—a testimony to the fundamental value of this approach in zoo medicine.

To make the best assessment of their behavior, I have always preferred to view animals when they are unaware of my presence. Binoculars are essential for animal observations in zoo medicine, and video monitoring has become an invaluable tool in

Young koala jockey and Alsatian at Lone Pine, Australia

special situations in the captive management and reproduction of many species. The San Diego Zoo staff and the world have been able to view giant pandas via the internet on the "Panda Cam" throughout the births and infancies of the two giant panda babies born in 1999 and 2003.

The keeper who knows the normal behavior of animals is the vital link to health clues, breeding, and well-being. Some individuals are masters at reading their animals, while others simply suspect that something is "different" or "abnormal" about their behavior. Mixed exhibits can make observations more difficult, but, if interaction is the norm, these social situations can produce useful information relating to health about animals. My guess is that the future will bring more widespread technology to the monitoring and treatment of animals in zoos, including the selective implantation of telemetry devices that will transmit data on blood pressure, heart rate, blood sugar, adrenal hormones, and other important physiologic factors. The basic electronics are now in development and used in research institutions, and are getting smaller and more versatile. Individuals requiring long-term medications may even be managed with devices that monitor certain physiological parameters related to blood chemistries, cardiac performance, and blood pressure. Perhaps one of the most interesting applications could be the use of implanted drug delivery devices to medicate or sedate an animal gently without the stress of physical handling and tranquilizer darts.

Before a zoo opens up to the public each day, many animals are acutely conscious of people who are in the public spaces, but they relax when the familiar crowd starts to stir. If you step over a barrier where the public does not normally tread, most animals become alarmed. Great apes are perhaps the most amusing in their interaction with visitors and zoo personnel; they can pick a zoo veterinarian from a crowd of hundreds in front of their exhibit. After viewing animals from a distance, it is usually necessary to move up for a closer look, often when they are closely confined. I have always found this to be uncomfortable, since many animals find it so. They feel a sense of vulnerability and know that your gaze is different than the average observer, and they seem relieved as you depart, as if you were a predator cruising their neighborhood for food. Imagine how you would feel if someone stopped his car, walked into your yard, and stared at you with binoculars as you reclined on your front porch.

The bush dogs are near the top of a zoo veterinarian's animals-not-suited-for-captivity list. These small South American wild canines are an example of the zoo animals from hell. Nervous, busy, stressed-out little creatures, they are fond of running in circles. Skin problems, fighting, diarrhea, foot sores, and stereotyped behavior—you name the problem, and the bush dogs have it, again. They keep everyone forever busy with medical issues until their eventual departure to bush dog heaven or another naive zoo. Someone needs to do for bush dog medicine and husbandry what Australian fauna parks did for koalas and platypus—figure out what they need. If perseverance counts for anything, I am sure bush dogs are very competent doing what they do in the wild, since nothing will deter them from their chosen task, however self-destructive. For now, and for most zoos, they are still too tightly wound for captivity.

"I shouldn't, but I'm going to have the garbage."

11. FEEDING THE ARK

The Nutritional Wisdom of Animals

The cells of a Komodo dragon, elephant, and hummingbird require essentially the same nutrients for metabolic chemical reactions necessary for growth and maintenance. It is the myriad ways by which nutrients make their way into those body cells that provide many of the challenges and much of the fascination of comparative nutrition. What is food for one animal may be as nutritionally inert as a rock for another. At one extreme, termites eat and digest woody plant materials, whereas most creatures only build their homes and nests with such materials. The ways in which living creatures obtain, mechanically alter, digest, and assimilate foods vary in relationship to the environments within which they evolved.

The science of animal nutrition is the most basic, but historically one of the least applied, disciplines in zookeeping. Feeding practices often vary widely from zoo to zoo, based on tradition and pragmatism as much as anything to do with science. In the past, most zoo diets were empirically formulated, but animal nutrition technology is now defining and improving feeding practices in zoological gardens. The Nutrition Advisory Group was formed within the American Zoo and Aquarium Association in 1994 to coordinate the documentation and development of suitable formulas for feeding captive wildlife, including neonates. This growing body of information is now Internet-accessible through www.nagonline.net.

Zoo diets were historically determined by considering the natural feeding behavior of animals in the wild and the practices used in feeding comparable domestic species. Practical adjustments were made over time, based on the outcomes of the captive-feeding experience. Many of the historical husbandry problems were attributable to inadequate knowledge of animal nutrition. The first zoos to hire full-time animal nutritionists were the Metro Toronto Zoo (1975), the National Zoo (1978), and the Brookfield Zoo (1980).

The dietary requirements for specific nutrients can vary significantly between species. What is a minute, essential dietary substance for one species may be produced internally by the body in another from dietary precursors. By definition, vitamins are organic substances that are required in tiny amounts and, unlike proteins, fats, and carbohydrates, do not provide energy or protein-building units. Their role is to act as coenzymes or parts of coenzymes to facilitate key metabolic reactions. Some animals, for example, can produce vitamin C (ascorbic acid) in their own tissues, but gorillas, some monkeys, and humans must obtain it from the food that they consume. It has been known for three hundred years that citrus fruits protect against scurvy, an illness that was ultimately identified as a vitamin C deficiency; Englishmen were called "limeys" because their sailors commonly consumed citrus fruit to prevent scurvy, long before they knew the chemical basis of the disease. It was not until 1932 that ascorbic acid was first chemically isolated from lemons.

For most of the history of zoos, even the existence of common vitamins was unknown, let alone specific requirements for various species. Except for specialized feeders, many animals in nature eat a large array of foods, varying in abundance with soil, temperature, rainfall, and season. Unlike in captivity, there is a shifting interplay between animal preferences and food availability, resulting, overall, in acceptable levels of nutrition on a population basis (individuals are on their own). Whereas animals spend a good deal of their time in nature finding, manipulating, and consuming food, zoo cuisine often comes in several compact daily portions, distilling this food-acquisition activity into short periods of hyperconsumption.

The case of the gorilla provides evidence of the detrimental effects of certain human-imposed feeding routines in zoos. Some captive gorillas have commonly re-gurgitated and reingested (R/R) their food, a vice that has defied most efforts at de-terrence. This behavior is not observed in wild gorillas. Often, captive gorillas will vomit food on the ground in a matter-of-fact manner and then leisurely reingest it, sometimes joined in this activity by their exhibit companions. Needless to say, this behavior is not endearing to the public. A controlled study by several zoo researchers led to a significant reduction in these undesirable activities, focusing primarily on the traditional practice of feeding milk to gorillas. By eliminating milk feeding, substitut-ing a small volume of fruit juice, and increasing the proportion of fiber-rich dietary ingredients, R/R was reduced by nearly 40 percent. This behavioral modification may be particularly important in breaking the R/R cycle from generation to generation, since such behavior in young gorillas seems to have an important learned component.

Much of the current interest in zoo animal nutrition derives from the many years of work by Dr. Duane Ullrey, the former director of the Comparative Nutrition Lab-oratory at Michigan State University. His hundreds of published papers on animal nutrition, and the generations of graduate students that he has mentored, have pio-neered the research in this field. Surprisingly, zoos employ more geneticists and re-production specialists than animal nutritionists. Complete formulated rations were developed at the Philadelphia Zoo in the 1930s. H. L. Ratcliffe implemented the earli-er dietary work of Dr. Corson-White, a pathologist with the zoo. It would be many decades, however, before the first trained animal nutritionists were employed in zoos.

For most of the history of zoos, the public was allowed to bring food for the ani-mals as part of the entertainment experience, as well as to subsidize the zoo food budget. Most public feeding is now banned. This transition included various schemes to control feeding, such as providing vending machines with specific animal food, rather than having the public bring their own junk-food choices. The death of wide-spread public feeding of zoo animals was slow and painful, and it taxed the creativity of zoo staff, whose traditional approach was to post a "Don't Feed the Animals" sign. For many visitors, the feeding of animals was their link to animal interaction—a long-presumed right of zoogoing. In the final stages of banning feeding and other interac-tive public behaviors at the San Diego Zoo, a more amusing approach was taken that was better received than the typical "Don't" signs. A summer student was put to work observing negative public interactions with animals and was asked to make some suggestions. His product, a clever sign, has generated significant revenue through the sale of thousands of copies in the zoo gift shop and has helped modify public expectations and behavior.

Many zoos, including the San Diego Zoo, used to make it a practice to withhold all food from the big cats one day a week, and it was still in fashion when I first arrived there. I received interesting comments from some of the mammal keepers when I inquired about this practice. Since appetite is one of the more reliable indicators of how an animal is feeling, I was a little perplexed about the loss of this vital information on all of the zoo's big cats for an entire day each week. One keeper said that he thought the cats were supposed to be healthier because of it, but he wasn't sure why, except that it was considered "more natural" since the big cats don't eat every day in the wild. Another attributed it to cost-cutting, since tigers and lions are expensive to feed, and this had been done for more than fifty years. A third simply replied that they skipped feeding on Mondays because that was the main day when most of the regular keepers did their heavier cleaning and maintenance; skipping the feeding gave them more time for other chores. Inquiries at other zoos turned up similar, mixed responses. Instead of fasting, one zoo fed chicken necks to the big cats one day a week because they were cheaper than horsemeat, although they might have contributed to oral health by reducing dental tarter accumulation. It seems that skipping the feeding of carnivores once weekly originated primarily as a cost-saving practice and was rationalized by naturalizing it. We did away with the fasting custom, and all carnivores were fed daily after this brief survey.

Indeed, the cost of feeding animals, and carnivores in particular, has been on the minds of San Diego Zoo managers from the start. In response to criticisms about the cost of keeping a private collection of animals, just donated to the new San Diego Zoo, the *San Diego Union-Tribune* published the following commentary in 1917:

> When the question of the acquisition of these animals is broached to certain conservatives they appear stricken with fear at the enormous amount of meat the lions and tigers are supposed to consume, quoting figures they must have obtained from some farmer's almanac, and shrinking from joining the Zoological Society because of the supposed high cost of maintaining large animals. Some compromise by desiring the Zoological Society to only place on exhibit the local ground squirrels, gophers and field mice, thereby losing sight of the real function of a great zoological

garden, which is to house and exhibit, along with the local fauna, a representative collection of the large exotic species. When these people think of a lion eating 15 to 20 pounds of meat a day, they think of the cost in terms of beefsteak at the butcher shop. As a matter of fact, the meat problem at a zoo is far more simple than at a home as the animals are fed horse meat. Old horses cost from $2 to $4 depending upon their size, and one fair-sized horse lasts all the animals in the Zoo for one week.

Still struggling with the meat bills eight years later, an article with the following title appeared in the same newspaper: "Lions, leopards and tigers at Zoo are getting hungry—old nags wanted to feed them."

There is still a common, but misguided, belief that animals are born with innate nutritional wisdom that empowers them to choose a balanced diet from a cafeteria of foods. This cafeteria model works in the wild, where the menu is not human-made but one with which the animals evolved. Cafeteria feeding assumes that when provided with a blinding array of choices, animals know what is best for them and will select the correct ingredients and proportions to form a nutritionally complete diet. Why we would assume anything as presumptuous as this is hard to fathom, but it seems to derive from our abiding trust in the wisdom of Mother Nature. Take the following examples: man's closest animal friend is, indisputably, the domestic dog. Humans have spent thousands of years and millions of hours selectively breeding and teaching domestic skills to dogs, yet you can't trust dogs to watch your food. Give a dog a bath and it won't hesitate to roll in the first dead and decayed piece of protoplasm that it encounters. Dogs consistently prove themselves nutritionally incompetent—eating bones and garbage until they get deathly ill, and then doing it again only a few days after they recover. And one last thing about dogs—and this is why I don't understand why people trust animals to select a balanced diet—tie a dog to a clothesline rope on the porch, and most will remain there until they starve to death, never thinking that within seconds they could chew themselves free. I love dogs just the way they are, but I have no delusions about their critical thinking skills.

Studies have shown that animals naturally do what most people do: they have preferences for the most palatable rather than the most nutritious ingredients. In other words, they behave just like our children—and us. A feeding study with monkeys demonstrated that their zeal for junk food was as strong as in humans. Forget the tofu, broccoli, and brown rice they were offered when the equivalent of Twinkies, popcorn, and hot dogs was available. They consumed carbohydrates at the expense of protein, using palatability as the principal decision maker.

Since many contemporary zoos have had to survive at the mercy of municipal governments, the expense of feeding zoo animals has always been regarded as a burden. Particularly with specialized feeders such as many bird species, it is common to experience significant food wastage. The cost of feeding berries and cultivated insects to birds at the San Diego Zoo accounted for at least some of the financial anguish experienced by the zoo's comptroller.

The public brought its surplus food to the bear pits of old European city centers to support these charitable attractions, and this tradition carried forward into the twentieth century. Leftover bakery goods, second-class fruits, and vegetables from produce vendors and fallen animals from slaughterhouses and farms became the everyday staples for many zoo animals. Even in the year 2000, zoo animals in some locales were at risk from questionable food supplies. The deaths of twelve tigers at India's Nandankanan Zoo, for example, were caused by the consumption of decomposed and contaminated cow meat, according to an official pathology report.

Virtually no commercial zoo diets were available for zoo animals prior to the 1960s, and the quality of dietary husbandry varied widely. In a 1923 edition of the *San Diego Union-Tribune*, a crisis was declared when it was announced that the monthly feeding costs for the entire San Diego Zoo had exceeded an alarming three hundred dollars. A public plea was made for donations of mice and rats to feed the reptile collection, which was expanding rapidly. Requests also went out to farmers and ranchers in the region for donations of fallen and unwanted livestock to feed the zoo's carnivores. From these frugal, penny-pinching beginnings, the practices of feeding zoo animals took their formative steps. In fact, one need only travel to zoos in some less prosperous or enlightened countries to see the same problems today.

Many wild animals failed to arrive alive at their zoo destinations because they lacked wholesome and balanced diets to sustain them en route. Particularly with stress-prone or nutritionally specialized species, transitions from the wild into captivity often overtaxed their abilities to adapt as they passed through a complex custodial chain in the animal trade. When vitamin reserves are depleted and protein and energy intakes are below what is needed, the fasting body literally begins to consume itself. Glycogen reserves and fat deposits are mobilized and burned up, accompanied by the utilization of muscle for energy and for the protein needs of more vital tissues such as the heart. This catabolic state marks the beginning of an accelerating process that rapidly jeopardizes survival.

During episodes of the CBS television series *Survivor,* there were noticeable changes in the physical status of the competitors. What began as a general shortage of groceries eventually challenged the participants nutritionally. The physical and emotional effects of calorie deprivation and stress were apparent in all of the contestants—they got on one another's nerves, lost focus and ambition, and in some cases became emotionally vulnerable. In zoos, the signs of nutritional stress in animals may not be so readily apparent. A dwindling state of nutrition, coupled with chronic stress and poor sanitation, causes significant mortalities in wildlife before they can adapt to captivity. Younger animals with more demanding nutritional requirements, leaner body masses, and less resistance to common pathogens are particularly unlikely to survive unless special efforts are made to nurture and rehabilitate them. The lack of essential amino acids, vitamins, and functional enzymes to catalyze normal metabolic reactions results in immunosuppressed states similar to those characteristic of HIV/AIDS, where even garden-variety bugs can be fatal.

I can testify first hand to the insidious effects that malnutrition has on physical and psychological well-being. While working in West Africa before attending veterinary school, I experienced vitamin A deficiency after months of field research in the rainforest regions of Liberia and Sierra Leone. I had lived on a limited diet of rice, cassava, chicken, and other readily available village staples. The problem began as a loss of peripheral vision at night—a peculiar sensation of tunnel vision. A skin rash and psychological malaise followed, and I was at a loss to figure out what was happening to me. I languished for days before finally visiting a rural missionary clinic to see an English doctor. Shuffling through the queue of pregnant mothers, crying children, and old men with festering leg sores, I was immediately diagnosed with a vitamin A deficiency. The lack of dietary green vegetables containing beta carotene (the precursor of vitamin A) had depleted my liver reserves of this nutrient, but the problem began to resolve within days after I began taking vitamin A supplements. In many ways, zoo animal nutrition is also a largely unexplored wilderness.

When animals are collected in the wild by hunters, who bring them back to their villages and inexpertly attempt to keep them alive until they are sold, the mortality rate can be staggering. In the case of chimpanzees, it has been estimated that, even in the second half of the twentieth century, ten chimp deaths resulted from each import.

This starts with the shooting of the mother and capture of the young, the typical manner of collecting chimps from the wild.

Animals that are malnourished have abnormal behaviors. Low-protein feeding studies have demonstrated significant changes in social interaction, as quantified by alterations in eye contact and other indicators of anxiety. To the casual observer they may appear no different than animals fed normal protein diets, but there are measurable changes that, in highly social creatures, place their well-being at risk.

Some wild animals simply do not recognize domestic foodstuffs as edible, and they may reject everything that is unfamiliar. The confinement of captivity, separation from companions, and the abrupt alteration in their normal constellation of smells, sounds, and space can prove overwhelming. After a protracted period of anorexia and malnutrition, some seem unable to recover their former vitality under any circumstances. The stress of captivity may cause intractable indigestion, alteration of normal gastrointestinal flora, and inability to digest and assimilate nutrients. Microscopic changes to the cells of their damaged intestinal linings may unalterably compromise their ability to absorb nutrients and regulate water balance.

Notable among the difficult species to adapt to captivity are some of the specialized leaf-eating mammals, such as the colobus and langur monkeys, many of which have exhibited varying states of malnutrition upon their arrival at zoos. Their digestive systems have evolved to process plant fiber through the aid of symbiotic bacteria in their complex stomach and hindgut, just as gut flora are thought to help termites digest woody materials. Surveys of diets fed to captive leaf-eating primates have revealed that zoo diets are generally lower in fiber and higher in protein than wild diets, demonstrating that further efforts will be required to approximate natural diets more closely. Other factors requiring study include the presence of toxic secondary-chemical compounds in plant materials fed in captivity and their variations in concentration with season. It was learned with koalas (obligate folivores), for example, that eucalyptus browse can vary greatly in its content of cyanide compounds, a potential concern for captive koala feeding. As a precaution, when selecting eucalyptus species for cultivation in San Diego for koala browse, testing was done to eliminate those species with higher cyanide content. It is presumed that secondary compounds serve to protect plants by deterring excess browsing. Livestock intoxications by cyanide are well known in the Australian veterinary literature, particularly when eucalyptus trees have been damaged by fire and generate sucker growth that is readily accessible at ground level. There also is evidence that free-ranging primates avoid certain plants because of the presence of deleterious chemical compounds.

Some species are poorly represented in zoos because of failures in converting animals from wild to captive-diet substitutes. Concentration camp inmates of the World War II era sometimes succumbed to the well-intentioned efforts of their liberators, through the overwhelming stress caused by acute ingestion of nutritious foods. Similarly, providing unlimited amounts of certain foods to debilitated animals may overtax their ability to cope. Sudden dietary prosperity often causes indigestion, bloating, and death. Reversing serious malnutrition should be approached in a manner similar to that used to restore normal body temperatures in hypothermic patients—gradually.

The North American moose has been notoriously difficult to keep healthy in captivity and, for perhaps both nutritional and behavioral reasons, moose have never adapted well in zoos. Those that survive are often sorry-looking specimens. Despite efforts to develop diets that duplicate the composition of natural moose foodstuffs, it seems that moose are not yet destined to become a common zoo exhibit animal. Some years ago, a motion picture director and his Canadian animal trainer telephoned me from their woodsy filming location in Oregon. Both were in a panic about the concluding scenes of their movie and had been working overtime to finish it. Among the crucial animal stars in the final scenes of this drama were two tame moose, "Bullwinkle" and "Rocky," that had had diarrhea for the past five days. We discussed the history of these two creatures in detail—how well they were trained, the extremes that the trainers had gone through to condition them to riding in a truck, waiting calmly for a scene, tolerating lighting effects, and moving in and out of camera views as needed. After suffering through this lengthy history, we finally reached the current problem: persistent watery stools. Things had nearly come to a halt on the movie because neither moose could complete a scene without acting as though it was about to go relieve itself.

Not suspecting some infectious plague of moose, and fresh out of intelligent medical questions, I finally asked, "How do you teach the moose to do all of these things anyways?" The Canadian trainer said, "Aye, they will do anything for bananas and that's what we give the buggers." I said, "You mean you have to give them bananas to do everything." "Aye, just about, yes, we do," he said. "But they never get tired of them no matter what because we've been filming for seven days in a row now and they still like 'em." Cringing a little in anticipation of the answer, I asked, "And how many of these bananas do you suppose they have been eating every day for the past week?" "Oh," he replied, "I guess that would be between aboot fifteen and twenty pounds each per day, but yesterday they had more—we worked late, you know. Aye, do you think that might be the problem?" For a few moments I was speechless.

Many of the recipes for feeding animals that can keep them alive have been derived from uncontrolled experimentation, personal preference, food availability, and practical experience. The following is such a recipe for a baby elephant formula that we used in the San Diego Children's Zoo. Like many zoo diets, its origin is a mystery, but the elephants did well on it. There are now, however, diets for baby elephants that are somewhat more scientifically formulated.

Baby Elephant Diet

1 cup cooked rice
1 cup cooked barley
3 cans evaporated milk
1 tablespoon of calcium tribasic
4 tablespoons of honey (optional)

Mix ingredients and add sufficient water to equal 1 gallon.
Feed three times daily if animal is over 1 year of age and is eating other
   supplements. If younger, feed every 2–3 hours.
Continuous shaking of the bottle while feeding is necessary to prevent
   rice and barley from settling to the bottom.
Supplement this with Sudan hay and cut-up vegetables and fruits.

Feeding animals in groups poses additional challenges to proper zoo nutrition, for individuals vary in their nutritional requirements by age, sex, and reproductive status. This often makes it necessary to feed all animals in a group at a level meeting the nutritional requirements of the most demanding individuals present, such as the young and lactating females. Group social issues also add complexity to mixed species and age exhibits. At the San Diego Zoo, we experienced a series of deaths in one of the large walk-through aviaries, which housed dozens of bird species in a forest-like setting. The principal findings on postmortem examination were "malnutrition" or "starvation," but there was also evidence of trauma, as seen in bruises to the skin and underlying tissues. Several of the bird keepers took offense at these diagnostic labels because they consistently fed a substantial quantity and variety of quality foods and were far from neglectful. But the pathologists stuck to their guns. When activities in the large walk-through aviaries and at the feeding stations were observed closely, everyone, including the keepers, finally agreed that the problem lay with some birds aggressively defending their feeding sites. They simply prevented more passive species from eating and harassed those that tried. "Starvation" was probably an apt description after all. As soon as the numbers of feeder stations were increased and placed at different heights and locations, the mortalities dropped dramatically. The total amount of food fed was about the same.

In the wild, herbivorous animals spend large amounts of time foraging for plant foods, and it is desirable to parallel this behavior in captivity. However, few zoos are able to provide naturalistic exhibits with the variety of living food choices found in the wild. When cafeteria offerings of domesticated food items are provided, some individuals will monopolize favored feedstuffs, such as grains and protein supplements, at the expense of other animals in the exhibit. To overcome this problem, many zoos began feeding nutritionally complete pelleted diets along with hays, making it more difficult for dominant animals to overindulge on preferred feeds. As with the birds, multiple feeder stations also help to provide more equitable distribution of food. Nourishment of young, socially subordinate herbivores may be accomplished with "creep" feeders, which are designed to allow smaller animals physical access to more nutrient-dense food while excluding adults with less demanding nutritional needs.

Even animals with comparatively simple dietary habits, such as wild carnivores, have had their share of nutritional problems in captivity. Failing to take into account the nutritional contribution of all parts of a whole animal that would normally be consumed by a predator, many zoos have attempted to raise and maintain carnivores exclusively on muscle and fat. Meat alone has a low calcium concentration and an imbalance of the minerals calcium and phosphorus, which is ordinarily compensated for by consuming the non-muscle parts of prey. I once received a radiotelephone call from a South American ranch, where the owner's family was hand-raising several ocelots, small spotted felines from the region's forests. After bottle feeding and weaning, the cats had grown rapidly into beautiful little creatures with glossy hair coats. But they were becoming lame and having difficulty walking, all due to their unbalanced, all-meat diet. The owners readily accepted recommendations for adding calcium to the diet, and the ocelots made rapid progress in subsequent weeks and became quite normal.

In similar nutritional scenarios, dietary imbalances have been commonly identified in meat-eating birds, reptiles, and amphibians. The zoo carnivores that have experienced fewest problems are the ones consuming whole prey, such as hawks, owls, crocodiles, lizards, seals, and sea lions. This assumes, however, that if these carnivores are fed colony-reared rodent and avian prey or farm-raised fish, the diets of the prey species must be optimized with respect to their content of essential vitamins and minerals.

Other parallel pitfalls have been noted in reptiles and amphibians fed diets of crickets, mealworms, or wax moth larvae, which tend to be low in calcium as compared to phosphorus. The techniques of nutritionally adjusting the composition of these insect creatures to make them more suitable as a balanced food are now well known. They were dusted with supplement powders in the past, but these supplements are commonly lost as the insects move or groom themselves. Much more successful is the provision of a customized insect food that leaves a high-calcium, nutrient-rich residue in the insect's gastrointestinal tract. So when they are consumed by an insectivorous predator, the insect plus its gut contents comprise a nutritionally balanced meal. Calcium metabolism is also dependent upon the presence of vitamin D in the diet, or access to the sun or an appropriate artificial source of ultraviolet B (UVB) irradiation. Historical efforts to keep these animals healthy in captive environments were often compromised by a lack of understanding of these crucial factors.

Apes and most monkeys have nutritional requirements generally similar to those of humans, including mandatory requirements for vitamins C and D. Deficiency of the first will cause scurvy, and, of the second, rickets or osteomalacia. In climates where ample natural sunlight is available, captive primates can produce their own vitamin D from metabolic precursors. Many of the cases of rickets in zoo primates are in multiseason, temperate climates where indoor housing and the absence of proper amounts of direct sunlight are limiting factors. Window glass filters out the wavelengths of light that are required for vitamin D synthesis, and young animals with rapidly developing skeletons are more vulnerable to deficiencies than adults. For many years the cause of bone deformations in captive monkeys was not understood. Some interpreted the problem as being caused by confinement in small cages and called it "cage paralysis." The typical findings included bowed and thickened bones and collapsing vertebrae. Animals became crippled and immobile and were unable, or reluctant, to move about, even to obtain food that was placed in their cage. These invalids would often lie around their cage bottoms, losing use of their arms and legs, and their muscles wasted away for lack of use. Finally, in the 1930s, two vitamin D forms were isolated and their structures determined, and the role of this nutrient and sunlight in cases of cage paralysis eventually became known and incorporated into primate husbandry routines.

Two forms of vitamin D are found in foods: vitamin D_2 in plant and fungal tissues and vitamin D_3 in animal tissues. Although vitamin D_3 is most biologically active in the monkey species that have been studied, Old World macaques seem to use either vitamin D_2 or vitamin D_3 quite well, whereas New World capuchin monkeys, spider monkeys, howler monkeys, and tamarins seem to be significantly more responsive to vitamin D_3. Contemporary commercial primate diets now scrupulously include the D_3 form of this vitamin (and vitamin C), but baby monkeys kept indoors and that depend on their mother's milk (and little other food) for an extended period can still fall victim to rickets.

Zoo primates can be resourceful in supplementing their diets with the local bird fauna, and I observed this on a number of occasions in the San Diego Zoo. One small group of gibbons, long-armed and highly arboreal monkeys, lived on a small island exhibit and waited patiently on their elevated bamboo perches for birds. It was impressive to observe a gibbon stab its arm overhead into the air, snatch a surprised bird in mid-flight, and eat it. A male Barbary macaque monkey in the zoo was much more premeditated about his quest for sparrows and grackles around the monkey yard. Birds played an important role in his daily life. He was most successful when the public was in the zoo and birds were lulled into a false sense of security. Sitting by the wire front of his cage, he would place several small, carefully spaced morsels of monkey biscuits within his reach on the ground outside. Calculating and patient, he waited with his feet propped on the cage wire and his arm strategically placed within striking distance. Nonchalantly, he anticipated the arrival of his prey. As small birds hopped innocently toward his bait between him and the visitors, he grabbed them with lightning speed. To the shock of the visitors, he stuffed them into his mouth, and then fastidiously plucked out the larger tail feathers and discarded them on the floor. One horrified child, who I observed witnessing this microcarnage, recoiled from the sight and exclaimed, "Ooh, gross, mom!" In contrast, San Diego's first two gorillas, Mbongo and Ngagi, acquired as youngsters in the 1930s, were reported by Belle Benchley in her book *My Life in a Man-Made Jungle* to be observed gently holding a live chicken that made a habit of straying into their cage, making no attempts to harm or devour the bird. On the other hand, a keeper observed them playing with a feral rat by picking it up and dangling it by its tail. When the rat finally bit one of them, they tired of the game. The dangling rodent was dropped into their water pool, where they closely observed it until its demise. It alternately swam and sank until it finally came up no more. Mbongo then retrieved the body from the water and laid it out on a shelf near the keeper.

Animals sometimes survive in captivity even if they do not eat the food we offer them. The keepers at the zoo hospital were concerned because a small African carnivore, an aardwolf, had not eaten since her arrival. We weighed the animal to compare with her arrival weight, and to everyone's surprise she had actually gained a few ounces. One night when I came in to the hospital to tend to a sick animal, I walked quietly through the back animal ward, and in the subdued light I witnessed our little aardwolf chasing cockroaches and swallowing them like bits of popcorn.

The red and pink feather pigmentation of some birds, such as flamingos and roseate spoonbills, results from regular ingestion of natural carotenoid pigments that are present in their wild diets of crustaceans, insects, and algae. Early captive diets for flamingos often produced disappointing losses of plumage coloration. This problem can now be solved by providing diets containing somewhat costly synthetic or natural pigment products, such as the pigment roxanthin, found in red or dried powdered shrimp shells and carrot oils.

In addition to the inadvertent omission of important nutrients in zoo animal diets, the manner in which foods are processed and stored may also lead to malnutrition. Some of the fish species commonly fed to marine birds and mammals may be altered in nutritionally significant ways when they are frozen and stored—a common historical practice. Thawing frozen fish with running water results in loss of some water-soluble nutrients. Thawing in a refrigerator avoids this problem and inhibits microbial growth that might occur when thawing at room temperature. Of course, this approach, because it is slower, requires advance planning to ensure that thawed fish are available when needed. Another common fish storage problem has important implications for the supply of the B vitamin, thiamin, a dietary nutrient essential for health. Thiamin is present in generous supply in whole prey, such as fish, and is obtained through normal digestion and absorption. Freezing, storing and thawing fish, especially herring, smelt, and mackerel, may allow the enzyme thiaminase in fish liver to destroy thiamin, causing a deficiency in fish-eating zoo animals, such as seals, sea lions, and sea birds. Thiamin shortage can lead to neuromuscular weakness and cardiac problems. This can be avoided by placing thiamin tablets in the gills or mouths of fish or injecting them with thiamin solutions before feeding them.

Kenton "K.C." Lint, an elder statesman of bird curating at the San Diego Zoo, was a great lover of bird feeding recipes and anecdotal husbandry advice. In recounting some of the idiosyncrasies of living a lifetime with a bird nut, his wife, Marie, once complained to me about all of the strange things that she regularly found in his pockets before laundering his shirts and pants. These ranged from sunflower seeds to wriggling mealworms, crumbled crickets, and live anolis lizards. K.C.'s habit was to feed his favorite specimens as he toured his bird collection in the zoo. Years before, he had impressed his zoo curator peers by repeatedly breeding some rare macaw parrots for the first time. The "secrets" that were touted as the defining factors of his success were the nesting box that he provided in which these parrots reared their young—a used wooden whiskey barrel—and a diet that included fresh corn on the cob. For years, many zoos with this parrot species tried to emulate his accomplishment; whiskey barrels became common zoo parrot domiciles around the world. Keepers and curators from other zoos and private collections used to contact the zoo to be sure they were getting the correct barrel size and were using the same diameter opening through which the birds could enter. Some even wanted to know the brand of whiskey and the time elapsed since the barrel had contained liquor. Despite this passion for detail, nearly everyone else failed to replicate this breeding success, while these original birds continued to produce babies in their whiskey keg.

Such is the nature of popular recipes for success, whether they are birdhouses or diets. Transport those same successful birds and their whiskey barrel and corncobs to another zoo, however, and they might stop breeding altogether. However diligent our search for optimal ways of feeding animals, some in the zoo profession will undoubtedly continue to use a blend of folklore, witchcraft, and science, and there will be strongly held preferences, just as there are with the feeding of our most common household animals, our domestic dogs and cats. I can only hope, with our developing knowledge in comparative nutrition, that the rational application of science to the feeding of zoo animals will prevail.

While the longevity of zoo animals has steadily improved with better housing, management, disease control, and nutrition, the current nutritional trend is toward obesity in Americans. Contrary to the zoo experience, some experts are predicting that today's human children may be the first generation to have a life expectancy shorter than their parents.

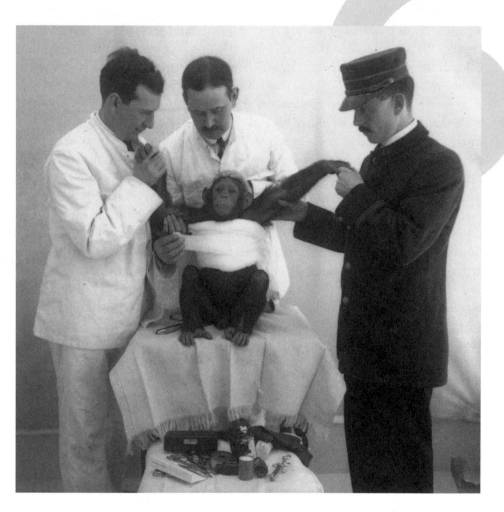

Chimp with pneumonia at the New York Zoological Park, c. 1905

12. GETTING CLOSER TO ANIMALS

Judas Goats and Alpaca Coats

Leave it to veterinarians to try to help animals only to have their good deeds backfire. Our single alpaca in the zoo had accumulated an enormous thick hair coat. These South American hoofed relatives of the llama are adapted to cold climates in the Andes Mountains at altitudes of fifteen thousand feet, where they have been domesticated for hundreds of years for fiber and food. When summer came, I started worrying about our heavily frocked alpaca, who I was sure would suffer under the hot San Diego sun. Alpaca wool, which is as soft as mohair, is often called the "fiber of the gods" and is one of the most luxurious in the world. Its superior insulating and working properties make it prized by wool fanciers. During the annual visit of our sheep shaver to shear the Children's Zoo sheep for the summer, we offered him the rare opportunity to groom an alpaca—something he could proudly talk to his children about, or at least within the social circles frequented by sheepshearers. He jumped at the chance.

Our mild-mannered alpaca stood less than four feet tall at the shoulder. Living without a mate of the same species, she managed to stay healthy and out of conflict with several llamas and vicunas in a mini-South American exhibit on the Hoof and Horn Mesa. Until shearing her, no one quite realized how small an animal resided beneath this huge mop of wool.

The shearer shaved to his heart's delight. The more he shaved, the smaller she shrank and the bigger the black heap of fleece grew on the ground next to her. However, no one was more shocked at her small size than she. We had transformed a statuesque animal into a Grinch-like waif. She looked around at herself in apparent disbelief at the alien she had become. No longer worried about heatstroke, we shifted our concerns to the alpaca's mental well-being. She behaved as if we had stripped her naked and tossed her into the public square. For days, she refused to venture into the exhibit area and hid in the seclusion of the back holding pen. From time to time she would peek out in front, as if to see if anyone was staring. It would be weeks before she would be anywhere near normal and several days before we could coax her to eat. Ordinarily, we don't imagine animals as being victims of vanity, but she shunned all human contact and seemed unable to stand to look at her own legs and body.

The wool, however, was eventually fashioned into a beautiful sweater.

Zoo animals do not always carry out their amorous acts in private, any more than your dog tries to be discreet about licking certain of his body parts or relieving himself on the lawn. As with our domestic pets, the reactions of people to these intimate situations in the zoo are especially different when in the company of small children, who demand an explanation for *everything* that's going on. Unlike many animals that have seasonal estrus periods, the primates, like humans, are in a relatively perpetual state of availability. The Monkey Yard and surrounding primate exhibits were in close proximity to the zoo entrance, and easily accessible to parents with children and teachers with young students. The baboons, in particular, are role models of promiscuity. They have harem-like social structures that attempt to assure that all eligible females are pregnant or nursing at all times. Teachers and parents automatically gravitate to the monkey areas because of their universal appeal. Only experienced and resourceful visitors have learned to navigate skillfully around the compromising situations offered up by the baboons.

If a mating scene spontaneously unfolds in the presence of children, some parents simply grab their kid's hand and drag them unceremoniously to the next exhibit without comment. Or they make a profound transitional pronouncement such as, "Hey kids! Let's go get some ice cream right now!" The most creative parent I ever witnessed in this predicament decided to stand her ground with her five-year-old and simply lie. Asked what the two monkeys were doing, she said, "Well sweetie, the little monkey on the bottom hurt her leg, and the big monkey on the top, well . . . he's trying to help her up on the tree so that she can rest." Promoting the appealing sentiment that animals are caring souls, the lie succeeded, and they moved onward to the next set of monkey cages, most likely with a parental prayer that they would encounter no more orthopedically challenged inhabitants.

The price of successfully breeding animals includes the responsibilities of rearing them and finding suitable homes for the surplus offspring. Wild sheep, deer, and goats are very prolific, and the job of rounding up these surplus animals for shipment to other zoos ultimately falls to the keepers and veterinarians, and this may not always be an easy task given the agility and herd behavior of these animals. Some can be trapped and funneled into crates, but others require trickery and chemical restraint for their capture. Just as the Pied Piper of Hamlin led the children away from their families, the zoos' "Judas goats," of various species, help to attract and march off their surplus herdmates. The biblical reference implied here refers to the infamous Judas, who betrayed Jesus for thirty pieces of silver, in a similar manner in which animals also forsake their own species and sometimes lead them to slaughter. Human trappers in Asia have used tame elephants to deprive wild elephants of their freedom. Similar techniques have been used for hunting wild animals and waterfowl, where live animals act as actual decoys or confidence builders, to attract animals to within a hunter's range.

A Judas goat in a zoo is a hand-raised animal that has lost much of its normal aversion to humans because of the taming, and often imprinting, that takes place when they have been bottle-fed since birth. Absent from their herd during critical socialization periods, they have greater affinities to people than to individuals of their own species. A Judas goat acts as if all is normal when humans are around, even when loading chutes, traps, and people await them in catch pens behind the exhibit. The Judas goat calmly eats its food and relaxes, deceiving his herdmates that nothing is awry. Then, when it's too late, the selected émigrés find themselves trapped where they cannot escape their fate. The modest reward for a Judas goat's behavior is its continued residence at the same zoo.

Things were not so easy with George, one of the San Diego Zoo's last remaining common chimpanzees, following a decision to specialize exclusively on pygmy chimpanzees and put the others up for adoption. Biding his time pending the move, George spent his days in a large two-story outdoor cage behind the Ape Grotto, overlooking a forested hillside. This off-exhibit enclosure was covered with heavy-gauge chain link fencing and could be approached at ground level. Intelligent, curious, and increasingly suspicious, George seemed to wonder what had become of his female companions, who had diminished one by one as they were sent off to other zoos. With the disappearance of his wives, his behavior suggested that he was beginning to question the sincerity of his caretakers, and so he moved to the opposite side of his cage at the slightest suspicion. Perplexed by his shrinking family, his wariness only grew.

When news came from the curators that a new zoo home had finally been located for George, Dr. Chuck Sedgwick and I contemplated how we would get him out of his spacious accommodations. Despite our earlier efforts, he had rejected all of our attempts to slip tranquilizing drugs into his foods to make him manageable for crating. Because the chimpanzee is among the strongest of the primates, pound for pound, this would require an intellectual and chemical, rather than a physical, exercise. We decided to start by paying social calls on George to size up his attitude and to find a way to exploit his vulnerabilities. It turned out that George's main weakness was for food—speckled bananas in particular. As we reduced his daily fruit ration of bananas, grapes, and apples, George grew noticeably concerned. The coup de grace, however, was for us to visit George while Sedgwick ate an apple and I methodically peeled a banana for myself. As we nonchalantly savored every morsel, George watched intently and lusted after the small brown paper bag from which we would ceremoniously pull out the fruit, leaving only a few token pieces if he approached us before we departed. When shipment day approached, we finally made our move. George was optimistic to see us with our customary bag of fruit, which by this time was becoming an obsession with him. He salivated as we extracted the fruit and ate it piece by piece, excluding him from the fun. No matter how much we hoped to catch him, this deceptive drama was tinged with a little veterinary self-loathing for our insincerity, as we had already determined the manner of George's undoing.

I removed a banana and slowly handed the bag back to Chuck. As I began to peel it, curious George approached us. Without a second's hesitation, Chuck nonchalantly reached into the bag, withdrew a capture pistol, and shot George in the leg with a dart. George was stunned and outraged at the deception, glaring at us in disbelief as he screamed in anger and yanked the dart from his leg. He wildly flung it at us, barely missing Chuck's head, jumping, stomping, and scolding in such a fit that made the hair prickle on the back of my neck. His eyes began to glaze over. We tossed him a small apple as a peace offering, but he threw it back at us like a baseball. His consolation for this insult was joining the company of other chimps over a thousand miles away. There he continued to father little Georges, who were probably equally fond of speckled bananas.

Veterinary rounds to the quarters of the great apes was always a special experience, shared on numerous occasions with their favorite keeper, Harold. The living accommodations were pretty simple, made up of barred cubicles with heated floors, laid out behind the public exhibit areas along a series of hallways, divided into separate zones for chimpanzees, gorillas, and orangutans. I preferred to visit in the early morning before the housekeeping chores were complete so I could see the evidence of the feeding and digestive activities of the past night. On some days the hallways were a gauntlet, depending on the family moods of each group. Everyone had names, which highly personalized the degree of feedback between keepers and veterinarians about the individual animals in contrast with larger groups of animals in the zoo. At close range, it was common for strangers to be sprayed with water from an orangutan's well-placed thumb over a running water tap. Other favorite missiles, flying through the bars in the service hallways, included scraps of leftover fruit and gorilla-sized handfuls of loose dung. One of the best ways to prevent such occasional assaults was to avoid direct eye contact. Staring, especially by strangers, is impolite and aggressive among the great apes. By emulating their habits, we were merely adopting the logical protocols that we expect of our fellow humans, such as hand-shaking, smiling, and other howdy-do pleasantries.

Only after making a matter-of-fact, humble entrance can you get to the business of looking more closely for reported medical issues of the day. As in many human cultures, you cannot do business with these intelligent animals before you socialize. This often involved direct contact with more approachable individuals to scratch their backs, rub their tummies or even hold their hands. Linda, the pygmy chimp, was a hand-holder and loved to have her belly rubbed. She was as trustworthy as any great ape could ever be; if she were truly ill, I wouldn't have hesitated to open the door to examine her. The mother of the entire colony, Linda, along with husband Kakowet and the rest of the pygmies, were an endless source of entertainment and companionship for the animal staff that cared for them. Several years after Linda was finally transferred to a primate breeding facility in Georgia, I had the occasion to travel to her outdoor compound by detouring from a trip to the Atlanta Zoo. As I parked my car and approached her enclosure, I could see her sit up and take notice of me from a distance. The closer I came to her, the more animated she became, until I was near enough to touch the hand that she extended to me through the heavy wire mesh. We were both glad to see one another. Two years had not diminished her affection for contact with an old friend.

Developing rapport with individuals helps greatly, but safety always remains a concern with these powerful primates. No neckties are allowed in proximity to the apes, as more than one behind-the-scenes visitor to zoos has been grabbed and thoroughly thrashed with such a convenient handle. Among the chimps and orangutans, my favorite befriending treat was sugarless cinnamon gum. Some of them never caught on to the idea of gum-chewing and would simply gulp it down. A few relished the taste and texture, though, and, on several occasions, when the time came to go up on public exhibit, they would sit contentedly and chew for several hours while they checked out the visitors across the moat. It became difficult to discern who was more intent on watching whom. The people saw black and red apes with shaggy hair gazing across the moat toward them. The apes saw tattooed bikers and their babes, serious punkers, obese goths, liposucked gangbangers, and botoxic rockheads staring at them. On balance, the apes were often more competent than their human observers.

Perhaps the greatest ape offender residing in San Diego was a newly acquired gorilla named "Abe," who arrived complete with extensive dental infections. Abe could spit like a champion tobacco chewer. His journey to San Diego from the Colorado's Cheyenne Mountain Zoo was a little unconventional, as he was the excuse for a well-lubricated gratitude party for volunteer boosters of the San Diego Chargers football team on the team's private Boeing 707 jetliner. The beer and champagne flowed freely for everyone aboard except the flight crew and our gorilla transfer team. While we left San Diego in warm sunshine, we could see wisps of snow in the overcast drizzle as we touched down on the wet tarmac at the airport in Colorado Springs. Several rows of seats had been removed to accommodate Abe's crate, which was shifted off of a forklift and into the side door of the aircraft near the food galley. Along with a sharp blast of cold air, the partying passengers got their first whiff of a genuine gorilla; every football locker room they would smell in the future would be tame by comparison. Abe was flying first class on this trip and sat calmly in his crate as the other animals partied their way back to San Diego. Back at the zoo, he became a spitter, targeting nearly everyone who approached him. As you walked down the ape bedroom-service aisle, the best strategy was to move fast, turn your head, and avoid eye contact. I can still recall the warm, slippery sensation of being hit on the back of the neck by Abe. Treating his dental problems slightly improved his breath, but it did not alter his behavior. Most people always gave him plenty of extra room.

Abe had been brought to the zoo to bolster the gorilla population since our long-beloved male, Albert, had developed health problems that eventually took his life. One of the most handsome gorillas ever born, he had a regal air about him that universally appealed to the staff and the public. Unlike Abe, who came across as sort of a vagrant, Albert had bona fide class. When Albert began to suffer from kidney and heart disease, it finally became necessary to sedate him and better define the causes. He was twenty-seven years old and had seldom been sick, and most of his veterinary experiences had been positive ones. When he caught sight of the blowgun, he cringed, but bent over and put his hands in front of his face, providing the easiest possible shot at the great muscles in his rear end. His surrender made me embarrassed to shoot the dart into him. As soon as he felt the prick of the needle, he patiently pulled it out of his rump and politely handed it back through the bars without malice, fully convincing me that he knew this intrusion was an attempt to help him.

After Albert died, a staff taxidermist from the Denver Museum of Natural History came to the hospital to make a plaster death mask and prepare Albert's remains for relocation. There was Albert, propped up in a sitting position on the necropsy table, with that handsome face covered in wet white plaster of Paris. I walked in to see how Albert and the museum man were doing as the technician slopped on another layer of plaster. He asked me if I had known Albert. Feeling some regret that my treatments had failed, I said, "Yes, I was his last veterinarian." The final time I saw Albert was several years later on a business trip to Denver. He had not yet been fashioned into a museum facsimile of himself, but his skeletal remains rested in several neatly labeled cardboard boxes on a shelf. I moved a box onto a table and took a peek inside to find plastic bags full of his carefully cleaned bones. Alone for a few minutes, I said my goodbyes and resolved to return in another year to see the results of their efforts to reassemble him to his former glory at the zoo—but I've never been back.

In our efforts to help animals, veterinary zeal has led to more than one animal's demise. This happened on an eight-hundred-acre island in New York, the unlikely location of the US Department of Agriculture's Foreign Animal Disease Center. Plum Island is located a mile and a quarter off the northeast shore of Long Island. The USDA complex is somewhat reminiscent of San Francisco's Alcatraz Island in terms of security. It was named for the wild beach plums that were seen on its shores by early explorers. A real estate bargain like Manhattan, it was sold by local Indians to a European man for "a coat, a barrel of biscuits, and 100 muxes (fishhooks)." While some may find animal research with infectious diseases disheartening, there is no question about the importance of protecting our agricultural economy from the devastating effects of these disease agents.

Zoo veterinarians are in strategic positions in the detection of foreign animal diseases in exotic animals that may have escaped interdiction during their original importation. A small group of zoo veterinarians was invited to Plum Island for a unique opportunity to see, firsthand, live cases of the world's most frightful animal diseases. These included foot-and-mouth disease, African swine fever, rinderpest, African horse sickness, avian Newcastle disease, and other scourges of the livestock planet that had previously been eradicated or largely avoided in the United States. One entire department of the research facility was dedicated to biological security, and the rules and regulations resembled a Marine boot camp in their inflexibility.

The morning routine involved a ferry ride to the island from the mainland. Visible name badges, closely monitored personnel checks, and an aura reminiscent of the Manhattan Project surrounded this transition from civilian life to the risky world of biological containment. Given the destructiveness of these pathogens to livestock, the mere thought that these dangerous viruses might accidentally infect America's herds and flocks due to the negligence of research workers was pervasively disconcerting. Permission to participate in this direct exposure to infected animals required formal preconditions, including signed affidavits and memoranda of understanding promising no contact with livestock or fowl for a minimum of two weeks after departure. All Plum Island employees are banned from keeping livestock or from visiting farms, fairs, or other venues in proximity to live animals.

Our small party of zoo veterinarians assembled on the boat dock and we were issued identification badges. Along with the employees, we shuffled aboard for the boat ride and disembarked through the island security gate, making our ways to appointed work areas. The morning of our first day was devoted to lectures on foreign animal disease, showing grim images of disease disasters from around the globe that all of these efforts were meant to protect against. After lunch, we were to see live animals that had been infected with hoof and mouth virus and African horse sickness and the dreaded Newcastle poultry virus. Study animals for the research arrived from specially monitored, disease-free supply farms.

To enter the disease containment area, we were directed to remove all of our clothing and accessories and take showers. Exiting naked to a separate suite, we were provided with sterilized coveralls, footwear, gloves, caps, and masks to wear while in contact with contaminated animals. Everything that left the building, except people, was sterilized or incinerated. All ventilation and liquid waste systems were filtered and treated to assure that the possibilities for extramural contamination were virtually nil. Emergency power generators were in place to assure that a power failure would not compromise the lab's mission. It was an awesome operational discipline.

The cattle, pigs, horses, and chickens were segregated in their own subunits of the containment area and had been experimentally infected with livestock disease agents. We went from unit to unit, observing animals with blistered feet and gums, diarrhea, depression from virus fevers, and neurological tremors, physically examining individuals to test our growing knowledge of foreign animal diseases. God, please spare us and our animals from these problems.

We had a rigorous day observing the dying and the dead, the victims of diseases that most veterinarians would only read about in textbooks, some of the most destructive and costly animal diseases known to mankind. Afterward, before exiting the building, we went through a supervised series of decontamination procedures. Stripped naked again, we dropped our clothes into an autoclave hamper, blew our noses three times, coughed up and discarded phlegm, and took the first of three mandatory germicidal exit showers. Finally, we emerged into our original locker rooms and were reunited with our street clothes and personal belongings. The experience was somewhat extraterrestrial, and, slightly dazzled, we walked out into the late afternoon sunshine, quietly congratulating ourselves on our good fortune to have been entrusted to witness these infamous animal plagues.

As we stood beside this disease-fighting fortress looking out toward the nearby Long Island Sound, we observed a lone seagull with an obvious limp and a drooping wing struggling along the edge of the parking lot. Picking it up to examine its problem, we passed the fortunate patient around the group—the collective knowledge our elite group of zoo and wildlife veterinarians would surely help this poor bird. Then reality struck us simultaneously: we had committed a terrible crime. Minutes out of the poultry plague lab, we had violated our affidavits that forbade all animal contact and handled the first living creature that we set eyes upon.

One sheepish volunteer, seagull in hand, marched back to the fort, offered a contrite group confession, and handed over the unlucky bird for a complete necropsy and incineration. We would all hear about our transgressions in the next day's lecture.

13. SO, YOU WORK AT THE ZOO?

Employees, Visitors, and Fence Jumpers

Zoo tour bus driver/guides have a special place in the experiences of visitors, and their services offer a convenient alternative to hours of walking up-and-down hills in the San Diego Zoo. Drivers are expected to develop their own narrative routines, within the limits of fixed routes, stops, and good taste. Each tour begins with, "Welcome to the World-Famous San Diego Zoo," and continues with the formal admonition, "Please remain seated and enjoy your tour and keep your hands, arms, legs and small children inside the bus at all times." After that, the drivers and the passengers are on their own.

Only a few drivers are career employees. Most are college students filling in summers or weekends. Certain personalities seem to gravitate toward these jobs, as it requires a knack for rattling off statistics about animals, paying attention to stray human limbs poking out of the bus, and going through the same boring punch lines to the same jokes, day after day. Their closest competitors were probably the tour guides on the Jungle Safari River Cruise at Disneyland, minus the blank pistols that they used to scare away the mechanical hippos.

Since repetition breeds boredom, the bus drivers were always coping by being convivial party animals. Without doubt, they were the most socially motivated subculture within the zoo. Although plenty of tour-guide material was passed down over the years from driver to driver, each one tried to bring something fresh to the challenge. For some, it became a place for them to try their standup comedy routine talents on entirely captive audiences. Most of their statements ended with lilting tones and exclamation points. Accuracy often took a back seat to truth in search of the audible sighs that came from passengers when apprised of such stunning facts as "The cost of replacing the plant life in the zoo alone would exceed the value of the animal collection by thirty times!" (no reason was given, however, for such a radical proposal) and "It takes over two hundred thousand bananas, fifty tons of raw horsemeat, two million crickets, and five billion grains of rice to feed the animals at the zoo every year!" At least the visitors now understood why the admission price was so high.

Certain health fables were perpetrated to justify the interaction of the drivers with selected performing animals in the zoo. Even though the public was not supposed to feed the animals, the bus drivers regularly did so to amuse the riders and generate laughs. One myth was about the bear biscuits that they fed to get "Yogi" and "Boo Boo" to rub their bellies and pat their heads, or to salute "our loyal armed forces personnel on the bus." The monologue would then continue, "These biscuits were formulated specifically for our bears by our zoo veterinarians. We feed them to be sure that they get all of the vitamins and minerals they need to keep them healthy." So their stories went. I stood on the sidewalk numerous times during my health rounds and exchanged eye contact with the drivers. They knew that this was a total fraud, but resumed their narrative in front of me anyway: "Feeding animals is not allowed in the zoo, but the biscuits that I am giving them are strictly for nutritional purposes." (Veterinarian grits teeth and rolls his eyes.) We usually broke off all eye contact at that point, and the bus moved on up the hill to the next bear exhibit, and a fresh handful of biscuits. One driver seemed particularly unnerved by my presence one day and fixated on me in his side mirror as he rolled forward to the next bear exhibit. His attention was abruptly jolted when several agitated riders yelled out to him, "Keep on moving!" He had failed to notice, while focusing on me, that the lone male spectacled bear that the bus was passing was engaged in a contortionist act of self-stimulation.

If a performing animal was asleep upon the arrival of a bus, a sharp blast from the air brakes or a well-placed biscuit to the skull brought it straight to its feet. Just as motorcycle-riding chimpanzees have disappeared from zoos and have been replaced by more high-minded activities, the feeding of the San Diego's bears and elephants from the buses gradually lost its defensible place in the consciences of the zoo trustees, and the tradition was allowed to die. This only placed an even greater burden on drivers to attempt verbal antics in order the win the loyalty of their passengers.

Most of the corny jokes were cute and benign: "These peccaries to your left are very piglike, but they are not really pigs. They are also called javelinas—that's hava lee' nahs. The name of the big handsome one on the left is Gregory Peccary (laughter) and the smaller, prettier one, on the right is Olivia De Javelina (more, less spontaneous, laughter). Gregory is the one who has the stinky odor. . . . " "That cute little carnivore hiding behind the log on your right is a wild cat called a lynx—his name is Smokey. . . . "

On Hoof and Horn Mesa (where the zoo's deer and antelope play) it continued: "Hey, do any of you kids know the biggest medical problem of a giraffe? (momentary silence). A sore throat!" The kids laughed, adults groaned, and, as for the giraffes, they never got sore throats. To this same question, the best answer I ever heard a kid yell out was "nosebleeds!" The driver smirked with upstaged resentment and ignored him (he probably planned to use this on his next tour). The only things missing from these bus monologues were the pratfalls and rim shots.

Admittedly, the guides had a tough audience, since they tried to capture the attention of linguistically challenged foreign guests, distracted parents, sticky little children, and servicemen from the Navy and Marine bases. Another "humor spot" on the bus tour was along the zoo perimeter, where the buses stopped and the driver would challenge the passengers to name the species of wild animal behind the tall chain link fence. After a brief silence, and watching the audience strain to figure it out, the driver would chortle, "Those are the dangerous *Homo sapiens*, the wild all-American teenagers at Roosevelt Junior High School!" No matter how lame the joke, it always seemed to get a laugh (or a groan) from someone on the bus. The foreigners who didn't get it often laughed out of politeness.

If nothing else, the success of bus-driver humor is a vivid testament to the profound effects of vacationing in a warm climate on human intelligence. Almost anything works when people are relaxed and off their normal cynical guard. A spell descends over many people when they enter many zoos, and it dissipates only after they part with their last souvenir dollar in the gift shop and exit the turnstiles. The same phenomenon occurred when special visitors toured the San Diego Zoo hospital behind the scenes on VIP tours. I secretly thought that, surely, some of these prominent personalities and celebrities would take pity on our humble medical establishment and whisper some encouragement in the right administrative ears to fund a new zoo hospital.

At first, our facilities were most unimpressive, underequipped and understaffed. Yet, mesmerized by their proximity to a tiger or a koala, almost everyone, brain surgeon and board chairman alike, fell into a trance of baffled awe and thought that our hospital was state-of the-art marvelous. I imagine that for them it was like getting off a plane in Haiti or Cuba and being oblivious to the less progressive aspects of those countries while the tropical fragrance of plumaria and jasmine addle the brain. Some time later, when we built the new modern zoo hospital, physicians and dignitaries gazed around, now in more familiar surroundings, often complaining that their own human hospitals were not as nice or as clean.

Other driver jokes quickly got axed from the bus routines when visitors took offense to the material. Apparently some things do have the capacity of cutting through the spell of the zoo experience and crossing the reality line. After reciting numerous stunning animal facts during his tour, one standup comedian driver reached a little deeper for a "one-two" as he eased the bus to a stop in front of the giraffes. "What do you get if you lay all of the arteries, veins, and capillaries of a giraffe end to end around the earth's equator?" Everyone hushed while awaiting the answer, and the driver answered—"a long narrow mess."

One joke earned a driver several days' suspension without pay: "Over on your right, those handsome hoofed animals are the Somali wild asses. They are very rare in nature and live on the arid plains of northeast Africa. These animals cost the zoo over $10,000 each. . . . Now that's a lot of money to pay for a piece of donkey!" A few belly laughs blurted from the servicemen on board, accompanied by some stares of disbelief and indignation from parents accompanying children. The driver had the misfortune of hosting half a busload of church members on an outing with their families and would hear about it from his supervisor when he returned to the bus station.

The employees in the San Diego Zoo Security Department had an especially interesting subculture. Upon my arrival to the zoo, their mood was highly military, and many of the uniformed staff were former servicemen, police officers, and even a retired prison guard. Unlike some zoos that dressed their security personnel in whimsical pith helmets and shorts, the haircuts here were short, the uniforms crisp straight-arrow police style, and some of these guys looked as if they had taken a heavy toll on the enemy in their soldiering careers.

The zoo's perimeter fence had been wired with electronic surveillance sensors to detect intrusions. Various radio code words were used to communicate public misconduct or noteworthy circumstances, such as, Breach of Perimeter Fence Security, Inebriated Visitor, Injured Visitor, Pervert, Animal Escape, or Zoo Director on the Grounds—the director never had a radio and so he was isolated from much of this intrigue. Interlopers attempting to scale the fence for free admission were hunted down like escapees from a maximum-security prison. It was a friendly sport, but many of us puzzled at the overdedication of some of these officers in pursuing petty offenders. We were also perplexed that they were all so well-armed. Most of the nighttime trespassers were intoxicated Navy or Marine recruits who came over the fence on a bet.

Veterinarians had a special, peculiar bond with security officers as a group, and I could sense it when we had our animal capture guns on the zoo grounds. One day it dawned on me that this kinship was based on the fact that we were the only other zoo personnel who were armed. Altogether, the zoo security problems were pretty minimal for an annual visitor population of over three million people. Much of the credit was probably due to the total change of atmosphere, which seemed to attenuate many negative public behaviors. The lack of beer and liquor sales in the zoo then probably raised the average IQ a few points as well. Visitor screening started at the front gate. Here the tipsy, barefoot, shirtless, rowdy, and derelict elements were sized up and ushered out. The security force usually gave scantily clad women a pass, however, and I suspect they had a radio code for them as well. On peak days, the crowds created such an elbow-to-elbow experience that human behavior adopted a herd mentality, voluntarily surrendering to issues of interpersonal space and comfort.

We called one perpetually unsmiling security officer "Killer John" (not to his face, of course). Rumor had it that the only time he ever smiled was when he injured his foot one day. The night security guard, however, took the peculiarity prize for the whole force. I hardly ever saw him in the light of day, and I doubt that he was ever suntanned in his entire life. The zoo is a mysterious, sometimes haunting, place to be at night. Purposely lighted in a subdued fashion to permit animals to rest, the darkness is peaceful, except for the occasional roar of a lion or animals shuffling, snorting, or barking. Knowing the beasts that reside in the neighborhood can make walking alone in the dark a little intimidating to the psyche.

Officer Snyder was a stocky, balding man who dressed in dark clothes and wore a black stocking cap. He could see in the dark like a cat, and he lurked around the zoo like a nocturnal predator. His nighttime habit was to creep up behind uninitiated employees in his crepe-soled shoes, turn his eight-cell metal flashlight on the back of their head—at point blank range—while simultaneously shouting, "Who is it?" After one initiation like that, and a change of underwear, you were sure to call him on the radio to advise him of your presence when you next tended to a nighttime illness.

One evening Snyder offered me a midnight ride back from the nursery to the zoo hospital in his patrol car. We careened off of the front entry plaza in the dark like a speeding rock down a steep canyon road with all of the vehicle lights off. I felt as if we had dropped down a mineshaft and were certain to end up in the hippo pool at the bottom of the hill. Safely back at the hospital, I asked Snyder why he drove like hell in the dark like that. He said, "Doc, if you're going to catch someone in the zoo at night, you gotta take 'em by surprise." I asked, "Snyder, who are you trying to catch tonight?" A man of few words, he replied, "All of them, Doc!" And off he raced into the blackness to rejoin the other creatures of the night.

14. ANIMAL CASES AND CHASES

And Some Things Better Kept to Myself

When one is doctoring a large collection of wild animals, every day brings new problems and twists. After fifteen years at the San Diego Zoo, I often wonder what it would be like to regularly tend to animals in a smaller zoo where less changes from day to day. When I have visited smaller zoological gardens over the years, I have found a certain serenity in being in someone else's zoo for a change. Many of these smaller zoos actually have some open, grassy glades and quiet shaded benches to rest on while leisurely observing the animals. There is no perpetual crush of a crowd, no minefields of fumbled food obstacles, no intermittent screeching of tour bus brakes. In stark contrast, few days seldom went by at the San Diego Zoo without some event that stirred the staff's adrenal glands.

Shortly after I arrived in San Diego, we received an urgent radio summons from zoo security that one of the orangutans had escaped from the exhibit on Primate Mesa. Meanwhile, several hundred people milled around at the zoo entrance, readying themselves to start their visits to the animals. My boss, Dr. Chuck Sedgwick, and I frantically tossed capture equipment into two vehicles to head for the zoo grounds. This was going to be the big one! This was no Alexander Haig moment: the veterinarians were definitely in charge.

Each armed with a capture pistol or rifle, we hastily loaded a few tranquilizer darts while attempting to get confirmation about who had escaped, in order to determine the drug dose for the capture. But no one could tell us who had gotten out. The males are over twice the size of the females, so we loaded a dose that we hoped had enough safety margin to work for either. With emergency flashers going, I sped down the hill from the hospital in one vehicle and up the steep slope to the back service entrance of the ape grotto. Meanwhile, Chuck headed toward the front to defend the main zoo entrance. As I pulled up to the ape kitchen's loading dock no keeper was in sight, but strewn all over the ground like the aftermath of a tornado was the ape string's fruit and vegetable order for the day. I raced through the ape kitchen with the gun and a few spare darts, up a flight of stairs and down the hall to the orangutan holding cages. They were empty. Running up yet another flight of steps toward the public area, I found all but one of the orangs outside in the exhibit—a single female was unaccounted for. Just then a message barked from the radio that "Sally" was the escapee, and she was seen heading toward the main zoo entrance several hundred yards away. I bolted up the pedestrian incline walk from the exhibit in that direction, and after only thirty yards I spotted her—seven score pounds of flowing auburn hair walking about free on all fours.

A keeper in a pickup truck had just arrived on the scene and parked at the peak of the incline that I was ascending. Just then, Sally approached the truck and climbed into the cab through the passenger window, as the keeper dove out the driver's door. She seated herself behind the steering wheel, wildly swiveling it to and fro, like a kid mimicking an adult driver. Then she started to ratchet the gearshift on the steering column, as if she was ripping off a tree branch. I thought the next scene in this movie would have the pickup truck, orangutan at the wheel, jolting out of gear and heading for a downhill finale into the ape exhibits at the bottom. But, instead, she clambered out of the truck and continued her journey toward the front entrance.

By this time, several more employees had arrived in the area, taking cover in several nearby buildings, peeking out of doorways, trying to spot the escaped ape. I hoped that the security guards were taking this all in stride and would give us time to capture her unharmed before taking any extreme measures. As Sally left the truck, I followed her. She was so enthralled with her adventure that she didn't notice me trailing behind, and she stopped several times to pull up handfuls of flowers from planter beds along the path. She alternately knuckle-walked and ambled upright, passing the Bird Yard cages like a regular visitor.

Then, just as she lifted her leg to climb over a low wall along the Gibbon Island water moat, I fired the dart. It struck her in the hind leg below the right buttock. She swatted at what must have felt like a bee sting and puckered her lips. By the look on her face, she seemed to realize that her picnic was beginning to go sour. Reversing direction, she headed back toward the ape exhibits, a dart dangling from her leg. I was unsure if it had actually discharged its drug dose, and I quickly loaded up another. Within only a few minutes, however, the effects of the drug began to show; Sally began to look around overhead as if she were considering a vertical escape in one of the many surrounding trees.

As she stumbled her way toward a group of small aviaries, she chose one and scaled the front wire, having difficulty with her finger holds as she went. When she reached the roof, she had little zest left in her beyond bracing herself from falling over. Mired in a chemical meltdown and at the end of her freedom run, she was unceremoniously lowered down a ladder in a cargo net and toted back to her bedroom quarters. The next morning I visited her before she went back on exhibit and offered her a piece of cinnamon gum. She took it from my hand, stuffed it into her mouth, and began to chew. No hard feelings.

The cause of the escape was human error. Sally had not returned to the sleeping quarters the evening before and had spent the night topside in the exhibit. Missing the note from yesterday's keeper, the regular keeper entered the exhibit and started to clean. When he left to get some supplies, out the door went Sally. Unaware of the morning's excitement, the visitors awaiting the opening of the entry gate spread out for their own adventures in the zoo.

Zoo veterinarians sometimes have to be spoilsports to get their work done while providing for the safety of others. Until the construction of the new San Diego Zoo Hospital in 1977, it was difficult to accommodate hospital visitors because of cramped quarters and work areas. Special provisions were made in the new hospital to provide viewing areas behind glass walls to host special visitors and zoo staff while preserving safety. When we began to do a dental surgery on a tiger or work on animals such as a gorilla or a large crocodile, zoo staff members sometime came out of the woodwork to get a peek at one of these creatures up close.

On a day that we worked on a black cobra, the news traveled fast throughout the zoo. Most of our work on venomous reptiles was done in the main reptile house, and we never hospitalized poisonous snakes outside the holding areas there. Occasionally, though, one would come to the hospital for X-rays or some other diagnostic procedure. A researcher at the local medical school had made a special plea for a sample of cobra blood for his work on coagulation and cancer. I was unenthusiastic about handling poisonous reptiles to begin with, but, in the interest of science, I agreed to accommodate his request. My caveat to the curators was that the animal would be fully anesthetized to increase the safety of the procedure. The cobra arrived from the reptile house in what is called a "hot box," a sturdy, red, lockable carrying case for venomous snakes. It had metal-screened air holes, stout carrying handles, and a special lid with a double door—the first solid and the inside one screened.

The keeper carried the red box into the hospital's large procedure room and placed it on the floor next to the examination table, as if he were setting down a land mine. As we started to talk about the next step, a few onlookers crept into the room for a closer view. I asked everyone except the reptile keeper to leave the room—after all, this was a dangerous job for "experts" only. Now that the distractions were gone, the plan was for the keeper to remove the cobra from the box by securing its head in a straplike noose at the end of a snake handling stick, and then place the snake on the exam table. This would then allow me to insert a plastic tube into its windpipe (which in snakes is in the front of the mouth) and pump the snake's lungs full of anesthetic vapor.

Everything was going as planned until that point, and the onlookers were safely sequestered in the viewing area, noses pasted to the glass. Just as I was manipulating a forceps to spread the snake's jaws and insert the tube, it suddenly slipped from the restraint strap and slithered atop the anesthetic machine next to me. Drawing itself into a coil, it opened the hood on its head and neck in a chilling display. We jumped back and reconsidered our plan, while the onlookers, now grateful that they had been ejected, pressed harder on the glass.

After recapturing the cobra and placing it back in its box without further incident, I encased the whole container in a trash bag and filled it full of anesthetic vapors until the cobra was safely unconscious. While many venomous snakes have sizeable heads, some cobras have small ones in relationship to their necks, making the strap-restraint method less reliable. That was the last research cobra I agreed to handle. I limited my future research projects to more predictable rattlesnakes. Our zoo pathologists would not necropsy a venomous snake until it had first been decapitated, yet another luxury not enjoyed by the clinical veterinarians.

The San Diego Zoo, in keeping with its large display of poisonous snakes, had a fairly elaborate emergency response plan in the event of a venomous snakebite. As a first precaution, poisonous snakes were not to be handled in the reptile house unless two qualified keepers were present. In the event of a bite, the first measure to take place was the activation of the alarm system, which went straight to the zoo security office and to an alarm bell on the roof of the reptile building. The immediate priority, before any first aid treatment took place, was to secure the guilty snake in order to avoid injury to personnel that came to respond to the accident. It was also critical to determine the snake's identity with absolute certainty. The local medical center supposedly had at least one staff physician on duty in the emergency room who had been briefed on snakebites, and written protocols were kept in notebooks in the hospital emergency room.

It was up to the zoo to maintain its own stockpile of exotic snake antivenin and essential that it be within the product expiration dates so that the physician would not decline its use. These biologicals are often produced by repeatedly inoculating horses with small doses of venom and harvesting the serum from their blood which then contained antivenin properties to neutralize the effects of the toxins. In the event of a bite, a detailed evacuation plan was in place, including access for an emergency ambulance to the reptile house. The snake-bitten person, along with the cache of the appropriate antivenin, was to be transported to the hospital to find (hopefully) a knowledgeable and willing physician awaiting their arrival.

Despite all of the ludicrous folklore about tourniquets, cutting, suctioning and poulticing bites to remove snake venoms, the basic procedure is to keep calm, keep the affected area elevated, and seek prompt emergency care. However, in the 1930s, lacking competent knowledge, most of today's prohibitions about bite treatment were actively promoted. The San Diego Zoo reptile department's old advice to the public concerning rattlesnake bites was published as follows:

- Make a cross incision over each fang mark to the estimated depth of the fang puncture
- Suck for at least half an hour
- Do not give whiskey or alcohol in any form
- Give a cup of strong coffee or a teaspoonful of aromatic spirit of ammonia
- Do not place a dead chicken, tobacco juice, gun powder, or any other remedies on the bite
- *Always cut and suck.*

Very wrong about everything else, they were correct about the chicken, tobacco, gunpowder, and whiskey.

No human emergency room ever finds venomous snake bites routine. In some cases, physicians have declined or delayed giving the antivenin because of unfamiliarity, or for fear of causing allergic shock, especially after reading the labels, which warn "Do not administer to patients allergic to horse serum—this may precipitate a fatal anaphylactic reaction!" Faced with a choice, most reptile keepers would rather take their chances on the risk of death by horse serum allergy rather than by snakebite. Some of the most toxic snakes can have lethal effects within only minutes from cardiac, respiratory, and muscle effects, making medical complications from a product more academic than real. Virtually all zoos in the United States decline to house a venomous snake for which they do not stock or have ready access to antivenin in ample quantities. Reptile keepers in zoos are a special breed, marching to different drums than bird and mammal keepers. A few of the San Diego reptile keepers enjoyed driving out into the local desert in the evening to see how many rattlesnakes they could apprehend warming themselves on rural highways in the desert night and then simply release them—just for fun, of course.

The giraffe is one of the few animals in the zoo that is known to never utter a sound, making no audible vocalizations even when a mother is stressed and agitated by separating it from its offspring. If you were led blindfolded throughout the animal barns in the zoo you would be know immediately when you arrived at the giraffes, since they have a unique, pleasant odor entirely distinct from elephants, zebras, rhinos, and other herbivores. Occasionally, giraffes have mishaps and injuries in their exhibit areas, but treating sick or injured giraffes is one of the least desired of zoo veterinary tasks, for obvious reasons of size and altitude.

Their inconsistent responses to immobilizing drugs also make them high risks, and a drugged giraffe can topple over, causing serious injuries to itself and to those trying to break their fall. Our largest San Diego Zoo giraffe was a male named Topper, who stood seventeen feet tall. One of his ongoing problems was the notable overgrowth of his hooves, which were getting uncomfortable and unsightly. Despite our desire for a special restraining chute to attempt to whittle away at his problem feet, it would be some years before one became a reality. Such specialized equipment has helped greatly to move, handle, and crate animals such as apes, elephants, and a variety of antelope species. The only chance I had at trimming Topper's feet came on a moment's notice, when a radio message alerted me that Topper was unconscious on the ground. By chance, I was about a minute away from the exhibit, and on arrival I saw the big giraffe stretched out flat, his overgrown hooves staring me in the face.

Topper had fallen after becoming entangled in a rope and pulley that had just been installed on an exhibit palm tree earlier in the day by a creative zoo gardener. The intent was to facilitate hoisting his plant browse up a tree for him to feed. Despite their long necks, it is difficult for giraffes to feed off the ground, and drinking water in the wild is also an awkward maneuver for them. Like all other mammals, giraffes have only seven cervical bones (vertebrae) in their necks; they just happen to be very long ones. Captive giraffes are given elevated feed bunks and drinkers.

Topper, however, managed to place his head and neck between the ropes and the tree and panicked as he turned to leave. Lassoing himself and losing his footing, he knocked himself out cold when he hit the ground. The keeper and I ran to Topper's side, and I took his pulse as I supported his huge head in my lap to check the pupils of his eyes. My first thought was that he had broken his neck, but as I watched, his breathing began to return to normal in a few minutes. He rolled his eyes and flicked his huge eyelashes as he slowly moved his head. I sat there on the ground staring longingly at his overgrown hooves—my hoof-trimming tools were in my truck nearby, but the opportunity was fading. As Topper regained his faculties, he raised his head above us and succeeded in stumbling to his untrimmed feet with our assistance as we pushed on his rump. In lieu of chemically restraining him for footwork, we installed a specially roughened concrete slab in his favorite feeding place, and his foot overgrowths gradually subsided to a manageable level as the slab wore them away. The restraint chute didn't come until later, long after our aging Topper went to that big giraffe savanna in the sky.

A telephone call came late in the afternoon on my day off that Freckles, our female giraffe, had stepped backward into the outdoor exhibit and tumbled into the concrete moat that separated the exhibit platform and the public viewing rail. Stunned and confused, Freckles was in a panic. When I arrived at the zoo I received an account from a visitor: "She was just standing there, dozing off and chewing her cud. I was watching the wad of food travel up and down her neck, then, without warning, she seemed to forget where she was, stepped backward, and fell like a tree."

Slightly banged up with some visible abrasions on her head, Freckles was pacing to and fro, trying to figure out how to extricate herself from the moat to rejoin her mates. The moat itself was five feet deep and shaped like a U in cross-section; it had been constructed by laying wire mesh over shaped earth and spraying it with concrete. It had no exit, coming to an abrupt stop on each end of the exhibit perimeter. She made several futile attempts to climb out, but gave up in frustration after taking several pathetic tumbles for her efforts, adding more bruises and scratches to her legs and feet.

As night fell and we all stood and watched, Freckles paced the moat. Given the coming darkness and her spooky demeanor, it would be impossible to rescue her that evening, so we set about preparing for an overnight vigil, spreading straw over the moat bottom and trying to comfort her with some of her favorite treats of carrots and apples. She was far from being in the mood to eat. Finally, in exhaustion, Freckles collapsed on top of her bruised and spindly legs, and gave up. At first, her recumbence came as sort of a relief to us all, and she seemed to recover from some of the excitement. Her breathing became more regular. But after an hour, I became concerned—her immense weight upon her legs, combined with the hard concrete beneath her, spelled impending trouble in the form of nerve paralysis, which could make it impossible for her ever to stand again. Surrounded by our flashlight-toting rescue party in the moat, she lay there and resisted our efforts to push and prod her back onto her feet. Meanwhile, her lower legs began to feel cold to the touch.

Running out of time, I resorted to a piece of equipment that I had never used—an electric cattle prod. This device looks much like a flashlight, but instead of a light on the end it terminated in two metal electrode points. I retrieved it from a storage drawer at the zoo hospital and installed fresh batteries, hoping this would be the stimulus that would get Freckles up. Climbing back in the moat with her, the first shock applied to her rear got her attention, but still she wouldn't stand. Going for broke, I inserted the probe into her rectum and pressed the on button. Contact! Her eyes opened wide. As I switched it off and on, her ears twitched wildly, and she rocked herself free, staggering to her feet. She remained standing all night long. When dawn came we built an incline ramp out of plywood and hay bales, and she gladly clambered back into the exhibit to rejoin her companions in the barn. The moat was then partially filled with dirt to reduce its depth to only three feet, which was safe enough—even for a narcoleptic giraffe.

Many other animals have had encounters with zoo moats, including the San Diego Zoo elephant shown at the beginning of this chapter. Fortunately, she climbed back

Elephant climbing out of moat after a fall at the San Diego Zoo

into her exercise yard without serious injury. The moat hazard was later eliminated from the exhibit.

Some of the medical problems involving zoo animals are more like detective mysteries than combat adventures. For reasons that were only conjectured, the zoo's polar bears were turning green. Furthermore, this was not the first time that they had taken on this verdant hue—it seemed to happen annually. To complicate the plot, there were anecdotal reports from zoos in Europe and Australia of the same phenomenon, yet no one had a factual explanation for it. For lack of a more definitive title, I referred to it as "The Green Polar Bear Syndrome." One idea was that there was too much chlorine in the water, which was distorting the hair color chemically. Another was that green algal slime around the wet parts of the exhibit was rubbing off onto their hair coats.

To put these speculations to rest, I fashioned a hair-collection device from a wooden pole by attaching a saw blade from a small carpentry tool to one end. I snagged hairs from our two green polar bears, Frieda and Caspar, while they were confined to a small back holding area. In the hospital lab, there was no question that the hair contained green pigments, but it was difficult to make out exactly what was taking place under a normal light microscope. Sticking with the algae theory, I was fortunate to find one of the world's experts on algae, Dr. Ralph Lewin, at the nearby Scripps Institution of Oceanography. With his expertise we identified the cause of this puzzling, but harmless, phenomenon.

The green color was indeed due to algae, which had taken up housekeeping *inside* the hollow shafts of the larger guard hairs of the animals' pelage. This hollow hair architecture is designed to provide efficient insulation for the bears in their Arctic homelands. Using the scanning electron microscope, we found crystal clear images of the little round green single-cell algae living contently in these spaces. Cultures from the hairs produced nearly pure colonies of a common freshwater blue-green algae called *Aphanocapsa montana.*

After discussing our findings with other zoo veterinarians, I was sent fresh hair from polar bears at another zoo three hundred miles away, as well as from a zoo in Australia. The results were the same—the hollows of the nonpigmented hairs were colonized with algae. This translucency allows light to pass through the hair surface and support the growth of algae through photosynthesis. Normally hollow, zoo polar bears' guard hairs tend to wear from abrasion on hard exhibit surfaces, opening the chambers to colonization. Unlike the zoo hairs, the ones that we obtained from wild polar bears and museum specimens were intact and algae-free. Only a few other animal species (several types of seals and sloths) have been shown to have algae on their hair coats, but these are surface, rather than internal inhabitants.

Shortly after our findings were reported in the journal *Nature* and in *Time,* I walked by the polar bear exhibit to discover that Frieda and Caspar were now snow white. I had intended to do some controlled tests by adding salt to their water to be able to prescribe how zoos can safely and scientifically turn their polar bears white again. I was curious about what had taken place to preempt the plan. The bear keeper was behind the exhibit in his kitchen, washing up after preparing food for the animals. "Jim!" I called out. "The bears are white—what happened?" "Doc," he said, as he scooped out a cup of white powder from a can under the sink, "when it gets too green, I just throw about a cup of this stuff in the pool and in two days they look great." "What is it?" I asked, trying to conceal my disappointment. "Dishwasher powder from the zoo restaurant." Then I asked, "How long have you been doing this?" He replied, "Oh, for a few years, I guess, but I always forget about it until someone complains." "What brand of dishwasher soap is it Jim?"

Zoo animals have been transported by every imaginable means, and some individuals make their living doing just that. When I first started as a zoo veterinarian, I met a few Neanderthal-style animal shippers and I was pretty appalled by their attitudes. Let's just say that the bad guys are mostly gone from the business, and good riddance to them. Nothing offends a veterinarian more than someone who has little or no regard for the safety and well-being of animals. I evicted one such individual from the zoo hospital compound (not physically, because he was an ex-professional wrestler) when he attempted to assist in loading several lions into his animal trailer with an electric cattle prod. I refused to have any direct dealings with this individual again in my career, and told him so on the spot. As he departed he quipped, "I don't really give a damn what you think, Doc—I buy and sell vets every day!" I assured him that this would not be the case on my watch.

Some years later, and still doing business with dozens of American zoos, he finally achieved his moment of infamy on the CBS television program *60 Minutes* for his role in the unethical sale of surplus zoo animals at live animal auctions. His most memorable TV video cameo, however, was on the grounds of the San Francisco Zoo, when he spit on a Channel 5 news reporter while she attempted to interview him about his animal transactions with shooting ranches as he departed for parts unknown with a fresh load of surplus Axis deer. Subsequently, he was dropped as a registered animal dealer with the national zoo organization.

The largest donation of animals to the San Diego Zoo came through the personal agent of Welsh singer Tom Jones. Having gone through an expensive divorce in England, Gordon Mills was liquidating his assets at his plush country estate in Weybridge near London. To our surprise, his private zoo included three full-grown male gorillas, one female, and seven orangutans. In anticipation of the long-distance shipment of the whole lot, we set about building ape crates that would be suitable for such formidable inhabitants. We finally settled on ten-layered marine laminated plywood as the perfect compromise between strength and weight, and lined them with sheet metal to render them impenetrable to nearly anything that would fit into them.

One of the most frustrating details of the entire trip was assuring that vital equipment and drugs for sedating them could all be properly cleared through security and customs upon arrival in London. Despite dozens of phone calls to American and British authorities, the best that I could do was to have the equipment permitted entry as professional tools and supplies, as is done for manufacturers' representatives who sell, demonstrate, and service equipment. The interesting condition under which the drugs could enter the country was that the permit holder was responsible for assuring that they all left the country as well. This, of course made no sense at all, since we had every intention of using the drugs on the apes. Nonetheless, that was the best that I could negotiate in the bureaucracies that I ran up against. I rationalized that, in any event, the used drugs would be present within the bodies of our apes that would accompany us, and their mere presence in the crates would have to be ample proof that they were used for that purpose.

I had expressed some concern about practicing medicine in another country without a veterinary license, but I was assured that a well-known English zoo veterinarian would be in attendance to assist, so not to worry about that detail. Finally, we seemed to have everything right—our permits, our arrival plans in London, our trip to the estate, the local trucking logistics and our Lufthansa reservations for nine apes and our small entourage, which would include four of us from San Diego and two employees from the estate who would accompany us back.

After a brief stayover in London, we took the train to Weybridge. Greeting us in a battered Volkswagen van upon our arrival was a young, energetic animal keeper who had a thick Cockney accent. It was disorienting enough to be traveling English-style down the opposite side of the street in a van, but Jeremy drove like a certified maniac. We looked back and forth at one another as he tailgated and rammed from intersection to intersection on the left side of the road, talking a mile a minute and cursing everything in his path. Arriving at the estate, we unloaded our gear in the carriage house. Our new silver-painted crates had arrived exactly one week beforehand as planned. Just then another caretaker came to the carriage house to fetch us to have a look at the male gorillas that had been in a scrap and inflicted some minor bites on one another. The tension of the impending move seemed to be building with the animals.

The estate was a spacious property with several residences for hired staff and big grassy paddocks where zebra, camels, and other hoofed animals had romped before the divorce. Separate buildings, now nearly vacated, had housed the carnivores and the great apes. Nearby, sheltered by winter-bare hedges, an impressive thatched two-story family manor house, where we lodged, stood amidst lawns and formal gardens. The remnants of the staff and family at the estate had a demeanor that fell somewhere between the personalities in *The Osbournes* and *The World According to Garp*—friendly but conspicuously eccentric.

Upon our arrival, Jeremy announced that the movement of the apes from England to San Diego had set off a big stir among the zoo people in the United Kingdom, raising concerns that someone might petition the customs ministry to halt the transaction at any moment. To make matters worse, no one had heard from the English vet who was to be our local facilitator in this project. Rumor had it that he might be a no-show, given the controversy that the ape deal was creating among his zoo clients. I called up a veterinarian friend in England for his input, and he advised us to simply go full speed ahead and outpace the bureaucracy. Here we were with our staff, crates, drugs, and airline tickets, and, English vet or not, we were determined to get on with bringing the animals back to San Diego. Our newly formed team of Englishmen and Americans started off fresh in the morning by laying our plan of attack on the crating up of the apes. All food and water had been withdrawn the evening before, and we had kept ourselves as discreet as possible around their quarters.

We started with the gorillas and darted them with sedatives one by one, toting them on canvas stretchers in the VW van. (Jeremy drove with uncharacteristic care.) At the garage where the crates were assembled we boxed them up and secured their doors. Male gorilla number one went smoothly, and he slipped into the box nicely. People who are unaccustomed to coming into intimate contact with a sedated gorilla have highly variable reactions. Even those who work with them daily often find it disconcerting to have no barrier between them and such a formidable creature. Gorilla number two, however, gave several of the inexperienced helpers a panic attack. As we slid him out of the van next to his crate, he reached out and touched someone. Not aware that apes under typical sedatives sometimes make aimless motions, several people panicked as we started to stuff him into his box filled with loose excelsior bedding. On the verge of hysteria, the team discipline disintegrated. Some began shoving him every which way. He wouldn't fit into the box. "Give him more drugs! Give him more drugs! He's going to run way! This is crazy!" shouted the worst-stricken of the helpers. It was painful to see the fear on their faces. "OK, everyone listen up," I said. "Stop wetting your pants and get all of that packing material out of his crate. No one's going to get killed!" With the crate now entirely empty, we easily slid gorilla number two into place in a sitting position and packed the stuffing around him like a Buddha statue. When the guillotine door was dropped closed and the bolts were in place, a noticeable relief came over the excitable members of the group, who now looked at each other in embarrassment for losing their composure.

With everyone finally secured and all nine crates occupied, our truck and forklift arrived at dusk, as scheduled, and we loaded up for our rendezvous at Heathrow Airport. In the Lufthansa cargo assembly area, our silver boxes were neatly lined up in a row. One of the energetic young orangutans swayed to and fro in his box, causing it to inch forward in a surprisingly straight path across the room. Curious freight handlers lingered as they passed, perplexed by the creeping box and the musky odor of gorillas that permeated the air. With only two hours before loading, we impatiently bided our time, expecting the government to arrive and seize our shipment at any moment. We watched more befuddled freight handlers pass by and dragged the orangutan's box back to its starting point every fifteen minutes. But, finally, we were loaded and airborne. Because of the pungent aroma of our nervous gorillas, I was concerned that the passengers on our DC-10 "combi" aircraft would be overcome with the smell recirculating from the gorilla passengers. The forward portion of the plane carried passengers, while that rear half was configured for cargo. To our amazement, no odor at all could be detected in the passenger cabin—a compelling statement about the air-handling system in the plane.

All of our apes arrived in excellent condition and, after several days of acclimatization, Jeremy and his girlfriend departed for their return to the empty zoo at the English estate. Some months later, Jeremy had a serious accident in the VW van. According to his girlfriend, his head injuries caused him to lose all memories of ever working with gorillas or accompanying them to the United States.

If you have qualms about shipping a pet anywhere by air cargo, trust me, your fears are well founded. Over the years, I have heard of and witnessed a number of incredibly dumb things that resulted in animal transport deaths from pure negligence. First of all, there is the possibility that the aircraft cargo hold may accidentally lose its pressure, which can be fatal to animals, as it was to a full grown Siberian tiger we received from the Soviet Union via a prominent German air carrier. This animal was a valuable first generation captive-born male, dead on arrival in San Diego. A rare Mongolian wild horse stallion inadvertently had his entire shipping crate wrapped with plastic sheeting by a major air carrier in Korea, and it suffocated on its flight from San Diego to China, where he was to play an important role in a breeding program to reestablish wild populations. In yet another fatal shipping mishap, an endangered Arabian oryx antelope, traveling to Jordan in the Middle East for release in the wild in a conservation breeding program, was accidentally liberated from its shipping crate in Tel Aviv, Israel. To prevent it from interfering with active aircraft using the runway, it was shot and killed by an El Al security officer.

When the San Diego Zoo initiated contacts with Chinese zoos and several animal trades quickly followed, we had a close call on an aircraft on the inaugural shipment involving two southern white rhinoceros in a Boeing 747 cargo plane. Confined in substantial rhino shipping crates, the animals became agitated during the flight and began to jostle about in their containers. The pilot became alarmed that they might break out of their crates and could feel the handling characteristics of the airplane change when the animals began to thrash about. Although accompanied by zoo staff, no veterinary personnel were along to provide any chemical alternatives to the problem. Matters became grave when the pilot finally warned that if the two animals did not settle down he was considering decompressing the cargo hold at their 35,000-foot altitude, if that was what it took to protect the safety of the aircraft. Fortunately, the animals and the pilot both settled down, and they eventually arrived fully intact at the Canton Zoo, where I caught up with them several days later.

Shipping problems also arise from using improper crates. We once received two hyenas at the zoo hospital that had just arrived by air cargo from Africa. After a first glance at the crates my concerns grew, since the ventilation holes looked inadequate for grown animals of this type. As I strained with a flashlight to look at the crates' inhabitants, a strong odor of ammonia burned my nose and eyes and the animals were uncharacteristically quiet. Quickly, we opened the crates and unloaded their semiconscious cargo, which was probably close to succumbing to the noxious fumes created by fermenting urine in the waste pans in the crate floors.

For flighty animals such as small antelope, narrow, snug crates with nonslip footing serve best to avoid injuries. Larger animals need space to change positions and avoid problems from being too cramped. An animal dealer from Africa once told me that because of the small commercial aircraft available, it was difficult to ship larger animals out of his country. He devised a creative, though risky, solution to his problem. In the case of several juvenile forest buffalos that were hand-reared, he trained them to live in their shipping crates at night by giving them food rewards. As they grew larger, they gradually learned to crawl into the crates on their stomachs. And, finally, the day came to ship the animals by air—a date determined by their maximum size that allowed them to fit in the crates in a lying-down posture. When the new owners arrived at their airport to retrieve the animals and saw the small size of the crates, they were annoyed and attempted to call him to complain—after all, they had been promised that the animals were going to be at least half grown. When they opened the crate doors to release them, however, they were stunned by the size of the animals that exited the crates and stood up to their full height.

It is common practice to condition many animals in advance of their travel crates in order to reduce the degree of alarm that they might experience when shipping time comes. We did this with several shipments that I personally accompanied involving okapi. Okapis have been known to the Western world only since 1901 and are costly to acquire. This particular male was going to a zoo breeding program in Colorado, and we carefully mapped our route for the two-day trip, arranging to overnight the animal and truck at the Rio Grande Zoo in Albuquerque, New Mexico.

As part of this carefully laid out plan, we carried big plastic jugs of San Diego water and all of the familiar foods that our okapi would need for at least ten days. Two animal keepers accompanied me and the animal, including Ernest, the zoo's senior okapi keeper. We loaded our truck with the crated okapi and our supplies and began our journey via Arizona and New Mexico. To monitor his well-being at all times, Ernest rode nearly the entire distance in the back of the truck with the side door open to alert us up front if there was a problem. Given the remote areas through which we were traveling, the extreme value of the animal and the narcotic tranquilizer drugs that we possessed, the last item to be loaded into the truck was a double-barreled .12-gauge shotgun—"just in case."

Everything went smoothly the first day, and we arrived at our destination tired, hot and hungry. Our contact at the zoo met us with one of their experienced hoofed stock keepers to maintain a watchful eye on our animal all night long. We gathered our personal belongings and medical bags for our ride to the hotel, and I wrapped up the shotgun discreetly in a blanket to carry it along.

To our surprise, our Albuquerque hosts had booked us into the upscale Hilton Hotel, where there was a formal party in progress. An elite social event was underway when we arrived, and dozens of people dressed in evening attire were assembling in the hotel lobby. I began to feel a little out of place in rumpled blue jeans and T-shirt, not to mention the shotgun-in-a-blanket. I refolded the blanket around the gun so that the barrels wouldn't peek out as we entered the hotel. The fleeting thought occurred to me that someone could mistake this for a robbery, but we proceeded anyway.

Heading straight for the registration desk, we got a better look at this interesting assortment of guests. On closer inspection, the men looked like extremely well-dressed cowboys with expensive, tailored Western suit coats and polished dress boots. I handled the shotgun nonchalantly while the keepers checked us in, nearly dropping it when I juggled my possessions to sign the guest register. Relief began to come when we finally moved away from the festivities toward the elevators and the privacy of our rooms. As we pressed into the small crowd on the elevator and pushed the up button, one of the well-dressed gentlemen aboard looked me square in the eyes and asked, "How's the huntin'?" Floored by our apparent transparency, I said "Uh, just great! Fine party you're havin' here tonight!" "Don't beat huntin' though—good luck tomorrow," he replied. Later the next day, we safely delivered our rare animal cargo to its destination at the zoo in Colorado Springs. I flew back to San Diego while the keepers drove back with the gun.

Some animals require a different magnitude of equipment than most of our patients, especially the elephants. In order to work with such imposing animals, training and handling are essential to providing the regular care that these animals need. The two elephant species, the Asian and the African, have superficial resemblances, but quite a few differences in their training capacity and reliability. Despite the more trainable nature of the Asian elephant, any elephant can take control of the scene if injured or frightened.

Elephants have the largest appetites in the zoo, and consume more than a hundred pounds of hay daily, along with perhaps twenty-five pounds of fruits and vegetables. This results in a sizeable amount of labor to clean up the digested remains of this forage, not to mention the liquid by-products of the prodigious amounts of water that they consume. Elephant keeping is hard physical work!

Lucky and Maya were our two large Asian elephant cows. Almost all elephants in zoos and circuses are females. Male elephants can be held only in specialized facilities after they become mature, due to their unpredictable, aggressive tendencies. Since these two ladies were inseparable companions and of similar size, we noticed earlier than normal, by her profile, that Lucky was losing a significant amount of weight. Our facilities had no scales, and so this weight decline was based on our observations and from photographs over time.

One of the worrisome diseases of elephants, usually contracted from other animals or people, is tuberculosis. This a slow and persistent bacterial disease. As a veterinary student on a visit to the Detroit Zoo, I remember well how they baked isoniazid medicated bread loaves for their elephants to get them to take their daily doses of antituberculosis drug. Fearing TB, we skin-tested both Lucky and Maya, and to our relief both they and their keepers tested negative. Intestinal parasites, another potential cause of declining condition, are nearly nonexistent in established zoo elephants. As we stepped over melon sized balls of elephant dung on our regular visits to the elephants, I don't recall who noticed it first, but Lucky's droppings were noticeable coarser than Maya's.

Because of the physical differences in the stools of the two animals, it seemed most likely that Lucky wasn't digesting her hay properly. I was able to do a cursory dental exam on her because she had been given some fundamental training by the elephant keepers. She was used to standing and picking up her feet for routine care of her soles and toenails, and Lucky did so willingly for rewards of apples and carrots. As she stood focused, munching on her apples, I slipped one hand and forearm inside her mouth and could feel the molar teeth back alongside the cheek on each side. As I ran my fingertips along the enamel ridges, I came upon an oddly shaped tooth about the size of a small bread loaf. Lucky had a major dental problem, and the distorted shape and position of this tooth was the likely cause of her weight loss.

Elephants have dentition quite unlike all other animals. The teeth that do all of the work of mastication develop throughout their lifetimes and emerge in their huge upper and lower jaws in the rear jaw area. Stacked and cemented together like oversized piles of poker chips lying on edge, the teeth erupt slowly and gradually migrate forward as they disintegrate on the front edge. The forward end of the tooth flakes off in segments, gradually expending its chips as another tooth starts its journey in the same manner. For unknown reasons, one of Lucky's molars became stuck along the journey and was being rear-ended by its replacement tooth, causing it to twist sideways. This had caused a malocclusion with the opposing tooth in the jaw. Thus, the hay remained poorly chewed and only partially digested, depriving her of nutrition.

Though little zoo work had been done with elephant dentistry, it was clear that the tooth had to go, and it was up to the zoo veterinarian and his dental consultant to figure out how. Fortunately we had several good drugs for sedating elephants. One in particular, etorphine, is a powerful synthetic narcotic estimated to be ten thousand times as potent as morphine. It would allow us to lie an elephant down completely on its side for dental surgery.

I drove to the maintenance warehouse and went through all the power tools that they had, looking for the right implements for the job. I finally settled on an electric jackhammer that was used for chipping concrete on repair jobs in the zoo. It came with handy chisels of various widths and sharpness. A few crowbars, hammers, chisels, and hacksaws rounded out the tools that we needed for the job. As we arrived on the day of the big dental procedure, the keepers looked with skepticism at the tools that Dr. Dave Fagan, our dental consultant, and I brought along—an array of medical bags, oxygen tanks, ropes, winches, hammers, crowbars, and demolition tools.

Whenever a large-scale animal procedure is about to get under way, zoo veterinarians typically go over the game plan with the key participants—a sort of preflight briefing. We walk through the expected sequence of events for the anesthesia and surgery, including emergency and safety precautions. Among the critical aspects of this particular dental procedure was the imperative that Lucky needed to end up lying down on her right side. If she went down on the left side, we would be unable to physically move her to work on her left upper molars, and that would scratch the surgery for the day, making her more wary in the future. Despite our efforts to conceal the preparations from Lucky for her impending sedation and surgery, the fact that she was locked inside and her companions were out in the exhibit yard was ample warning. She refused to lie down on command so that she could be sedated while recumbent, and instead I had to give Lucky her injection of M-99 into a foreleg with a hand syringe.

With large ropes placed around her neck and her legs and the help of several "come-along" hand winches anchored to the massive barn beams, we were able to give her physical guidance. Shortly after her injection, Lucky made a slowly controlled stretch and came to rest on her chest on the straw-padded floor. Just as we started to pull her right leg forward to position her on her side, she reached out suddenly with her trunk and gave me a whack that sent me hurtling into the wall. I'm not sure that I have ever experienced a blow so solid—it was like being hit with a fire hose that had snapped free of a hydrant.

To save face while the pain slowly subsided, I pretended it didn't hurt, and we proceeded with the surgery. After nearly an hour of prying at the molar, the seven-pound tooth was finally delivered—a brown, comma-shaped baguette. The gallery of keepers looking on smiled in approval. Just ten minutes after administering the drug antidote into an ear vein, Lucky rose to her feet, looked around her barn, and accepted an apple. With time and supplementary feeding, her weight loss was stabilized. Without these drugs it would be impossible to handle many of the pachyderm problems seen in zoo practice today.

15. ZOO REGULARS

Coworkers Without Titles

She arrived at the gate just before it opened each day, as precise as an atomic clock. She was a bona fide "Zoo Regular." The San Diego Zoo is open every day of the year without fail. I am not sure that anyone alive remembers a single day when the shades on the ticket booths did not roll up to meet a brand new queue of visitors. The San Diego Zoo is so widely known that if it closed its doors for good there would still be people who didn't get the word and would show up twenty years later to visit. As in the television program *Cheers,* every major zoo, public museum, and library has a central cast of characters that are referred to as "The Regulars." These are the devoted and sometimes lost souls who make that institution a focus of their daily existences, dutifully going there as if it were their place of work. By foot, bus, taxi, or limousine, they showed up at the zoo every day, some frequenting select geographical niches on the zoo grounds, others roaming widely to offer their daily greetings to specific gorillas, elephants, or giraffes.

In many zoos, in the vicinity of the great apes or other charismatic species, you often encounter self-appointed docents who know all the animals by name, the details of their family history, their individual idiosyncrasies. At first you might mistake them for employees as they enthusiastically interject answers to questions that arise as newcomers discuss the animals before them. In order to keep official docents in predictable synchrony with zoo policies, many zoos have established formal training programs for them.

Zoo regulars speak to certain staff members every day, but they may silently pass by others for years. When they gave you a wink, a wave, or a knowing nod, you know that they had accepted you as part of *their* zoo. Regulars are above and apart from the rest of the common crowd, who are, after all, ignorant of the true inner workings of their private little world. They always have favorites among the animals and the zoo staff, and they often hang out near the keepers at their coffee breaks to learn the latest gossip in the trials and tribulations of the keepers' and animals' personal lives, or for an update on the progress in treating medical problems in individual zoo animals. One "zoo nut" always wore a hat and safari vest that sagged under the weight of scores of zoo souvenir pins that he had faithfully collected in his travels to other zoos, wearing them like campaign medals from far-off wars. Some offer impromptu lectures about their beloved animals to the other visitors from favorite vantage points.

Unlike docents, who usually undergo structured training and follow established guidelines, the regulars are self-appointed freelancers who choose their own turf and make their own rules. In contrast, a "decent docent," according to La Jolla biologist and poet Dr. Ralph A. Lewin, has limits:

Doozen don'ts for docents
There are things a decent docent doesn't do,
Such as feeding alligators at the zoo.
You should leave the meals of monkeys
To the keepers and their flunkeys,
And they'll leave the nuts for visitors, and you.
There are things a decent docent doesn't dare,
Such as cosseting a bison or a bear.
You should leave the panther-petting
To the guys behind the netting
Who are trained for bearding lions in a lair.
There are things a decent docent doesn't do,

For you have to give the animals their due.
If they butt or bite, or nibble,
Or, like dromedaries, dribble,
You may lack the prime prerogative to sue.
A decent docent doesn't nag a gnu.
The ranks of rank transgressors must be few
Though there's just a tiny po'cent
Who debase the name of docent,
And who sometimes, inconspicuously, do.
So, although responsibilities accrue
In the service of a docent at the zoo,
When they let you go inside,
Let your conscience be your guide:
There are things a decent docent doesn't do.

One San Diego visitor, who always kept entirely to himself, and whose chosen outer garment was a trench coat, was dubbed "the Tortoise Guy." He came to the zoo only to observe the mating behavior of the giant Galapagos tortoises—an irregular regular of sorts. Leaning against the concrete block fence every day, he stared for hours as they carried out their propagatory duties. The tortoises milled around and clambered upon one another, making low grunting and hissing sounds as the tortoise man stood patiently and imagined the unimaginable (we imagined). Despite his otherwise harmless behavior, at least in the zoo, his final visit was on the occasion that a security guard noticed he was naked under the trench coat. Years later, while researching this book on the Internet, I stumbled across this sort of fantasy—apparently, the World Wide Web has brought about new networking possibilities for similarly afflicted "zoophiles" and "animists," offering chat rooms where they openly discuss their emotional and physical attractions to nonhuman species.

Less complex than the Tortoise Guy, "Harvey" always wore a helmet to the zoo, or at least that was the way someone dressed him to go there. Eventually the helmet acquired a telephone number that was neatly stenciled on the back, but Harvey never realized that he was a marked man. It didn't exactly shout "How am I driving?"—but that was clearly the intended message. Harvey had his good and bad days, but it was the bad ones and the phone number that caused his retirement from the zoo.

He often stood at the bottom of the steep hill in front of the old hippo exhibit, where the zoo tour buses regularly stopped for driver commentary. On some days his mission was as self-appointed sidewalk tour guide, and he would educate pedestrian passersby with unintelligible pronouncements. The drivers never stopped near him when he was in the zoo, since his disjointed ramblings and admonitions to passengers occasionally broke into obscene expletives. But Harvey was patient—he stood and waited for his audience. For the most part, the buses stopped short of or past him to avoid his salutations. It was a game of dodge-Harvey, and most of the time, they made sure that Harvey missed the bus. When bus traffic was backed up on busy days, however, Harvey would finally score—there was only so much roadway in which to evade him. Drivers sometimes purposely foiled coworkers in a following bus by stopping in a location that forced a dose of Harvey upon them in a fraternal right of passage for new drivers. Fortunately, his epithets were difficult for most visitors to understand, but his outbursts became more animated. It was surmised that his stenciled phone number must have been his undoing after several offended patrons reported his final transgressions.

Elderly, neatly dressed, dignified, and carrying a small black umbrella, apparently to avoid the San Diego sun, Miss Elisabeth, a thin, gray-haired matron, made her daily zoo rounds. Like most zoo regulars and the zoo's animals, she too was a creature of habit. For years she arrived in a taxi, strode through the same chrome turnstile with her senior pass, and was off on a precise route to visit her favorite animals. She rested on particular benches that gave her exacting views of people, animals, and events that she monitored daily. Her favorite bench was next to the Flamingo Lagoon, near the outdoor perch of the zoo's blind cockatoo, King Tut, a 1925 gift from the legendary animal collector, Frank "Bring 'em Back Alive" Buck. She always said good morning to Tut and then settled down on her bench.

Clutched in her hands every day, until the final bans came into effect on pigeon feeding in the zoo, was a small sack of bird seed and leftover bread. She was obviously much more of an animal than a people lover, strictly keeping her own company with the birds. Perhaps it was the no-feeding rule that contributed to her relatively rapid demise, but no one knows for sure. The zoo and surrounding Balboa Park, were plagued with pigeons and something had to be done. The presence of feral pigeons defecating parasites amid a priceless bird collection and swarming antelope feeders like locusts was untenable, never mind the costs of cleaning their messes from park facilities.

At the height of the "pigeon crisis" an employee at Balboa Park's landmark California Tower, an ornate bell tower attached to the Museum of Man, called me to recruit support for his own anti-pigeon crusade. He led me to the tower's interior and up the steep, winding iron staircase to witness the carnage. Amid nests on nearly every step of this metal helix in the bowels of the tower were scores of dead and moribund pigeons. The babies (squabs), unable to fly out of the vertical abyss, lay in random heaps. Something had to be done about the park's pigeon holocaust!

The clandestine efforts of the zoo's pest control technician, a top-secret program of poisoning the pigeons, was ended abruptly after several acutely intoxicated pigeons, apparently with terminal cardiac arrhythmias, crash-landed into a crowd on the zoo's main entry plaza near the Big Olaf ice cream stand. When the pigeon problem came up in staff meetings, I pointed out that pigeons were rare in neighboring Tijuana, Mexico, and, to no avail, suggested a fact-finding trip there to learn exactly why.

Then a very promising pigeon trapper, an enterprising Vietnamese refugee, learned of the problem and volunteered to help. He live-trapped the birds and the numbers started to drop; we were all impressed and hopeful. The masses of pigeons gorging themselves on antelope grain thinned noticeably. But, just as tangible gains were being made, the news came from the city health department that our trapper had been busted and would not be returning to the zoo. Inspectors discovered that he was serving up barbecued park pigeons in his family's local restaurant. Our trapper went out of the pigeon business, and the population rebounded.

Miss Elisabeth never learned of the behind-the-scenes warfare directed at the burgeoning pigeon population. In hindsight, some people thought that she had seemed more agitated than usual lately. She complained relentlessly about the feeding ban. Her once-loyal pigeons had abandoned her for fatter pickings at the snack stands and hung out instead with the tourists, who carelessly dribbled buttered popcorn wherever they went. I can only surmise that she became bitter about this radical change in feeding policy, and heartbroken that her birds had forsaken her. Still, no one realized that Miss Elisabeth was about to snap.

On her final visit to the zoo she meandered around on her regular rounds. It was a beautiful, sunny morning, and she was nearing the end of her walkabout. The mist had cleared from the zoo entry plaza and a clear blue sky was burning through the morning overcast. With the pavement still damp from the morning hosing of the groundskeepers, a small raft of tourists filtered past King Tut's bench toward the monkey yard. It was when she turned the last corner to take up her post that it finally happened. Laid out upon her favorite bench were a diaper bag and infant accessories—a woman was sitting with her back to the public thoroughfare nursing her baby.

According to an eyewitness, our mild-mannered senior walked up to her, screaming "This is my f—g bench!" and then whacked the still-nursing mother with her umbrella. It was an awkward scene by all accounts, and a security guard soon arrived to deal with the altercation. Resigned to her fate and without protest, Miss Elisabeth was gently, but officially, escorted from the zoo, rumpled umbrella in hand, never to be seen inside the turnstiles again. The park pigeon population was fed contraceptive bait and its numbers stabilized. We speculated that that Miss Elisabeth managed to find more grateful pigeons elsewhere in town.

A few people become so obsessed with certain animals that they become an endless annoyance to both keepers and the medical staff. One such woman was the "Tiger Lady." This dementia came about when we had a major series of Siberian tiger births in the zoo. One after another, the tigresses became pregnant, and the births exceeded the capacities of the mothers to care for them. The windfall for the public was that the Children's Zoo was awash in cute tiger cubs. They were stuffed in cribs, playpens, and incubators, and the visitors were a crush at the viewing windows to see them nursing from bottles, playing with dangling toys, and tussling with each other on the ground. Along with the tiger boom came lots of neonatal tiger medical problems in the form of infections, diarrhea, and gastrointestinal upset. Many sleepless nights were spent by veterinarians and nursery attendants treating sick, dehydrated, and hypothermic babies.

The Tiger Lady arrived early every morning, and she knew the names of the babies better than most of the employees. Naming new tigers became a creative chore; she lobbied for her nominations. Because of the public's strong interest in tigers, the nursery staff managed to do better than they did with the naming of three orphan rhea chicks that wound up with the backstage names Diarrhea, Pyorrhea, and Gonorrhea. The zoo hospital staff received more health reports from the Tiger Lady than from the nursery attendants. She ambushed the veterinarian on daily rounds with a list of who was sneezing, off of their formula, had loose stools, and should be treated—in her ever-humble opinion. Standing in front of the nursery, she informed visitors about the health status of each baby tiger in the window.

When she didn't manage to trap a veterinarian in the Children's Zoo, she called and left detailed messages at the hospital. Standing for hours, she alternately focused on the tigers and the baby pygmy chimpanzees that also occupied the nursery. Since tigers graduate from the Children's Zoo more rapidly than chimps, she eventually shifted her attention to the chimps, and then to their transition to the main pygmy chimpanzee group in the zoo. It was a relief to be accosted in the main zoo about pygmy chimps instead of tigers for a change. The tigers had made their way to homes in other zoos, but the Tiger Lady had morphed into the "Chimp Lady." I immediately began to lay a plan of contraception for the lion pride to avoid a rerun of the Year of the Tiger.

"We had to let the animals go. No one informed them of their rights when they were arrested."

16. ETHICAL CAPTIVITY

Animal Well-Being in Zoos

"What's popular isn't always right, and what's right isn't always popular."

—Howard Cosell

Is it humane to keep animals in captivity in zoos? We could ask similar questions about keeping dogs, cats, and horses as pets; some animal rights organizations do, but not mainstream ones. Zoos themselves are sometimes ambivalent about the term "zoo," and now often designate themselves as wild animal parks, wildlife conservation parks, and wildlife conservation centers. The former New York Zoological Society is now called The Wildlife Conservation Society. These and similar efforts are intended to cut away from the past and its lingering images of zoological confinement. Indeed, public attitudes about the confinement of wildlife in captivity have changed faster than the quality of their enclosures in zoos, placing steady pressures on zoos to change.

One of the biggest detours in the ongoing debate about the ethics of exhibiting animals or conducting research on them is the confusion between the terms "animal rights" and "animal welfare," which have been spun and counterspun and politicized in the public-relations wars between organized and well-funded animal interest groups. While the lines are most strongly drawn between animal rightists and biomedical animal researchers, zoos often find themselves confronted on related issues by the same animal-advocacy groups. There are fundamental differences in the "rights" and "welfare" concepts that I will explore later in this chapter. It is likely that this subject will remain confusing for the average person, inasmuch as it is constantly blurred and misconstrued by media superficiality.

The principal style of these so-called animal-ethics debates, by both sides, has been typified by sweeping allegations about one another's actions and motivations. This is followed by minimal analysis or dialogue about the veracity of these assertions on either side's part. They seldom actually appeal to each other in their communications, but instead play strictly to the audience—the general public. The battles between the extremes of the animal-rights movement and the extremes of the biomedical research community are battles of images, with both sides staking claims to our emotions—images of abused research animals on one side and sick children awaiting research breakthroughs on the other. The public often observes these media spectacles with as much true enlightenment as watching a tennis match being played with an invisible ball.

My simplest answer to the opening question above is: Yes, it is humane to keep animals in captivity in zoos—if they are properly cared for and purposefully exhibited. I can offer lots of reasons that justify the existence of zoos, but amusement for its own sake is one of my least favorite. I prefer to view the keeping of animals in zoos as bolstering a higher cause that includes the cultivation of compassion and understanding about animals and nature. Entertainment, however, is part of the alchemy needed for the survival of zoos. Another measurement I would make of a zoo is the degree to which it encourages average citizens to support efforts to maintain and respect wildlife and wild areas. This should not be limited to faraway lands, but involve the very communities in which zoos reside.

Perhaps the measure of an "unemployment rate" could be devised for zoo animals as a yardstick of the success of keeping them in captivity. Just as with us humans, a high animal unemployment rate would reflect badly on zoo leaders. In the wild, as I have said, most animals are preoccupied with foraging for their food, interacting socially, and avoiding predators. What will substitute for these age-old daily behavior patterns when they become irrelevant or marginalized in the zoo? How can the success of animal enrichment programs be assessed to gauge the relative success among zoos? One method being evaluated involves the field of behavioral endocrinology, utilizing assays of stress hormones (corticoids) in feces and urine to quantify physiologic dysfunction.

How do you really judge which zoos are the best: by their self-proclaimed successes, by their reputations in the media, or by more quantifiable review processes which do not yet exist? Despite our competitive American tradition, the notion that zoos can be ranked like football and baseball teams is pretty unrealistic anyways, since the subjective playing fields vary so enormously from zoo to zoo. People often tend to determine what they like by objecting to what they don't like, and zoogoers are no exception.

The San Diego Zoo had its opponents at its outset in the early 1920s, when critical letters to the editor were published in the *San Diego Union-Tribune*, titled, for example, "The Zoo is a Disgrace and a Crime" and "The Zoo Should Be Disbanded for the Good of the City." Given the reports of the questionable housing facilities at San Diego's pre-zoo exposition menagerie, from which some of the zoo's animals originated, it isn't a total surprise that some individuals wanted to thwart the building of a permanent facility of that standard.

Some of the early criticisms of the San Diego Zoo had to do with the public feeding of snakes, such as "Diablo" the python, which was such a spectacle that it was announced in the *Union-Tribune*: "San Diego Zoo will give 'Diablo' first meal in five months; 23-foot python will be forcibly fed at Seal Lagoon this afternoon."

At a culmination of the early public debate on the humaneness of the zoo in 1925, matters were taken to the San Diego Humane Society and the *Union-Tribune* by several citizens. A Mr. Richard Wolfe and a Miss Kay Dillenbeck complained about the conditions for the elephants, including their chaining. Miss Dillenbeck led by stating, "I never go to the zoo because I don't like it. Dr. Wegeforth [the Zoological Society President] is just trying to shut us up by having our president [of the Humane Society] on his board of directors [of the Zoo]." She continued, "You will print only defenses of the zoo. A veterinarian should be in charge of the zoo, not a vivisectionist like Dr. Wegeforth. Untold cruelty is going on up there all the time. The forcible feeding of the anaconda is terrible." Miss Dillenbeck was interrupted at this point and told that it was a kindness to force-feed the big snake in order to save its life. "That may

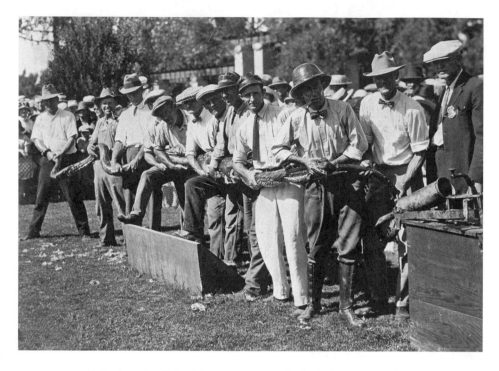

Diablo the python being fed with a sausage stuffer in the San Diego Zoo, 1925

be true," she said, "but it need not be done in public. It is humiliating for the ana-conda to be fed that way. After all, a serpent is a serpent. You will see that one of these days there will be strict laws that will prevent keeping any animals in captivity. There will not even be goldfish in bowls. And the worst is yet to come. The zoo says it is going to put up a hospital for animals. The tigers died from neglect and so have other animals. That hospital will not be for sick animals. It will be for vivisection, for ex-periments on our dogs and cats. And we will soon be hearing the heart-rending howls of anguish from that hospital when we go to the park. Oh, I know all about that place!"

Only a few months later, zoo troubles continued in the same paper, which head-lined a report: "Tormented chimpanzees spit water at lawless zoo visitors; special po-lice protection is asked for animals; rule breakers face arrest."

And shortly afterward, perhaps acknowledging Miss Dillenbeck's admonition to involve a veterinarian, a story led with: "Zoo's veterinarian alleviates deer's pain by extracting ulcerated tooth."

Perceptions and values were a bit different in those days compared to now—in fact, quite different. They were also affected by the economic hardships of the Great Depression. For example, in the early 1930s, in an unsuccessful effort to generate extra income, the San Diego Zoo offered taxidermy mounts of deer heads for sale to the public from the surplus members of the zoo deer herds. In 1934 it was casually acknowledged in the zoo veterinarian's annual report published in its own *ZooNooz* magazine that "in order to reduce maintenance costs a number of less valuable, easily replaced exhibits (animals) were destroyed." Like many other zoos then and afterward, the San Diego Zoo fell on hard times. Charles Schroeder, then the zoo's veterinarian, made frequent trips to nearby Mexico to buy low-cost horses that were then shipped to the zoo as animal food.

An allocation to the zoo from the city's property tax revenue that began in 1929 was reduced in 1934, causing the zoo leaders to call foul. A castigating article in *ZOONOOZ* magazine in June 1934 took issue with the San Diego city manager who implemented the cuts. He informed zoo and society staff that "if the zoo workers didn't have the time to water the trees, the zoo had too many trees," and added that the zoo should consider replacing zoo workers with welfare workers to save money. (Years later, when the zoo experienced a union labor contract dispute, director Dr. Charles Schroeder made a similar threat to hire vagrants from downtown when the threat of a strike drew near.) That same year, again in the *ZOONOOZ* magazine, troubled times stimulated desperate appeals to the public for zoo support and management lamented to subscribers: "To those who inquire 'What have you done with the things in the Zoo, the baby walrus, the elephant seal, the great pythons?' shall we say to them 'Oh, we just sat by and allowed politicians to kill them'. . . . Now is the time for all good citizens to come to the aid of their zoo."

A popular, but misguided, promotion at the San Diego Zoo in that era was the Annual Snake Contest, which began April first and ended September first. The grand prize for delivering the largest number of live, "undamaged" snakes was $20, second prize was $10, and $5 went to the person bringing in the largest number of other reptiles (lizards and turtles). The announced intentions of the contest were, ironically, to have "a wonderful exhibit of our local specimens and a renewed interest in the reptiles of our own county." The contest advisory suggested that children should not try to catch rattlesnakes, and therefore placed no premium on them above other species.

Meanwhile, back at the financially distressed John Ball Park Zoo, in my hometown of Grand Rapids, Michigan, most of the animal collection was being given away to other zoos, and the deer and buffaloes were being butchered to feed the poor, leaving only a few aging specimens on the zoo grounds. In 1935, at the depth of the Depression, many municipal zoos took advantage of federal efforts to reduce unemployment, which resulted in the creation of the Works Progress Administration (WPA) and funding for zoo construction projects throughout the country. Local governments were required to supply the project materials while the federal government paid the workers.

Every living person is a walking contradiction in his or her personal actions toward living things. Do you swat flies, squash spiders, or clean the bugs off of your car windshield that you have annihilated by the dozens? Have you ever set a snap trap or placed a little brown and yellow box of D-Con poison bait in your garage for mice? Do you consume milk, meat, fish, or eggs? Have you worn leather shoes, belts, or watchbands? Do you suppose that you have consumed many products that have ingredients of animal origin in them? (Would you necessarily know if you had?) Have you ever had a pet in your life? Do you hunt or fish? Is there anyone in the world who has not done one of these things?

The point of this list of animal uses is to demonstrate that the use people make of animal life is measured in degrees, not absolutes. Based on our culture and experiences, we find some uses and actions to be acceptable, and we reject others. Horse-racing fans, by and large, find bullfighting repugnant, but we all know what happens to many failed equine contenders. Qualifications and distinctions are drawn to justify individual ethical positions, such as whether an animal is regarded as a "sentient" being or not—in other words, whether it is capable of emotion, thought, and suffering. This automatically accords status to more taxonomically privileged creatures, and denies, or qualifies it, with regard to so-called lesser species. Even animal-rights icon Peter Singer, the author of *Animal Liberation*, believes that such distinctions could be drawn "somewhere between a lobster and an oyster," and in general that "all animals capable of experiencing pleasure and pain should be given moral consideration."

The "mirror self-recognition test" used by some researchers takes this approach to the next level. It involves placing a mirror in front of an animal and evaluating its response to its own image. In the case of primates, a red dot is placed on an individual's ear, and the animal's reaction to it is observed. An animal that reaches for its own ear, as opposed to the image in the mirror, is deemed to have a capacity for self-consciousness. Chimpanzees, orangutans, and gorillas have all qualified in this form of test, and, like humans, respond directly to their own reflections. Overall, few animals seem to recognize their reflected image as their own (cats and dogs most often take it for another animal or show lack of interest altogether). One investigator has reportedly done the same test on one Indian elephant (with a very large mirror) and claims a response similar to that of apes.

As a consequence of the mirror test and claims that chimpanzees share over 98 percent of their DNA with humans, a new standard is being proposed—particularly by animal-rights lawyers—that would afford apes the constitutional protections accorded to children, the mentally retarded, and the infirm in human society. While the 98 percent argument sounds compelling, mice have been reported to have 97 percent of the same genetic material as humans, and mammals in general over 90 percent.

One of the more articulate spokespersons on this subject is animal rights attorney Steven Wise, who recently wrote the book *Rattling the Cage*. His objective is to open the door for organizations and individuals to file lawsuits on the behalf of animals—especially the great apes—in order to remove them from the custody of zoos, research labs, and circuses. Vocabulary-recognition and image-association studies demonstrating that young apes have the potential to develop their intellectual capacities to that of four-year old humans have been used to support the arguments calling for changes in the legal status of chimpanzees, orangutans, and gorillas.

At least one organization, Zoo Check, based in the United Kingdom, has dedicated itself exclusively to the total eradication of zoos, and it appears to make no exceptions. Its mission and philosophy are stated in its organizational literature: "Zoo Check is dedicated to investigating the plight of captive animals, exposing and alleviating their suffering and campaigning to phase out all traditional zoos." ("Traditional zoos" appear to be defined as zoos that have animals.) Zoo Check further proclaims: "Wildlife belongs in the wild" and "Most zoos remain little more than collections of animals held captive in unnatural conditions for public entertainment."

If one took Zoo Check's principal criticisms and accommodated them point by point, zoos that did the following should be acceptable to the group, if we overlook the small detail that they don't believe there should be any zoos at all:

1. Conserve endangered species.
2. Take part in coordinated breeding programs to preserve endangered species for eventual release into the wild.
3. Fund conservation projects in the wild.
4. Preserve a gene pool.
5. Protect animals from danger.
6. Educate the public.
7. Take part in scientific research.
8. Ensure that animal welfare is of the highest standard.

Unfortunately, there are still many dismal zoos around the world that provide boundless cannon fodder for their complaints. For example, in 2003 a visitor to the Bucharest Zoo in Romania had the following to report: "I had to leave before going round all the exhibits due to my children (and myself) being upset by the sights we saw. . . . Bears in cages they could not stand up in—rocking to and fro! Idiots were feeding cans of beer to the primates. I tried to find staff to do something about it—but no one around!!! I wrote to the director of the zoo offering to assist with the zoo on a charitable basis—no reply at all."

Animal-rights advocates and their opponents reach the ultimate impasse when their arguments enter into the realm of religion. The Christian faiths generally teach that nonhuman creatures were placed on earth for the benefit of humankind, automatically giving people dominion over them. This fundamental position cuts short the possibilities that animals are likely to be accorded equality with humans any time in the near future. Nonetheless, the sentience arguments keep the debate very much alive and in the public forum, and seem quite effective in needling the conscience of society in general with respect to its obligations to animals.

A May 2003 Gallup poll which measured public reaction to animal rights goals concluded that a majority (71 percent) of Americans believe that animals deserve protection from harm or exploitation. Surprisingly, 25 percent responding think that animals also deserve the same rights as people, although 48 percent of this group rejected bans on medical research on animals. Women were found to be more likely to support animal rights than men, although few differences were identified by age groups. One area that is clearly on the rise is an interest in improving conditions for agricultural animals. Efforts to ban hunting, however, have not met with the same support from the general public.

Despite many zoo employees' abhorrence of culling practices for the surplus animals born in zoos, there seems to be little outcry when petting zoo baby chicks or rodents are transferred to the reptile house as afternoon food for snakes and lizards. One popular exhibit in the San Diego Children's Zoo was a giant loaf of bread displayed in a glass tank called the Mouse House. Once or twice a week a new loaf arrived and the keeper cut a few small doors and windows in the crust to allow easy entry to the resident mice. Adults and children alike delighted to see this busy house, teeming with rodents like a scene out of the movie *Willard,* in the process of being reduced to a heap of crumbs. The stabilizing factor in the Mouse House exhibit was the existence of hungry reptiles just around the corner. Snakes have to eat, too, and, as long as there is a logically connected purpose, the public seems content to accept the fate of the mice. In sharp contrast, a recent incident in eastern Michigan caused caustic public outrage toward a Detroit animal control facility when an animal caretaker was discovered feeding indigent puppies to an indigent python in their care.

In examining my own behavior, I have to admit that my sensitivities also vary on a taxonomic basis. For example, I am able to place an earthworm on a hook without much soul-searching. I have also been able to catch fish and place them on a stringer or in a cooler (or the bottom of the boat) without contemplating how the fish might feel about it. But, frankly, such things have begun to trouble me a little as I grow older. I mostly catch and release fish nowadays, but some object even to that. I used to hunt deer and rabbits but now find it distasteful, although I am not quite ready to contemplate the ethics of duck hunting. When I see a moth struggling in vain against a lamp, though, I invariably liberate it outside into the night. Is it because I am growing soft and sentimental, or is mortality finally tickling my conscience and causing me to grow? We seem to pick and choose our prejudices and privileges when it comes to animals, but then we humans have always done this with members of our own species.

From their inception, the perspective of modern zoos has been heavily weighted toward the preservation of species, rather than individual animals, though one should not underestimate the importance of individual animals in zoos, particularly the popular or endangered ones. I find the keeping of wild animals for zoological display and education to be acceptable and justifiable, although I have misgivings about the propriety of their close confinement purely for entertainment. I have come to accept and live with my ambivalence, however, and would much rather be conflicted on this whole subject than complacent, so as to be constantly reminded about the obligations that we place on ourselves when we place animals in captivity.

A number of studies have been conducted on the motivation and behaviors of today's zoo visitors. Two of the earlier public surveys were published in 1976 by Neil Cheek in *Leisure and Recreation Places* and by Stephen Kellert in the 1979 *AAZPA Annual Meeting Proceedings*. They concluded that zoo visitors, while not generally the most informed among so-called nonconsumptively oriented wildlife groups (for example, campers, hikers, ecotourists, and birdwatchers), are above average in education and income compared to non-zoogoers. (Though going to the zoo will not automatically raise your income, I fear.) Given the rising cost of visiting most tourist attractions, these statistics may partly reflect the financial barriers of admission prices.

Some interesting conclusions have been drawn about the animal types to which zoogoers are attracted, which include, in particular, exotic and charismatic species such as gorillas, tigers, and pandas—especially the mammals, but also some of the predatory reptiles. Zoo visitor patterns are family-oriented in character, with emphasis upon a combination of three primary motivations—entertainment, education, and socialization. Unlike going to a movie, these visitors often share their experiences as family groups explore the zoo grounds together. Surveys have also demonstrated that, more than the average, zoogoers generally have strong affections for wildlife, as opposed to mere intellectual curiosity. In other words, there are huge opportunities to influence this audience in the realm of environmental conservation, if those opportunities are maximized. The effectiveness of graphics, signage, and other exhibit communication methodologies in educating the public are still not well enough understood and require ongoing study. There are parallel risks of alienating this public against the mission of zoos if animals are poorly displayed, explained, or cared for. Recent polls of visitors have shown that only 38 percent of them consider zoo and aquariums to be conservation-oriented institutions, as opposed to places for amusement. They need to be both to succeed.

The keeping of animals in captivity is a tradition that derives from humankind's innate curiosity and fascination with living things, and anthropocentric curiosity about how people and animals might share common attributes. Outside of books and before television, movies, circuses, and zoos were the usual extent of what average urban dwellers experienced with exotic wildlife. The public's appetite for wildlife and wild places was well demonstrated in the 1920s and '30s by the popularity of the motion picture documentaries produced by the celebrities Martin and Osa Johnson from their travels to Africa and the South Pacific. Most major, and even moderate-sized, cities built zoos as a form of both public entertainment and education. Just as a city of any status was expected to have a library, museum, and public transportation system of some merit, having a public zoo became the norm for any self-respecting metropolis. However, municipal zoos often became the stepchildren of city park departments and fell into a pecking order that frequently favored the public golf links and other, more familiar, operations. The management of zoos has always been a thorn in the side of many municipal administrations. Zoo directors often were political appointees, not biologists or educators. Zoos also occasionally became dumping grounds for civil service employees who graduated from other city bureaucracies.

The founders of the San Diego Zoo expressed this same concern about city-administrated zoos in the early 1920s. According to accounts in the *San Diego Union-Tribune*, the trustees believed that "the history of zoological gardens in the United States shows that municipal zoos have been failures, while those managed by zoological societies have been uniformly successful. San Diego Zoo supporters contend that where city officials or commissions have control, politics creep in, with an impairment of efficiency, while public-spirited citizens who devote much of their time and thought to the direction of the zoo through a society invariably attain the best results. Boston and Los Angeles are cited by society members here as examples of what happens to the zoos when politics are permitted to enter in the management."

Thus, like the New York Zoological Park, the San Diego Zoo's resolve to be operated through a nonprofit zoological society was ingrained from its founding. In recent decades a number of municipal zoos (Birmingham, Bridgeport, Buffalo, Cleveland, Columbus, Fort Worth, Lowry Park, Seattle Woodland, and Toledo) have been converted to similar models of nonprofit society management, while others have hybridized their structures to have strong private zoological society involvement.

Zoo administrators overall have been a heterogeneous brew as a profession, but have steadily improved in quality as trained personnel have assumed management roles in recent generations. That growth and maturation has come in no small part as a result of the leadership of many individuals within the American Zoo and Aquarium

Association. With a membership now approaching 5,500, this organization seeks to co-ordinate cooperation among zoological gardens and aquariums and raise standards for animal care, improved management, and scientific progress in conservation biology. Some old-timers still feel that there is too little regard for the history of zoos and an understanding of how zoos reached where they are today. There are also some concerns among other zoo professionals (not so old) that many key administrative positions in zoos are being filled with non-animal people whose expertise is top-heavy in marketing and theme park management at the expense of biological acumen, forcing the animal experts into the back seat in influencing institutional priorities.

Zoos have an early history of being net consumers of wildlife instead of being their conservators. Much of that has now changed. In earlier times this was well-illustrated by the first major attempts to import orangutans to zoos. According to the late Lee Crandall, a curator at the New York Zoological Park (Bronx Zoo) and author of *Mammals in Captivity,* orangutans first arrived in Europe in the year 1640 and in America in 1825. Additional accounts by Frederick Ulmer describe how a Dutchman brought 102 Sumatran orangutans to Europe in 1927–28, thirty-three ultimately destined for the United States. Nearly all of these animals soon died of various causes, even if they arrived alive at their destinations. It took time, and more orangutans, to succeed in providing the minimal conditions for the survival of this relatively hardy species in captivity.

The historical mortality rates in acquiring animals for zoo exhibition were high, leading some early leaders in the zoo profession to doubt the prospects for keeping many species in captivity. For example, in 1915 the director of the Bronx Zoo, William Hornaday, stated: "There is not the slightest reason to hope than an adult gorilla, either male or female, ever will be seen living in a zoological park or garden." It would be some time before gorillas became common in captivity—the first captive birth of a gorilla was at the Columbus Zoo in 1956. Gorillas now live and reproduce in scores of zoos around the world.

In 1923, during its formative years, the San Diego Zoo hired Frank Buck, the colorful and controversial animal dealer, as its director. His time at the zoo was limited and he soon fell into disfavor with the zoo's founder, Dr. Harry Wegeforth, over issues of managerial autonomy. The fact that Buck was hired in the first place was indicative of the high priority given to bringing affordable animals to San Diego to build an extensive animal collection. Seldom did zoos organize collecting expeditions of their own. Rather, they relied upon animal dealers, who offered animals for sale to the

Young gorilla captured in 1930 by Martin and Osa Johnson

highest bidders. Wegeforth was put off by the outrageous prices demanded by animal dealers—enter Mr. Buck. But within a matter of months Buck was fired. In his unsuccessful breach of contract complaint in San Diego Court, Buck countercharged that Wegeforth had been responsible for the deaths of 150 snakes that had been force-fed with a sausage stuffer. The press photo of this stunt being applied to a large python made sensational publicity in the newspapers. Several thousand people turned out and paid a special admission to see the big snake being fed.

In 1930 Buck published a popular account about his animal collecting exploits entitled, *Bring 'Em Back Alive*, avoiding all references to his San Diego fiasco. Apparently, bringing them back alive was often the exception rather than the rule. Indeed, many animals and even whole shipments were lost from capture and transport before they ever reached the gates of a zoo, which Buck acknowledges in his book. One of San Diego's early chimpanzees, named Dinah, arrived at the zoo as a crippled youngster and died prematurely at the age of eleven. Her postmortem examination revealed that she had been wounded in the head, probably at the time of her capture, and a hole larger than a quarter was discovered on the right lower side of her skull, the likely cause of the disability she exhibited in her left leg and foot.

During the exploration of Africa by Westerners in the 1850s, American hunter-adventurer Paul B. DuChaillu provided the original insights into capturing gorillas. He was the first white person to see a gorilla in the wild and published the first authoritative artist sketches of this species. He killed a number of gorillas, which, in those days were vigorously sought after and purchased as specimens by major museums. DuChaillu was troubled but undeterred by his killing of this unique species, and he wrote in his 1861 book, *Exploration and Adventures in Equatorial Africa,* about the capture of a three-year old gorilla:

> I profess that I felt almost like a murderer when I saw the gorillas as they ran on their hind legs. They looked fearfully like hairy men, their heads down and their bodies inclined forward, their whole appearance like men running for their lives. Take with this their awful cry, which fierce and animal as it is, has yet something human in its discordance, and you will cease to wonder that the native's have the wildest superstitions about these wild men of the woods. . . . Instantly they [the hunters] made ready to fire, and none too soon for the old female saw them as they raised their guns and they had only to pull triggers without delay. Happily they wounded her mortally. She fell. The young one, hearing the noise of the guns, ran to his mother and clung to her, hiding his face and embracing her body. The hunters immediately rushed toward the two, hallooing with joy as they ran on. But this roused the little one, who instantly let go his mother and ran to a small tree, which he climbed with great agility, where he sat and roared at them savagely. . . . One of the men received a severe bite on the hand, and another had a piece taken out of his leg. . . . He constantly rushed at them, so they were obliged to get a forked stick, in which his neck was inserted in such a way that he could not escape, and yet could be kept a safe distance. In this uncomfortable way he was brought to the village.

Carl Akeley, the well-known naturalist/taxidermist with the American Museum of Natural History in New York City, gave a compelling account of his 1920s collecting activities in pursuit of gorilla specimens for a mounted display in their new Hall of African Mammals in his 1923 book *In Brightest Africa.* Since the capture of young apes for zoo exhibition involved the killing of the mothers and other family members, his experi-

Museum mounts of DuChaillu gorillas specimens in Melbourne, Australia

ences were probably typical of what took place in the forest in the process of procuring animals. Akeley eventually became conflicted about the taking of mountain gorillas and feared for the future of these noble animals. He wrote: "The black fur ball that I fired at was the four-year old son of the female that we had shot previously. As he ran about one of the guides speared him. I came up before he was dead. There was a heartbreaking expression of piteous pleading on his face. He would have come to my arms for comfort."

Some zoos started out solely as extensions of the egos of individuals, more than for any public purpose. The best zoos make education a central priority, not only to justify their public status in their communities, but also for the greater social obligations concerning animals. They should also make significant efforts to bring environmental messages to the public about their responsibilities as stewards of wildlife and natural resources. Such concepts are sometimes a challenge to sell to some city hall administrators and boards of trustees, who still may think of the zoo as a civic diversion or whimsical retreat rather than a catalyst for nature conservation and social enrichment.

World War II had practical implications for zoos, when hostilities disrupted the supply of animals and bombing devastated some of the best-known zoos in Europe. When I did research into the life of the Dutch naturalist, Johann Büttikofer, who conducted important wildlife field research in Liberia, the trail to his records ended in the bombed-out Rotterdam Zoo where he had been the zoo director. As a result of war disruptions, the animal collections of many zoos began to show the impact of inadequate, and often nonexistent, programs for reliably propagating their own animals. This shortage elevated the importance of developing breeding programs and alliances with other zoos, largely to assure a continued supply of animals for exhibition.

Other philosophies, such as those of New York Zoological Park director William Hornaday, may have influenced some industry priorities on the merits of breeding animals for exhibition. For many, replacing animals was less complex than reliably propagating them. In a vision that is a far cry from today's prestigious New York Zoological Park, he wrote in his annual report for 1920: "The first, the last and the greatest business of every zoological park is to collect and exhibit fine and rare animals. Next comes the duty of enabling the greatest possible number of people to see them with comfort and satisfaction. In comparison with these objects, all others are of secondary or tertiary or quaternary importance. The breeding of wild animals is extremely interesting, and their systematic study is fascinating, but both these ends must be subordinated to the main objects."

At the national level in the United States, some leaders of major public institutions are still not attuned to the logical roles of zoos as educational and research organizations. In 2001, for example, the new head of the Smithsonian Institution, the first nonscientist ever to hold that post, ordered the closure of its Conservation Research Center (CRC) in Front Royal, Virginia. This wildlife breeding and conservation research unit is directly affiliated with the National Zoo in Washington, DC, a unit of the Smithsonian. Its proposed elimination was justified by his interests in freeing up budget resources for making aesthetic improvements to public exhibits in several Smithsonian museums. Insiders, however, believe that this short-sighted proposal was symptomatic of a more fundamental philosophical agenda that resents pro-environmental activities ranging from studies of acid rain, nuclear power, and endangered species to the opposition to oil drilling in wilderness regions. While the underlying credibility of organizations such as the Smithsonian is based largely upon their research and preservation programs, the new director became viewed as considering animal conservation research to be both vague and expendable. Fortunately, a national outcry from scientists, museum directors, conservation organizations, and congresspersons reversed this decision, and this program barely survived—so far.

No consensus exists as to what the priorities of a zoo or aquarium should be. Are they principally for entertainment, education, or conservation? For that matter, the motivations of our culture for conservation initiatives in general are fraught with contradictions, as demonstrated by the following case: There is a proposal currently in the works for a large project to salvage southern California's Salton Sea. This large, salty, unnatural body of water was formed around the turn of the last century in the desert region between San Diego and Arizona, when the Colorado River overflowed its banks and those of off-branching irrigation canals, filling up a huge desert basin over a four-year period. Since then, the salinity of the sea has gradually risen to the point of becoming marginally habitable for introduced saltwater fishes. The causes of its hypersalinization include evaporative losses, as well as chronic salty water runoff from extensive agricultural irrigation in the region. The inflow from one of the world's most polluted rivers from across the border in Mexico, the American River (no less), is compounding the problem. While hailed as a major resource for waterfowl, the Salton Sea has also become a death trap for many migratory birds because of botulism and red tide, related to deteriorating water quality.

Current plans for the Salton Sea, originally championed by the late Rep. Sonny Bono, involve a proposal to spend more than $400 million to construct a series of dikes that would move water to evaporation impoundments in order to desalinate it. $400 million could establish and maintain dozens of national parks in critical wildlife habitats throughout the developing world. I'm not entirely (but mostly) against the Salton Sea restoration project, but this clearly illustrates the chaotic manner in which society allocates resources for conservation. We spend a fortune on an unnatural attraction while real wonders perish. Perhaps this inconsistency was best articulated by zoo critic Dr. Dale Jamieson, a philosophy professor at Colorado State University, who attributes misplaced conservation salvage priorities to "the peculiar moral schizophrenia of a culture that drives a species to the edge of extinction, and then romanticizes the remnants."

The existence of zoos probably cannot be justified and supported without some customized mix of entertainment, education, and conservation. This is reflected in the ongoing push and pull between conservationists and administrators within the zoo and aquarium profession. Administrative financial pragmatists are put off by fiscally vague, idealistic conservation and breeding programs, whereas conservationists are troubled by the pragmatists' lack of passion and purpose for being in this line of endeavor. Even when lists of mutual criteria may be acceptable in principle to all of those in leadership positions in zoos, disagreements often follow about the priorities of where the efforts and resources should be allocated. This confusion has occurred, to a large degree, because of the historical lack of consensus among zoo professionals and imprecise local goals of individual institutions. It is further exacerbated by the commonplace shortfalls of sufficient resources, both human and financial.

Zoos take root in many different soils, with disparate perceptions and locally biased priorities. Zoological gardens have been extraordinarily difficult for local politicians to fathom, engendering a consensus void that frequently leads to inadequate insight and to inertia in many local decision-making circles. Zoos have an aura, an arcane mystique, and a proprietary intangibility that make them different from the other assets that community leaders and administrators typically manage. In frustration, politicians may be skeptical of proposals, interfere in operational matters, and be confounded by what seems to be more complex and expensive undertakings than they had imagined or planned for.

The evolution of zoos has required the acquisition of both knowledge and experience, not only in caring for and exhibiting animals but also in the wherewithal to fund these undertakings. It has mandated the coevolution of zoo directors, veterinarians, curators, and animal keepers through their respective professional organizations. It has also required creativity in recruiting public and private benefactors to support their programs.

Some zoos and aquariums use animal-training exercises as substitutes for overt entertainment shows in order to attract visitors, and to a lesser degree some have become stationary circuses. Petting zoos, pony, elephant and camel rides, and shows involving birds of prey, seals, and talking parrots, still widespread in zoos, are gauged to fill the gap in the range of visitor tastes and create a synthetic bridge between captive animals and humans.

Fortunately, most of the crassest examples of ball-balancing bears and motorcycle-riding primates have now been abandoned. The San Diego Zoo had its own flair for flamboyant publicity in its formative years, including such antics as painting elephants for parades and public demonstrations of how the zoo's young apes had been taught table etiquette. Contemporary animal zoo and aquarium performances are couched in terms of necessary training (for example, of elephants and killer whales) or as education demonstrations, often using rehabilitated or rescued wildlife. The utility of training for animals must not be readily dismissed, however, since this cultivates important cooperative skills that can benefit their medical care. The modern-day versions of trained-animal shows use terms such as "natural behaviors," playing down the Big Top themes in a sort of greening of circus acts. For examples of old animal shows in zoos, one need only peruse the vintage postcards on ebay.com to get a flavor of yesteryear's animal performances. Historically, the St. Louis Zoo wins hands-down as the most prolific producer of lion, chimpanzee and monkey shows.

Even Disneyland, which seldom features live animal displays, has been affected by public sentiments and pressures that are changing the way that society relates to animals. After ongoing criticism of Disneyland's well-known Adventureland Jungle Cruise boat ride by animal advocates, the safari-clad guides were disarmed and instructed to stop shooting blank pistols at the mechanical hippos when they suddenly reared out of the water and threatened passing boats. A kinder and gentler pseudo-safari came to the cruise, just as East African photo safaris replaced shooting safaris. This armistice closely coincided with the 1998 opening of Disney's new Animal Kingdom attraction in Florida, perhaps because of the perceived contradiction of the corporate preservation of animals in one venue, and the practice of shooting at them in another. In reporting this change, the *Los Angeles Times* quoted Jamie O'Boyle, a Philadelphia-based cultural analyst and Disney consultant, who explained: "New generations grow up with new ideas. This is the way society evolves its norms, and Disney has to reflect that."

When the first giant pandas came to the San Diego Zoo from China for temporary exhibition in 1987, elaborate preparations had been made to accommodate the animals and the crush of visitors expected to view them. The efforts to secure a panda loan began more than six years earlier, when I accompanied a group of zoo trustees and curators on a friendship mission to Chinese zoos, not long after the country opened up to outside visitors. Pandas were obviously on the top of the list for potential loans and acquisitions. While pandas have always been rare outside of

Robotic hippos threaten the Jungle Cruise at Disneyland

China, we attended an entertainment event at an opera house in Beijing that included a trained panda dressed in colorful costume, along with other acrobatic performers. Panda life in the Chinese zoos that we toured was threadbare by contrast with the plush new accommodations that would be built in San Diego. While the financial requirements for the panda loan were staggering, the revenues from the increased attendance handily offset the expense.

A rather shocking surprise developed when the Chinese entourage arrived at the zoo with the pandas and began unloading various circus props—a large toy airplane, candy-cane colored logs, a panda tricycle, and other paraphernalia that were in gaudy contrast to the intentions of their new conservation-themed exhibit. While pandas were still used in traveling performances at home in China, these individuals were two of only four animals in the entire United States at the time. Subsequent panda exhibits in San Diego have shed the circus throwback themes as the status of pandas in China has shifted to an emphasis on their conservation as a unique element of China's national heritage.

Exhibiting family or social groups of animals rather than isolated individuals, is the accepted and desired norm in today's zoos, although there still is no precise methodology to assess the well-being of zoo animals. Paradoxically, this sometimes conflicts with the natural solitariness of some species, which come together only seasonally for breeding and baby rearing. Family groupings display more natural social behaviors and fewer stereotyped behavioral pathologies that can be a function of captivity. Emphasis is commonly placed on environmental enrichment of animals' living areas, with more comfortable resting spots, opportunities to retreat from the public and exhibit-mates, innovative feeding routines, and varied enclosure furnishings. Overall, exhibits are transforming from hard concrete surfaces to multidimensional mini-habitats—at least that is what is being attempted.

The San Diego Wild Animal Park is perhaps best known as an innovator of wide open spaces for captive wildlife. Opening in 1972, it improved significantly on the drive-through lion safari park and initiated programs to sustain their animal populations. Launched with both public funds and a steady infusion of cash from its operator, the Zoological Society of San Diego, the park set a new standard that was strikingly unique at the time but is now emulated in many ways by other zoological facilities. Captive breeding of rare and endangered species became the theme of the park, rather than a behind-the-scenes activity. Its major attractions, aside from entertainment shows, include spacious mixed-species exhibits, comfortable transportation to gain proximity to the animals, and extensive horticultural embellishments.

For some zoos, which have been through their nadirs of public approval and miscellaneous animal fiascos, reinvention of their programs and facilities has turned them around for the better. Often, however, it does not become apparent that things are as bad as they really are (to politicians anyway) until an exposé finally drives the problem to the front page of the local newspaper. In some cases nothing changes until zoo regulators, such as the US Department of Agriculture, impose sanctions or threaten to suspend their federal exhibitor registration. Another constructive pressure that has caused change in the living conditions for animals over the past twenty years is the accreditation process of the American Zoo and Aquarium Association. The failure to achieve or maintain this status has been the threshold event that has caused some municipalities to act to improve or close their zoological gardens.

Many of the problems in zoos arise not simply from the ignorance of zoo management, but from municipal foot-dragging in failing to provide realistic budgetary allocations. Some of the uncomplimentary zoo headlines around the country have read:

City Audit Stomps on Zoo
Zoo Loses Accreditation
Director Confirms Animal Sales to Shooting Ranch
Zoo Crumbles—Deferred Repairs Taking Toll
USDA Cites Inadequate Animal Care—Threatens to Shut Zoo
Third Zoo Director Leaves—Who's in Charge?
Keepers Accuse City of Neglect

While zoo public-relations people try to keep much of the news on the lighter, more upbeat side, no one can ultimately control the press. Not all animal headlines, however, are as accusatory as those above and add some needed levity:

Elephant Dung Made Into Electricity
The Bear Who Wrestled James Bond Dies at 25
Beavers Chew Way to Top of Pest List
Girl's Nightmares After Seeing Horses' Heads Fed to Tigers

The opening question to this chapter was, "Is it humane to keep animals in captivity in zoos?" In my mind, the answer to this question is complex and conditional. Intentions aside, for me it comes down to the fundamental perception of whether confinement constructively communicates our compassion for our fellow animal species, or simply displays our ability to control them on our terms. Animals that are poorly kept, insensitively displayed, and ineptly managed undermine all justifications for a zoo's existence.

Many roadside zoos have been closed down as a result of the federal Animal Welfare Act for failing to meet the most basic requirements for humane animal care. These tacky little throwbacks to early zookeeping are a lingering embarrassment to legitimate zoos and a continuing source of misunderstanding and confused identity with the zoogoing public. The concerns about the pejorative "roadside zoo" have reached such a level of concern that the American Zoo and Aquarium Association recently appointed a task force to deal with the dilemma caused by its trashy shirttail relatives. A few animal rights groups, however, take generous license in blurring the distinctions between well-operated facilities and these outcasts. Affirming this sleazy stereotype, some years ago Roadside Zoo was even adopted as the name of a rowdy roadhouse drinking spot for a while.

Some privately kept exotic animals live lives that exceed what many zoos can provide for their animals. One of the best-maintained groups of big cats in the United States probably does not live in a zoo at all but belongs to Siegfried & Roy, the popular Las Vegas performers, who feature white tigers disappearing in incredible illusions at Steve Wynn's Mirage Hotel casino. The care of these performing animals—their housing, feeding, and socialization—are unsurpassed in any zoo I have visited. On the several occasions that I have assisted in tending to medical problems in this animal entourage, I was impressed with their living quarters, exercise areas, and swimming pools in their large, landscaped compound at the Siegfried & Roy residence in a Las Vegas suburb. In particular, I was awed by the daily commitment of time, energy, and money that the performers themselves (not just assistants) invest in the well-being of their animals. The human contact and performance lives of these animals seem not to have interfered with their sense of well-being, and the birth of many white tiger babies seems to bear this out. Is this extraordinary display of live tigers in a hotel casino inappropriate? Given the care that they receive, I think not; if placed on other hands, probably so. Siegfried & Roy are not pretending to be conservationists per se, but the beauty that people see in these animals can only build the public's esteem for the world's tiger species. Sadly, the future for this show is in serious doubt with the serious injuries suffered by Roy Horn when he was attacked by a white tiger during a performance in the fall of 2003.

While many are reluctant to credit them publicly, animal welfare organizations, overall, have made significant contributions to the improvement of animal care in zoos and in the lives of laboratory animals used in biomedical research. Unfortunately, because of some of the outrageous excesses of the extremist elements of some animal activist groups, a middle ground for both zoos and some animal welfarists has been only marginally attainable. When it was suggested to one zoo trustee that a dialogue should be sought with animal advocate groups, his automatic response was an old military adage: "Never retreat when you are under fire!" My only reply to this ossified view was: "That's exactly what General Custer thought, and look what happened to him." Moderate forces for animal welfare deserve, and generally have, the respect of the zoo profession. Radical forces will write their own historical epitaphs.

The animal welfare movement in the United Kingdom has a longer, more contentious, history than in the United States. As a measure of the public's strong disapproval of marginal zoos, the London Zoo, founded in 1828, was nearly closed in 1992. Faced with growing criticisms of its outdated facilities in lacking sound financial counsel, it almost shut its doors for good. Saviors stepped in at the last moment to rescue the zoo from extinction. An earlier example of a distressed zoo was the Los Angeles Zoo, which had a spotty record since its creation in 1913. Many years later a new zoo came about through an $8 million bond, following brutal criticism by civic groups, city council members and other detractors. In the early 1960s the *Los Angeles Daily News* called the zoo an "inadequate, ugly, poorly designed, and under-financed collection of beat-up cages." The groundbreaking for the construction of the new Greater Los Angeles Zoo took place in the fall of 1964. It rained that day. Still struggling to reinvent itself in 2001, the zoo opened a $13 million Animal Health and Conservation Center, and the zoo is gradually undergoing another generation of transformations.

In the mid-1980s, faced with similar staffing and facilities problems, the Atlanta Zoo began a program to reinvent itself. In 1984 *Parade* magazine named the Atlanta Zoo as one of the ten worst zoos in the America. With the support of civic leaders and the community at large, Dr. Terry Maple, an experienced primate behaviorist, was appointed as the new zoo director, and projects and programs were launched to reverse the zoo's decline. Such efforts take large doses of financial resources, but, more important, even larger doses of informed introspection, determination, and hard work. The catalyst for the initial changes at Zoo Atlanta was a series of embarrassing animal-welfare debacles involving charges of mismanagement, poor animal care, and the death of an elephant. As president of the American Association of Zoo Veterinarians at the time, I met with a commissioner of the city of Atlanta who was desperate to find outside counsel to resolve their problems. The best advice that I could give her was that the real solutions rested locally, in the hands of the community and its leaders, and that only local commitment could turn their situation around from its present dismal state and avoid shutting the zoo. The humiliating problems that were haunting them with humane societies and the US Department of Agriculture were symptomatic of the lack of civic support and vision for a first-class zoological garden. Starting with the recruitment of Maple as zoo director, they assembled an entire new professional team which dramatically changed the culture of their organization and the course of the zoo. Zoo Atlanta is now a focus of community pride and had to make no apologies when Atlanta later became the host for the Olympic Games.

In 1971, in an article describing the then decaying Central Park Zoo in New York City, Eugene J. Walter, the former editor of the New York Zoological Society's magazine *Wildlife Conservation,* wrote in *Venture Magazine*: "While it might be a great place to buy a balloon or frozen custard, it is nearly everything that a dreadful zoo can be. It is an animal slum where the remarkable products of millions of years of evolution are condemned to an irrelevant, bankrupt, freak-show existence in buildings that are eyesores and nose sores. The animals here relate to nothing. Suppose you placed the finest stars of the Metropolitan Opera—isolated singly or in pairs—in a series of cramped, bleak tenement rooms, each furnished with a rickety chair and a bare light bulb. Would you then expect to step out into the hall and see and hear Carmen? Small wonder that people hoot and snicker at the animals. Ultimately the spectators become the real freaks. The dozens of pathetic little menageries like Central Park's suffer not merely from lack of money or space but from poverty of imagination." Subsequently, the management of this zoo and of New York's Prospect Park and Queens zoos was assumed by The Wildlife Conservation Society, and needed improvements followed. As of 2003, however, the city budget crisis was causing cuts in funding to these facilities, and thoughts of yesteryear's problems came back to old-timers' minds.

Some advocates believe that animals have rights akin to humans. Parallels have been made to slavery, women's suffrage, racism, and other social injustices over the centuries. On the surface, many people react to this deceptively simple notion by agreeing that animals, indeed, should have "rights." However, accepting this premise leads to other obligatory extensions that are both illogical and self-defeating. Nonetheless, some municipalities are now considering and even adopting proposals that prohibit domestic dogs and cats from being regarded as private property and, instead, require that humans be designated as their "guardians."

The animal welfare movement itself is factionalized, just as most other social movements are. On one extreme, some animal groups equate animals to people, object to eating animal products of any sort (veganism) and believe that using animals for agriculture, disease research, pets, or exhibition is immoral. (Remember Miss Dillenbeck and the goldfish.) Some are even on record as believing that discovering a cure for AIDS could not justify the loss of a single rodent's life in research.

Dealing with informational requests from adversarial animal-rights groups and reporters can generate quicksand for the unprepared zoo spokesperson. Since the intentions of such requests to zoos are sometimes unfriendly in today's climate, it is interesting to observe how they have been handled. One of the more innovative responses came from Dr. Lucy Spelman, director of the National Zoo in Washington, to a writer for *The Washington Post* and several animal-rights groups that had requested copies of the medical records of a giraffe that had died in the animal collection. (Bear in mind here that a primary tactic of the more aggressive animal rights groups is to achieve legal "rights" for animals, as we accord human rights to persons.) Spelman's reply was that the disclosure of these medical records would constitute a breach of the animal's "right to privacy"—leaving animal rights petitioners in the unenviable position of now having to argue that animals had no such rights. The initial response to her statement from the biomedical research community was horror—a key official in a major zoo was conceding that animals had some rights! In the final analysis, however, most had to agree that her position was a tactical, if short-lived, victory, as it shifted the request from an administrative one to a contradictory ethical one. The records of most public institutions require a practical degree of transparency, however, so long as this access is not used to disrupt normal operations unfairly.

The next positions toward the middle of the animal welfare free-for-all are held by yet another set of advocates who may forego some of the more extreme demands; they find pet animals acceptable, may support compromise (imperfect) vegetarianism, and have a wide range of views on biomedical research, farming practices, and zoological gardens. More in the mainstream, overall, are the general populace and the major animal humane societies in the United States. Rather than being absolutist in their objections to a particular activity (for example, zoos, research, or farming) as a class, they have developed attitudes that attempt to measure and improve the outcomes of these activities and to require and assess rationales for utilizing animals. In other words, they support the justifiable use of animals for human objectives and are more pragmatic in their approach. They believe that there should be limits on the use of animals for human purposes and often propose to accomplish this by regulations and laws. Opponents of more regulation, however, believe that the direction and management of even mainstream animal welfare organizations is being coopted by their infiltration with radical animal-rights elements. Collaborative efforts between animal welfare organizations and biomedical researchers have advanced further in the United Kingdom than in the United States, where inquiries by animal welfare groups are usually treated with suspicion and mistrust.

A polarized group wants to eliminate zoos and biomedical research from the face of the earth, whereas a centrist group argues that animals should be humanely and justifiably utilized. In the extreme approaches, tactics are designed to be controversial and confrontational in order to leverage media coverage. Centrist groups seek to modify and selectively correct and improve shortcomings and are moderate in their publicity methods. One of the most radical elements, sometime called "animal liberation" groups, have more of a car-bombing mentality. They set animals free from labs, zoos, and farms, burn and vandalize research facilities, toss red paint on fur wearers, and clandestinely threaten individuals. They often operate as isolated cells and use other, less radical, groups as their spokespersons. Several threats against farming interests have even implied the possibility of bioterrorism to thwart animal enterprises. The FBI is probably looking for them now, and the renewed efforts to combat terrorism following the World Trade Center attacks should cause them to re-think some of their tactics, for their day in court will be different than before.

On the opposite extreme of the animal liberationists are those who believe that humans have absolute dominion over animals in every sense and find no objections to animal fighting, staged trophy hunting, and even illegal activities. One of the more trivial contributions to the antagonism of animal rights folks included the formation of a counter-PETA pseudo-organization called "People for Eating Tasty Animals. " The original PETA (People for the Ethical Treatment of Animals) was so cyber-illiterate to begin with that the tasty animal founder preemptively purchased the domain name "PETA.org." At his newly launched web site, the virtues of consumptive animal uses were extolled, *bon vivant* recipes were shared for preparing meat, and a cyberfinger was wagged at all "animal rights wackos." A lengthy dispute to obtain the right to use that domain name ensued, with the animal-rights organization's trademark-infringement claims prevailing over the "free speech" claims of the parody site. PETA got its name back.

Those individuals and groups who reject regulation of any sort, and who believe that they alone know best how to use and care for animals, are as unproductive as the animal-rights extremists. This was the attitude of a relatively small group of zoo people after the passage of the Animal Welfare Act in 1966, but it never persisted in the manner that it has lingered within the field of biomedical research, where a few individuals still hold to the conviction that their lofty goals require full attention to their work, unfettered by so-called bureaucratic red tape. Like the National Rifle Association, they steadfastly view all regulatory initiatives as calculated to prevent them from engaging in their lawful activities. The hardliners will not publicly acknowledge that much, if any, benefit has ever come from animal welfare regulation. While they are a tiny minority, their attitudes influence policy within their professional groups and institutions and engender residual ambivalence about the need for competent animal care and use programs in research institutions. Moreover, by their strong and inflexible opposition to the regulatory process, they exclude and alienate themselves from joining in the formative deliberations to negotiate the very standards that they will have to live with, viewing this as braiding their own hangman's noose.

The most credible spokespersons in the animal ethics dialogues seem to be those who refuse to become trapped into the "rights" vs. "no rights" backwaters, and who simply believe that humans have obligations to treat animals with respect and kindness and that the use of animals for research and exhibition should be monitored, measured, and carried out with a minimum degree of stress or discomfort. They also believe that zoos and research institutions should assure the quality of the lives of their animal charges, and not be above justifying their existence to society; and that scientists, zoo managers, farmers, and the like should be able to support programs for the welfare of animals. After all, regulation is not only necessary to protect animals, but also the credibility of their professions and enterprises. But, most obvious of all, zoological gardens, agriculture, and research organizations cannot thrive in the absence good animal care.

In the early 1980s I testified in a landmark legal action that gave rise to PETA. The 1981 incidents that brought this case to court involved a research laboratory in Silver Spring, Maryland, which was conducting neurological studies of stroke, using a group of fifteen macaque monkeys. Much has been said and written about these events since then, and it has had a profound effect on the manner in which animal research is now conducted in the United States. These particular complaints involved charges that a researcher had failed to provide adequate veterinary care, as required by local humane regulations and the federal Animal Welfare Act. The research in question involved surgically severing sensory spinal nerves, resulting in complications, particularly sensory deficits, in the forelimbs. The monkeys often proceeded to self-mutilate themselves and developed serious infections in their hands and wrists, resulting in deformations and, in some cases, amputations.

Because of my background in zoo primate medicine and the reticence of the district attorney to obtain counsel from veterinarians within the research establishment, I was asked to examine the monkeys and document their condition. They had been "kidnapped" from the research facility and held in seclusion by PETA founders Alex

Pacheco, Ingrid Newkirk, and others in the basement of a private suburban residence. This specific incident was the genesis of the PETA organization. Along with another zoo veterinarian and local police officers, I sedated and examined the animals. The evaluation of the monkeys began with a meeting with police and the prosecuting attorney to review their evidence and the documentation of their investigation. Among the police photographs that were shown to us was a deceased whole monkey, its hand still bandaged, weighted down with an auto crankshaft in a barrel of embalming fluid, unsanitary conditions in the animal facility, and the mummified hand of a research monkey being used as a paperweight on the researcher's desk. If nothing else, considering the delicateness of using primates in research, this researcher was guilty of bad taste. Claims were later made that Pacheco had staged some of the photos, perhaps by skipping some cage cleanings, but the whole truth of these matters may never be fully known.

The bandages on the hand of the monkey in the barrel were apparently used to manage an infection. Even though inadequate veterinary care was the principal issue in the trial, the defense (wisely) never pointed to the crankshaft monkey with the bandage as evidence that medical care was being provided. No medical records were available to document the animals' medical care. A contract veterinarian occasionally visited the facility but left no evidence of his evaluations or treatments. The trial ended in a conviction for violating animal humane laws in Maryland; however, the researcher's conviction was reversed on a jurisdictional basis (it was claimed that this was a federal, not a local, matter for adjudication). Since funds from the National Institutes of Health were being employed in this work, a federal review of his research ensued, resulting in the withdrawal of his federal grants on NIH's evaluation of the facts. Nonetheless, several loyal science research organizations came to the researcher's defense and issued public statements contradicting the Maryland and federal findings.

Only a few years later, at the Head Injury Laboratory at the University of Pennsylvania, another shameful incident of monkey abuse and insensitivity unfolded, with video images that made national television and newspaper news. Baboons were shown being sadistically ridiculed and teased by research technicians after they (the monkeys) had been subjected to head trauma. Coupled with the Silver Spring fiasco, this continued the erosion the public's perception of animal research, enraged several congressmen, and further fueled the growth of PETA, which has used the Silver Spring monkey incidents as a fundraising tool for more than twenty years. The public's approval of biomedical research and zoos is not unconditional, but based on credible assurances of humane animal care and use. And as one candid community zoo supporter once put it to me: "Loyalty to the animals always; loyalty to the zoo when it deserves it."

In 1985, largely because of these two research incidents, new amendments were made to the Animal Welfare Act that were intended to substantially improve the oversight of animal research by mandating a system of research oversight committees called Institutional Animal Care and Use Committees (IACUCs). Even today, however, a few vocal holdouts believe that the Silver Spring incident wrongfully criticized this research. If they had been open to the basic sensibility of animal welfare regulation, knowledgeable of the facts of this case, and able to set their agendas aside, however, they may have been spared the extraordinary success of antagonists such as PETA. One of the reasons that part of the public remains skeptical, or at least ambivalent, about animal research is the self-serving manner of a few diehards in the profession who demand secrecy and "intellectual freedom" at the expense of public scrutiny. This lingering intransigence resembles the manner in which autocratic governments operate—resentful and intolerant of criticism, egotistical in their mission, and patronizing to the public. Like most governmental bureaucracies, they operate more effectively, and in the public's best interest, when illumination and transparency are abundant.

Fortunately, zoos—and the vast majority of biomedical researchers—have taken a different path. While there was initial resistance to the Animal Welfare Act (AWA) of 1966 as a knee-jerk reaction to government regulation, it never took on a significant level of intransigence. This legislation requires standards for a variety of animal enterprises, including research institutes, animal breeders, dealers, zoos, and circuses. Some argue that they are still inadequate. The initial uncertainties about the reasonableness of the regulations gradually abated in zoos and research facilities. Many zoos realized early on that they now had an outside agency whose reports could be used to augur for changes in animal care and facilities through their municipal governments. Zoo veterinarians and many on zoo staffs quietly applauded the new Animal Welfare Act.

Without the AWA, progress in animal care would have been much slower in coming. Its absence could have had a significant, negative impact upon the reputations and credibility of zoos. Meeting these basic requirements demanded some catching up on the part of many zoos, and the process is ongoing. Of the zoo industry problems related to humane issues, several of the most uncomfortable incidents have been due to the dealings that zoo personnel have had with unethical elements of the animal trading industry. Some zoos have been caught up in questionable sales or trades of surplus animals that have found their way to wildlife auctions, back yards, shooting ranches, and roadside zoos. A recent study by the United States Department of Agriculture demonstrated that, despite assurances to the contrary, surplus zoo animals are still finding their ways into inexperienced and unscrupulous private hands. The most dismal account of this problem is found in the 1999 book *Animal Underworld*, which is reviewed in the annotated bibliography at the end of this book.

The dilemma of what to do with surplus animals has been a significant ethical issue as zoos have become victims of their own successes in animal breeding. Animals are living longer in zoos and having more babies, resulting in surpluses of many species. The capacity of zoos to accommodate many of these, such as baby tigers and lions and myriad hoofed animals, has been stretched to the limits in many locations. In some cases the offspring of certain prolific species have been humanely destroyed at birth, but this can cause dismay to zoo personnel and the general public because it may be viewed as contradicting zoos' ethical positions on revering and nurturing life.

Part of the proposed solution to the care of these unwanted animals has been the proliferation of so-called animal sanctuaries or rescue societies. Unfortunately, this randomly spawn assortment of organizations has also been had its share of humane problems. Often started by individuals with sparse resources and credentials, some have themselves turned out to be part of the animal industry problem, housing animals in substandard conditions and on occasion breeding and disseminating exotic animals into private hands for profit. Overdue efforts are underway to improve the credentialing of legitimate sanctuary operations in the United States.

New emphasis is being placed on controlled breeding and contraception. The American Association of Zoo Veterinarians has a standing group named the Reproduction and Contraception Committee. Coordination of breeding is taking place in a cooperative fashion as various groups have formed within the American Zoo and Aquarium Association to manage certain species as collective populations in order to promote genetic diversity. Founded in 1971 as an autonomous organization, after years of affiliation with park management associations, the AZA has greatly expanded the scope of its interests and concerns over the past thirty years. It includes subgroups on captive breeding, field conservation, education, and, in 1980, zoo and aquarium facility accreditation. By 2003 it had 208 member facilities in North America, out of a total of an estimated 2,300 animal operations that represent themselves to be a zoo of one sort or another. Its stated mission is "to promote the welfare of zoological parks and aquariums and their advancement as public educational institutions, as scientific centers, as natural science and wildlife exhibition and conservation agencies, and as cultural recreational establishments dedicated to the enrichment of human and natural resources." Other players in the zoo profession internationally include the World Association of Zoos and Aquariums (WAZA), renamed in 2000 from its former designation as the International Union of Directors of Zoological Gardens, which first organized in 1946 and now numbering two hundred member institutions. The European Association of Zoos and Aquariums (EAZA), headquartered in Amsterdam, has 289 institutional members.

Despite the unpleasantness of the subject of euthanasia, it is a necessary topic for inclusion in a veterinary-oriented book on zoos. The term itself means "good death," which to me suggests that it should involve the least amount of pain and discomfort possible. This will mean different things to different people, and zoo personnel can be as conflicted about the indications and justifications as uninformed outsiders might be. In general, it is the practice of killing a hopelessly sick or injured animal as an act of mercy. The technology of euthanasia itself is sufficient to assure a humane process in most cases. Most are carried out using a lethal dose of potent anesthetic agents.

Often, however, the decision to euthanize an animal may involve a largely subjective judgment of an animal's state of well-being, and considers their discomfort level against the realistic prospects for constructive recovery and quality of life. In practice, an animal's condition leading up to the actual decision to kill it humanely can result in significantly more discomfort than any act of euthanasia, and involve pain and discomfort both from the illness or injury itself, as well as from stressful treatments. A decision whether to euthanize should be largely a medical judgment, although human sensitivities, personalities, and politics certainly weigh heavily into the process. Zoo staff members occasionally lobby for the continued treatment and surgery of marginal and painful cases where the prognosis is poor or even hopeless. In the interest of maintaining harmony in the ranks, there are probably times when redundant, unpromising, and even painful treatments have been continued by the medical staff to preserve people morale. Perhaps part of the concerns that promote this sometimes questionable practice relates to avoiding ad hominem aspersions of insensitivity on the part of medical caregivers. In these cases one can only hope that professional judgment will prevail over sentiments that serve the concerned person(s) more than the suffering animal. Such confusion may be avoided to a significant degree by developing euthanasia policy criteria on what constitutes "quality of life" in general and open discussions with staff that focus first on the animals' well-being. Simply because a procedure is technically feasible should not by itself be sufficient justification to carry it out. With such fundamentals in place, judgments on euthanasia can become more uniform and judicious, and, more important, better serve the humane interests of the animals involved as well as their caregivers.

During the 1980s, in an effort to address the surplus animal problem, one zoo director proposed that zoos should not artificially rear certain species and thereby compound their dilemma with marginal or unwanted individuals. Misappropriating a concept from biologist Charles Darwin, he advocated that, "just as in nature," either they prevailed on their own—the survival of the fittest (in captivity)—or were left to their own devices or euthanized. This policy drew upon the premise that zoo animals should be managed on the basis of populations, which is the norm in wildlife management practices, and minimize the consideration given to individuals. The staff reaction to this new policy was chilly and the public was appalled, prompting a local and industry-wide controversy about surplus animals which continues today. Many felt that it was the inadequacies of the artificial environment of the zoo that was mostly responsible for these failures to thrive, not flawed survival propensities. Fairly or not, some regarded these practices as Kevorkian in style; they were reversed in that zoo's subsequent administration.

Other zoos have had straightforward policies of euthanizing surplus animals of certain species, more often males, at birth, although this always remained a delicate and low-profile activity. Zoos have now turned extensively to various forms of controlled breeding, such as separating animals during fertility periods, selectively sterilizing individuals through ovariectomy and vasectomy, and various forms of chemical birth control. The San Diego Zoo was the first to use the Norplant contraceptive implants to control births in orangutans from material supplied by the World Population Council. We placed them under the skin of the females on their upper arms, and the implants were effective. An important part of breeding programs for endangered species also involves the collection and cryopreservation of sperm, ova, and embryos in order to conserve valuable genetic material for future breeding programs.

In response to public qualms and concerns about animal welfare in zoos, professional groups began to work to develop standards for their member organizations. In 1981 the American Zoo and Aquarium Association launched the Species Survival Plan (SSP), and cooperative animal breeding programs began to flourish in American zoos. There was new emphasis on self-sustaining captive populations and the management of genetic diversity. Focusing particularly on rare and endangered species, and directed through studbooks and breeding consortia, the ultimate goal is to manage these resources as collective rather than strictly private resources. Another significant advance of the 1980s was the initiation of a program of zoo accreditation, with the goal of elevating the standards of AZA member institutions. The American Association of Zoo Veterinarians has also established standards for programs of veterinary care in zoos.

All improvements to zoos aside, the scope of worldwide environmental degradation as opposed to the limitations of zoos' capabilities does not offer realistic hopes that their efforts will make the critical difference for most species. Zoo publicity efforts and an optimistic press have sometimes suggested such a grand role, and this has probably served to lull some of the public into a false sense of complacency, relying too much upon the potential of zoos as safety nets for species extinctions.

Only a relative handful of zoos have extensive conservation initiatives taking place in the field, where animal extinctions are actually occurring. However, the numbers of extension research projects and conservation collaborations are growing and involve zoo personnel on many levels. The consciences of zoos have been transformed in many ways over the past fifty years, and their ethical evolution seems to be securing roles for them as bona fide wildlife conservation and education organizations.

17. WHAT A ZOO SHOULD BE

And Ought Not Be

What should the mission of zoos be, and how can these priorities integrate and reconcile themselves with issues of conservation, education, entertainment, and ethics? Don't expect universal agreement—consensus involving the highly emotion-laden realm of animals is unlikely and unrealistic. Every zoo must decide on the scope and character of its own mission, based on the inclinations and commitment of their managing boards and available resources.

One thing that is very clear, however, is that today's visitors expect more of zoos' animal care and exhibit efforts both in front and behind the scenes. The types of exhibits shown in the following illustrations are now the expected norms for zoological gardens or conservation parks. There is simply no option of maintaining the status quo or turning back to the past.

In 1841, *Punch* magazine delivered the following account of the summer weekend scene at London's Surrey Zoological Gardens, all elements of which can still be found within zoos today:

Wild beasts in cages; flowers of all colour and sizes in pots; enormous cabbages; Brobdignag apples; immense sticks of rhubarb; a view of Rome; a brass band; a grand Roman cavalcade passing over the bridge of St. Angelo; a deafening bark of artillery, and an enchanting series of pyrotechnic wonders, such as Catherine-wheels, flower-pots, and rockets; an illumination of St. Peter's; blazes of blue-fire, showers of steel filings, and a grand blow up of St. Angelo. . . . Such are the entertainments provided by the proprietor. . . . Numerous picnic parties were seated about on the grass; sandwiches, bottled stout, and (with reverence be it spoken) more potent liquors seemed to be highly relished, especially by the ladies. Ices were sold at a pastry-cook's stall, where a continued *feu-de-joie* of ginger-pop was kept up during the whole afternoon and evening. In short, the scene was one of complete *al fresco* enjoyment; how could it be otherwise? The flowers delighted the eye; Mr. Godfrey's well-trained band charmed the ear; and the edibles and drinkables aforesaid the palate. Under such a press of agreeables, the Surrey Zoological Gardens well deserve the name of an Englishman's paradise.

There is no off-the-rack "mission garment" available for every zoo to wear. Each must be custom-crafted according to priority soul-searching. I see this as a multi-tiered exercise whereby smaller and medium sized municipal zoos have their primary purpose focused more locally, providing hands-on, tangible educational resources for teachers and community organizations, and connecting with pragmatic, regional conservation issues. Occasionally they may enter into joint ventures with other zoos and conservation groups on projects outside of their communities. It is both pretentious and impractical, however, for every zoo to assume the mantle of international crusader in the quest to thwart species extinction. Each, however, can be valuable information resources for their constituents on these issues.

In terms of common exhibit animals, zoos must collaborate in breeding programs to assure the availability of animals for all bona fide zoos. This involves planned breeding, genealogic management, and cooperation. The public has come to believe, often through the enthusiastic media-relations efforts of zoos and overreaching by the press, that the reintroduction of captive-bred animals into the wild is a key function of zoos, reminding me of the misguided adage that "the louder you sing, the better you sound." In reality, however, few animal species and fewer zoos will be involved in such efforts. The principal limiting factor for most species in the wild is the lack of undisturbed natural habitat, not the lack of viable breeding stock.

Zoos have played vital roles in several extreme cases, such as the near extinction of the American bison (Bronx Zoo), Arabian oryx (Phoenix Zoo, San Diego Wild Animal Park), and California condor (Los Angeles Zoo, San Diego Wild Animal Park), where the captive propagation of repository stock has been critical to their survival and the subsequent reintroductions into newly protected and managed habitats. From a world population of twenty-two birds in 1982 when captive-breeding efforts began, ten times as many California condors now exist. More than eighty condors are living in the wild under watchful human eyes and have begun to hatch and rear chicks on their own. On the other hand, human-imposed and natural obstacles have continued to plague reintroduced California condors, as they crash into high voltage power lines, consume carrion contaminated with lead from hunters' bullets, and fall prey to indigenous golden eagles and coyotes. Human activities, including settlement, livestock overgrazing, and shooting, have continued to affect oryx populations in their reintroduction areas in Jordan. A second self-sustaining oryx population has been now been established in the Mahazat as-Sayd region of Saudi Arabia.

The prairie grasslands, one of America's largest ecosystems that immigrants met upon their arrival to the Midwest, has now been almost entirely replaced by farms, factories, roadways, and residential settlements. American bison once numbered in the millions and were on the near-certain road to extermination in the 1870s when mass-market hunters sold their hides for $1.25, their tongues for $.25, and their hindquarters for $.01 per pound. In the early 1900s, New York's Bronx Zoo played a key role in propagating the survivors of this slaughter and saving this species from extinction. Captive-born stock was used to reestablish free-ranging populations. Sadly, far more people have seen video images of African lions in their authentic savanna habitats than of our American bison on natural prairie lands. The remnants of the herds of millions of bison that once roamed those seas of grass are now limited to comparatively token populations in several confined seminatural settings and on ranches. There is every reason to believe that the spectacular wildebeest migrations in East Africa could meet the same fate.

Giant pandas, forest elephants, bonobos, gorillas, Jentink's duikers, pygmy hippos, or the Somali wild ass? Which species will be next? No humans are alive who saw the last dodo bird or the last quagga, a relative of South Africa's plains zebras. The only quagga ever photographed alive was a mare in the London Zoo, and the last one died in Amsterdam's Artis Zoo in 1883, several years after the quagga was presumed to have become extinct in the wild. Efforts are afoot today, via DNA technology and selective breeding, however, to re-create the quagga (or at least a look-alike) from living plains zebras. This is an intriguing prospect, but one that rings somewhat hollow as countless other animal species face extinction in our own time.

What about the lesser ones that most of us have never even heard of? The clues can be found by examining the *Red Data Book* of the World Conservation Union, which maintains the doomsday list of species that appear to be on the path to oblivion. The number of basket cases for conservationists to work on is overwhelming. The primary focus should be more on the conservation of entire ecosystems, rather than the more common species-by-species approach—yet funding for conservation programs is often species-oriented.

Releasing captive-born wildlife into the wild calls for substantial financial and logistical commitments. For example, the resources required for programs such as golden lion tamarin (a tiny, golden-colored primate species) reintroductions in South America have been significant. Animals must be taught to feed themselves, climb trees, and avoid predators and a host of other obstacles that were not mastered in their captivity in zoos. Moreover, they require long periods of artificial feeding and postrelease management. It has been found to be more cost-effective to capture and release wild-born tamarins to establish new populations because of these labor and logistical obstacles. California condors destined for release into the wild are now put through short courses in power line avoidance. For many species, a significant period of gradual release and adaptation requires long-term commitments, unlike restocking practices used with hatchery-reared trout and salmon, which are pumped from a tanker truck into a lake or stream and left to their own devices.

Placing zoo animals into an area where indigenous populations are already present may interfere with existing populations and pose risks in introducing diseases that could jeopardize the welfare of the animals in the wild that the introductions are intended to bolster. Of all the mammalian types, the hoofed animals, especially open-country grazers, seem most naturally inclined to readaptation into the wild without intensive rehabilitation. Some years ago I was involved in discussions on the proposed release of captive chimpanzees into a Liberian rainforest. These animals had been used as research subjects, and most were captured years before as babies. They were to be released into habitat with an existing wild chimp population and in relative proximity to human settlements. The potential for disrupting existing populations and for disturbing rural agricultural activities weighed heavily against the proposal, and it was rejected. It was later learned that a caretaker in the chimp colony had contracted tuberculosis, which had gone undetected, and eventually caused several cases in colony animals. This example only reinforces the concerns that animal reintroductions must also consider the effects of introduced microflora and pathogens that accompany animals, which could decimate existing wild populations.

An innovative program of the Wildlife Conservation Society's Field Veterinary Program, based from their New York Wildlife Health Center, is providing veterinary insights into ecosystem health in locations around the globe. The proximity of people and their livestock to wild populations has created numerous disease problems throughout the world. For example, an outbreak of canine distemper virus, communicated from domestic dogs to Serengeti lions, resulted in a 30 percent loss of the lion population in a single incident. Tuberculosis introduced by domestic cattle is a serious problem in South African wildlife in the vicinity of Kruger National Park. For years, the disease brucellosis has been a serious problem shared by bison and grazing cattle around Yellowstone National Park. Gorillas in Africa are being monitored by Wildlife Conservation Society staff for diseases that could readily decimate these small populations. These and other examples of interchanges of infectious organisms between people's livestock and wildlife give rise to a whole vista of new and undiscovered problems that could affect the welfare and survival of animals and people alike. The science and politics of rural land use will have serious disease consequences for shrinking populations of wildlife. Studies that educate decision makers on these matters will be valuable in determining future actions that will regulate livestock and influence nature conservation strategies.

The motivation of average citizens toward environmental consciousness and stewardship should be paramount among zoos' objectives. Zoos should foster the application of global lessons of conservation biology in their own back yards. The greatest difficulty in all this is political. It is safe and comfortable to lament and criticize the cutting of African rainforests—the offended entrepreneurs and government officials have no practical capabilities for recourse or retribution. It may be quite another story, however, if a zoo goes up against entrenched corporate interests in its home region or takes critical positions against pollution and resource utilization where fault lies with local government and businesses. Indeed, it would be a courageous zoo that finds diplomatic ways to help identify or rectify local environmental transgressions.

In a recent address to the assembly of the World Conservation Union in Pretoria, South Africa, New York's Wildlife Conservation Society's former director, William Conway, observed:

> It is past time for zoos to stop arguing that enlightening children in New York or Tokyo about the plight of gorillas in Cameroon or Congo is responsive conservation. That's a lesson that I think we all know, but what I would like to ask each one of us to think about is "What are we doing about it?" If we really want to change the world and put in place the kind of new thinking that will really make the world a better and better place as the years go by, we will have to work a lot harder and to speak and act in such a way as to affect legislators, adult voters and the general public, in every way that we can.

When I was growing up in Grand Rapids, in western Michigan, and making forays to the Grand River, which runs through the center of the city, there was nothing at all grand about the river that I saw. The prevailing attitude was "that's just the way it is." This river bisects the former "Furniture Capital of the World" and had become a degraded body of moving fluid, oozing its way past industrial operations—the city's version of ancient Rome's Cloaca Maxima, or great sewer. Finally, the would-be Grand River dumped into Lake Michigan, which had become a toxic depository for mercury, polychlorinated biphenyls (PCBs), and agricultural chemicals from western Michigan watersheds. It was a pathetic sight to see drainpipes poking out along the river's banks, dribbling all manner of manufacturing waste. But why wasn't I compelled to action at the time? Where was the common sense of the average citizen or corporate responsibility while the degradation took place over many decades? Although much of this has now been significantly abated, thanks to enhanced environmental concerns and regulations, old bottom sediments in the Grand River and in Lake Michigan continue to contribute to aquatic ecosystem problems, including limits placed on the safe consumption of fish by people. It is remarkable and frightening how deadened our senses were that allowed our rivers to be polluted and our forests decimated in the first place. It took Rachel Carson's 1962 book *Silent Spring* to alert politicians and academics to the seriousness of our environmental problems, resulting in the establishment of the federal Environmental Protection Agency eleven years later.

The Grand River today, though never destined to be pristine, has been improved enough that salmon can make their way from Lake Michigan into the heart of the city, and fishermen stand elbow-to-elbow in spawning season in attempts to land a prized catch. Zoos have the potential to be catalysts for the conservation of their own community's streams, marshes, and woodlands. Some zoos have taken on the task of educating the public by creating hands-on laboratories that local schools can use to teach conservation biology. Kentucky's Louisville Zoo built such a teaching facility, the MetaZoo Education Center, years ago, and many other zoos have since followed its lead. In essence, the entire zoological garden should be an extension of school classrooms to complement their teaching resources. The Bramble Park Zoo in Watertown, South Dakota, for example, has embraced regional conservation issues by collaborating with the state Game, Fish and Parks Department and focusing on mixed grass prairie ecosystems. They have developed special projects for breeding the endangered black-footed ferret and swift fox, as well as conservation outreach programs that provide environmental instruction in public school classrooms.

As more resources become available through communications technology via satellite and the Internet, one can also envision zoo education programs establishing sophisticated multimedia centers that provide live connections to real-time, remote environmental imaging and video feeds from other zoos, sensitive habitats, and research projects around the world. An "electronic zoo" now under development in the United Kingdom proposes to use no live animals at all.

Larger zoological institutions can take on activities that are more global in scope, including in-house research programs and in-situ conservation programs in field locations far from the zoo itself. In some instances already, the traditional distinctions and barriers between academia, research, and zoos have diminished significantly. Although not every zoo can fund and administer programs of the scope carried out by the New York's Wildlife Conservation Society, the Zoological Society of San Diego, and a few others, every niche in between is available for projects and collaborative relationships in activities around the globe. The first zoo director to dedicate an institution to being primarily a conservation center was the Jersey Wildlife Trust's Gerald Durrell. Despite the small size of the Jersey Zoo, its departure from the zoo norm was revolutionary for its time. The staff likes to describe their organization as "the zoo that's not a zoo."

A growing number of zoos are creating small grant programs to assist in wildlife and habitat research. Though often modest in financial scope, such efforts have the potential to catalyze projects that kindle nature conservation activities in diverse locales. And catalyze is the correct operating term, since mere expatriate project initiatives, uncoupled to local capacity building (training in agriculture, ecology, and administration), are unlikely to foster enduring conservation programs. The *Annual Report on Conservation and Science* is published by the American Zoo and Aquarium Association (AZA), which lists the conservation activities of member institutions, is accessible on its web site (www.aza.org). International projects involving veterinarians and curators will challenge zoos to understand truly the limits and prospects of effecting conservation initiatives in foreign lands.

In some of my own work in West African wildlife conservation, I have had lengthy discussions with government officials about the risks of ignoring obvious signs of tropical forest degradation. To my surprise, one such official responded defensively, "You Americans used your country's natural resources to build up your country and to develop your economy. Now that you have your prosperity, you're telling us that we can't have ours." In other words, he had pretty much the same attitude about the exploitation of the environment as many of our ancestors did. Both perceived themselves as living on the edge. The surprise, for naive me, was that they, those few making the decisions, often choose to ignore lessons already learned in exchange for the short-term gains that they see in front of them. Outsiders offering advice are sometimes dismissed as "ecologic imperialists." His sentiments are not rare, and perhaps this reflects growing frustration toward expatriate "experts" whose suggested solutions may be incompatible with, or irrelevant to, needs on the community level, and whose projects may do little to build local capacity for environmental management.

Few officials of any stripe seem consistently disposed to implementing community capacity building for sustainable agriculture and environmental conservation. Such initiatives often conflict with political, ethnic, and private agendas. Frequently, there is a broad disconnect between ruling governments and their rural citizens. In developing countries, where more conservation opportunities exist, problems are rampant in the areas of benevolent governance, economic transparency, human rights, and even personal safety. Zoos will be wise to support programs that favor building local capacity, rather than simply supplying "experts" to study and recommend measures for foreign governments to implement and then leaving for home.

Thirty years ago, for example, a series of survey projects in Liberia was funded by an international conservation organization, recommending the protection of sensitive areas of forest and wetlands as nature reserves and national parks. Entirely lacking from these initiatives were significant plans to assist in the implementation of the recommendations. At the time that was that best that could be done, but, in the interim, significant conservation opportunities have been lost as the forest estate there has been subdivided. As conservation-grant programs proliferate (they are the simplest, most economic way for a zoo to be engaged in international field conservation), it may be wise for zoos to pool administrative resources or at least develop evaluative protocols to assure that the objectives of their conservation projects are clear, measurable, and are being met.

My fellow zoo veterinarians' numbers continue to grow, though their faces are changing rapidly. They contribute and depart, each passing on his or her experiences and observations in the manner of an endless relay race. The vision of their roles in collaborating in the conservation of captive and free-ranging wildlife is coming into clearer focus.

The Canada goose is an excellent example of the value and efficiency of collaboration. It is reported that a flock of geese traveling in a classic vee shape can fly much longer and faster because of the aerodynamic effects of formation flying. Like a sports cars drafting a leading vehicle, the energy required for the one following diminishes because of the vacuum created, which literally pulls the following object along. When the lead goose tires, the other geese take turns at the head of the column, which thereby is able to travel distances that a lone goose could not. Flying in formation, so to speak, zoos and zoo people can go much farther together than their individual efforts ever could in contributing to wildlife conservation.

Zoos have evolved from menageries to zoological gardens to conservation centers. Thirty years ago, most zoos were not involved in conservation work outside of their own gates, but it is not unusual now, even for modest-sized zoos, to have projects in South America, Africa, or Asia. South Africa's Johannesburg Zoo is now partnering with a Nebraska zoo and a Michigan college in its research and education programs. Johannesburg's promotional statement articulates what most people expect their hometown zoo to be: "It's a growl, a splash, a chatter of excitement, green trees, gardens, laughter and learning, a living classroom, a place for the family to relax—and much more."

Through the support and input of society, zoo veterinarians, curators, directors, and scientists will be expected to define and implement the "and much more" details. In that process, they will shape the character and course of the world's zoo community. Animals will be the ultimate judges of the performance of zoos by their ability to thrive in captivity and in the wild. History will judge zoos by their tangible contributions to understanding and conserving animals at home in their natural environments.

ANNOTATED BIBLIOGRAPHY
OF SELECTED WORKS ON ZOOS

Eric Baratay and Elisabeth Hardouin-Fugier. *Zoo: A History of Zoological Gardens in the West.* London: Reaktion Books, 2002.

A detailed review of the history of keeping wild animals in captivity, abundantly illustrated with reproductions of hundreds of old drawings, paintings, and photographs depicting the relationships between captive wildlife and people and the changing architecture of menageries and zoos. Overall, an intriguing but somewhat dark account of humankind's exploitation of animals for status, amusement, and profit. Originally published in French.

A. D. Bartlett. *Wild Animals in Captivity.* London: Chapman and Hall, 1899.

Compiled from his father's records by his son Edward Bartlett, this account provides interesting details about efforts to adapt many animals—from elephants to birds and serpents—to captivity. Though a taxidermist, not a veterinarian, Bartlett tended to the birds of the Queen of England and to many other ill animals at the London Zoo during his tenure as manager. He provides interesting anecdotes about animal keeping, including problems in trimming claws on lions, lancing abscesses on elephants, and generally nursing a wide range of creatures to help them survive their stays in captivity.

W. Reid Blair. *In the Zoo.* New York: Charles Scribner's Sons, 1929.

The author served for long periods as both veterinarian and director of the Bronx Zoo. A small section is devoted to some of the challenging medical cases in the first part of his career, and the rest of the book describes the manner in which many of the major species in the Bronx Zoo were acquired, acclimatized, and managed in their new homes in captivity. The text contains several interesting illustrations of veterinary care scenarios at the zoo.

Stephen St C. Bostock. *Zoos and Animal Rights: The Ethics of Keeping Animals.* London: Routledge, 1993.

Written by a Glasgow Zoo education officer, this work treats the ethics and value of keeping animals in zoos. Ranging from ancient times through modern-day transitions from barred cages to naturalistic exhibits, Bostock discusses the constraints of captivity and how they affect animal health, behavior, and public perceptions, with an emphasis on striving to improve these areas through evaluation and change. He provides arguments to justify the keeping of animals in captivity by illustrating the successes that zoos have had in education, breeding, and the reintroduction of endangered species.

William Bridges. *Gathering of Animals: An Unconventional History of the New York Zoological Society*. New York: Harper & Row, 1974.

William Bridges provides detailed insights into the history of the Bronx Zoo and its leaders as they struggled to fund, develop, and sustain one of America's largest zoological parks. There are interesting profiles of the strong personalities that founded the New York Zoological Society and the competing interests of exhibition, field research, and medicine that typified the subculture of this evolving zoo. The author, the zoo's curator emeritus of publications, explores these conflicts in an open and unapologetic style that provides candid insights into the political, scientific, and cultural factors that shaped the Bronx Zoo from inside and out.

Lee S. Crandall. *The Management of Wild Mammals in Captivity*. Chicago: University of Chicago Press, 1964.

This publication was once a standard on the keeping of wild mammals in zoos, dealing with husbandry and management issues group by group. Derived largely from his experiences at the Bronx Zoo, where Crandall held curatorial positions over a forty-five-year career, it was one of the few reference publications available for many years. Crandall wrote several hundred scientific publications and a companion book with William Bridges entitled *A Zoo Man's Notebook* (University of Chicago Press, 1964).

Vicki Croke. *The Modern Ark*. New York: Avon, 1997.

This book covers a range of issues, from the history of animals in captivity to the transformation of many old zoo exhibits into naturalistic ones. The author has covered zoo subjects for several media organizations and draws extensively on the experiences of directors, curators, and keepers to develop her discussions about conservation, ethics, behavioral aberrations of zoo animals, and the role of zoos in wildlife conservation.

Murray E. Fowler and R. Eric Miller. *Zoo and Wild Animal Medicine*, 3d ed. Philadelphia: W. B. Saunders, 2003.

The most widely used reference on zoo animal medicine and the first comprehensive text on zoo animal medicine, this is a taxonomic-oriented, multiauthor work created through the efforts of dozens of veterinarians who have made zoo medicine their life careers.

Alan Green and the Center for Public Integrity. *Animal Underworld: Inside America's Black Market for Rare and Exotic Species*. New York: Public Affairs, 1999.

A journalist attempts to describe the complexities of the trade in exotic animals involving zoos, dealers, private parties, and the animal-products industry. He concludes that in many ways, "animal laundering" resembles the manner in which drug money is laundered in our economy. Relating example after example of blurred chains of custody and ownership, he implicates many prominent zoos and a vast network of smaller players in his thesis. The recurring theme of the book is his contention that zoos irresponsibly reproduce animals and then dispose of many of them in ways that make it difficult to determine their ultimate fate in auctions, back yards, roadside animal brothels, and even restaurants and medicine shops. Depressing, tedious, and disorganized, the book offers as examples health certificates and other transport documents that illustrate shipments to nonexistent facilities and nebulous middle persons. Surely, many zoo staffers have checked the index in the back to see if they or any business associates made cameo appearances in the text.

David Hancocks. *Animals and Architecture.* New York: Praeger, 1971.

This is a well-illustrated history of zoological garden architecture, from old menageries to contemporary zoos at the time of its publication. It remains a classic in the literature of zoo design, in which Hancocks continues to play a prominent role.

David Hancocks. *A Different Nature: The Paradoxical World of Zoos and Their Uncertain Futures.* Berkeley: University of California Press, 2001.

An architect with diverse experience in designing and managing zoos, Hancocks has written perhaps the most important book to date on the history of animal exhibition and offers detailed opinions on the task before zoos that aspire to be important cultural institutions. Placing himself as an outsider, he takes some well-deserved shots at the tradition-bound leadership of the zoo profession, with the notable exception of specific individuals whom he holds out as innovators in the field of modern zoological gardens. Considerable discussion is devoted to the evolution of "landscape immersion" as the pinnacle of zoo exhibit methodology and how inept attempts to emulate it are fostering a new generation of failed animal displays, despite the rising costs of mega-exhibits. Taking zoos to task for their lack of vision, originality, narrow perspectives, and overstated accomplishments about their contributions to wildlife conservation, he describes the best and worst examples of animal displays and how opportunities are routinely missed to improve public awareness of real-world problems of environmental degradation and species extinctions.

Elizabeth Hanson. *Animal Attractions: Nature on Display in American Zoos.* Princeton, NJ: Princeton University Press, 2002.

A historian provides a very readable analysis of the role of zoos in American culture and how some of the larger institutions arose and changed over time. The activities of several zoo animal suppliers, such as Frank Buck and Carl Hagenbeck, are reviewed, as well as some of the larger collecting expeditions undertaken by zoos themselves. A discussion of moatless animal displays interestingly compares Hagenbeck's pseudo-geologic attempts at exhibit rock work to the detailed castings used in De Boer's efforts at the Denver and St. Louis Zoos in the early 1900s.

Heini Hediger. *Wild Animals in Captivity.* New York: Dover, 1950.

The former director of the Basel Zoo in Switzerland, Hediger is regarded as the pioneer grandfather of zoo animal psychology, writing numerous papers and books about the responses of wild animals to captivity. This book is a classic text for zoo animal behavior and discusses how exhibit design and environmental enrichment can exacerbate or blunt the behavioral aberrations brought on by confinement. In making his case for the effects of captivity on normal behaviors, Hediger points to the natural behavior of wild counterparts to encourage zoos to emulate more natural activities for animals in captivity.

R. J. Hoage and William A. Deiss, eds. *New Worlds, New Animals: From Menagerie to Zoological Park in the Nineteenth Century.* Baltimore: Johns Hopkins University Press, 1996.

Compiled largely from papers presented at the symposium entitled History and Evolution of the Modern Zoo, sponsored by the National Zoological Park and the Smithsonian Institution in 1989, this is a thorough analysis of the development of zoos in the nineteenth century as well as their predecessors in the menageries and zoos of antiquity. The overall depiction of modern zoos as institutions of education and science is emphasized, as well as some of the seldom recollected successes of animal keeping that predated modern technology and medicine. Interesting black and white historical illustrations complement many of the contributions.

Devra G. Kleiman, Mary E. Allen, Katerina V. Thompson, Susan Lumpkin, and Holly Harris, eds. *Wild Mammals in Captivity: Principles and Techniques.* Chicago: University of Chicago Press, 1997.

This is among the most useful single reference books on zoo animal care, medicine, nutrition, reproduction, genetics, and research to date. Several authors summarize strategies for unbarred, more naturalistic exhibit strategies. Each chapter carries detailed references to published literature, and the volume contains an annotated bibliography appendix to the major works and journals related to the science of captive animal management, now known as "zoo biology."

Linda Koebner. *Zoo Book: The Evolution of Wildlife Conservation Centers.* New York: Forge, 1995.

This well-illustrated book displays many examples of old and new zoo exhibits. It is a picture tour of many of the larger zoos in North America and features keepers, veterinarians, and zoo directors going about their duties running a zoo. The work of a number of notable zoo field workers is featured in the section on wildlife conservation initiatives being under taken by zoos in nature.

Terry L. Maple and Erika F. Archibald. *Zooman: Inside the Zoo Revolution.* Marietta, GA: Longstreet Press, 1993.

Dr. Maple's account details the trials and tribulations of the Atlanta Zoo, and his efforts as its director to rebuild the entire reputation and physical zoo facility from its nadir in the mid-1980s. Aside from the specifics of Zoo Atlanta, Dr. Maple discusses his philosophy of zoo management and the changes that he has strived to implement in Atlanta's exhibit methods, animal enrichment, education, and applied research programs. There are useful insights into keeping great apes in captivity and addressing the special social needs of these challenging, intelligent creatures. In his discussions comparing American zoos, he provides some intriguing statistics on their budgets, scientific accomplishments, and physical sizes.

Bob Mullan and Garry Marvin. *Zoo Culture.* Champaign: University of Illinois Press, 1998.

Hopscotching around the world from zoo to zoo, this book looks at how people view zoos and how zoos exhibit animals. The authors, one a social anthropologist, the other a sociologist, offer insights into how animals have been displayed and how regional culture has resulted in different interpretations of zoos in diverse places. Among the interesting topics are synopses of historical efforts to display native peoples in "ethnographic exhibitions" and some of the royal menageries that pre-dated modern zoos.

Bryan G. Norton, Michael Hutchins, Elizabeth F. Stevens, and Terry L. Maple, eds. *Ethics on the Ark.* Washington, DC: Smithsonian Institution Press, 1995.

This multiauthor text draws upon the experience of many knowledgeable spokespersons in the zoo field to review the state of zoos today and the issues of animal acquisition, exhibit design, captive well-being, breeding genetics, research, and euthanasia. The problems of surplus animals, animals as entertainment, and monetary vs. altruistic motives receive needed analysis, as do realistic expectations of zoos' roles in contributing to conservation of wildlife in the wild.

C. T. Robbins. *Wildlife Feeding and Nutrition,* 2d ed. San Diego: Academic Press, 1993.

A standard in the small library of works on zoo animal nutrition. Includes overviews of feeding strategies for both captive and free-ranging wild animals.

Nigel Rothfels. *Savages and Beasts: The Birth of the Modern Zoo.* Baltimore: Johns Hopkins University Press, 2002.

A well-researched account of the history of animal exhibition from early times to the birth of the trend-setting Hagenbeck Tierpark, near Hamburg, Germany, in 1907. Rothfels provides a detailed analysis of the Hagenbeck family, a long line of animal dealers and menagerie owners, and its extensive enterprises for supplying zoos and circuses and even exhibiting aboriginal humans. The returning themes of the book reveal the contradictions between self-promoted Hagenbeck images of the altruistic motives and methods of the family's animal activities and the well-documented evidence to the contrary (aggressive animal capture and training methods). Although patriarch Carl Hagenbeck has been widely credited for creating the model for the twentieth-century trends toward zoos without bars, the author concludes that his innovations in animal display techniques, such as open-moat panoramas of bioclimatic animal assemblies, were more for the promotion of animal sales and entertaining displays for the viewing public than for the benefit of the animals.

Colin Tudge. *Last Animals at the Zoo: How Mass Extinction Can Be Stopped.* Washington, DC: Island Press, 1992.

The thesis of this book is that zoos are an essential part of modern conservation strategy through their efforts at conservation breeding. The methods of breeding wild animals and the conservation of their genetic and behavioral diversity occupy most of this book, which provides overviews of a number of zoo projects related to propagating and reintroducing endangered species.

INDEX

adrenaline, 154 164, 167
Adventureland Jungle Cruise, 251
aggression: interspecies, 103, 117;
  intraspecies, 104, 115, 118;
  toward people, 45, 48, 57, 62.
  See also behavior, of animals
albinos, 92, 128
Albuquerque, New Mexico, 220
Animal Welfare Act (AWA), 254;
  implementation in zoos, 259,
  262; in research institutions,
  260, 262
American Association of Zoo
  Keepers (AAZK), 45
American Association of Zoo
  Veterinarians (AAZV), 27, 40,
  41, 256, 263, 266
American College of Zoological
  Medicine (ACZM), 41
American Museum of Natural
  History, 246
American Zoo and Aquarium
  Association (AZA), 39, 159, 172,
  253–54, 263–64, 266, 276;
  accreditation, 253–54, 263, 266;
  membership, 244; mission, 264
anesthesia: advances in, 30, 131,
  142–43; complications of, 135;
  early methods, 25, 53, 133, 135;
  experiments, 124, 138–39; ideal
  characteristics of, 143; purposes
  of, 139; risks, 53, 132, 138–39,
  151; variations by available
  space, 139. *See also* drugs
anesthetics: carfentanyl, 148;
  chloroform, 25, 133, 135–36;
  curare, 142; ether, 25, 133,

135–36; etorphine, 139, 147, 222;
  diprenorphine, 148; fentanyl,
  148; ketamine, 131; nicotine
  alkaloids, 142; phencyclidine,
  131, 132; M-99, 147–49;
  M50–50, 148–49; succinyl
  choline, 143; xylazine, 143–44
animal births, 51, 62, 115, 167,
  230, 265
animal-capture equipment: blow
  pipe, 142; Cap-Chur gun,
  140–41; squeeze cages, 48, 133;
  Telinject, 142
animal collecting, 13, 178; Frank
  Buck, 245, 281; gorillas, 246;
  chimpanzees, 245; Martin and
  Osa Johnson, 245; methods,
  178, 244; mortalities, 245;
  orangutans, 244
animal enrichment, 84–85,
  234–35, 248, 253, 257, 281–82
animal husbandry, 19, 112, 159
animal introductions, 115–16
animal rights/welfare, viii, 37, 71,
  234, 240, 254–55, 257–60, 262,
  266; and adequate veterinary
  care, 260; *Animal Liberation*,
  238; Animal Welfare Act, 254,
  259–60, 262; biomedical
  research, 259, 261–62;
  bioterrorism, 259; definitions,
  234; Disneyland, 13, 198,
  251–52; farming, 112, 258–59;
  fish, 238, 241, 257; Jamieson,
  Dr. Dale, 249; lawsuits, 239;
  lesser species, 238; media
  dynamics, 234–35, 259; People

for the Ethical Treatment of
  Animals (PETA), 259, 260–62;
  Rattling the Cage, 239;
  sentience, 240; Silver Spring
  Monkeys, 260–62; Peter
  Singer, 238; Tijuana Humane
  Society, 146; Steven Wise, 239;
  Zoo Check, 239–40
animals: dangerous (*see* deaths,
  of keepers), 5, 46–48, 71, 75–77,
  79, 133, 208; escapes, 6, 16,
  76–77; transporting, 48, 82,
  166, 209, 215, 218, 245
animals, mentioned by name:
  Abe, 192; Albert, 193; Barney,
  77; Big Al, 106; Bob, 65–66;
  Boo Boo, 198; Bullwinkle,
  179; Caspar, 214; Checkers,
  53; Chopper, 54; Chuny, 51;
  Diablo, 235–36; Diarrhea, 230;
  Dinah, 245; Dolly, 66–67;
  Dudley Duplex, 93; Freckles,
  211; Frieda, 214; George,
  189–90; Godzilla, 92;
  Gonnorhea, 230; Iki, 144;
  Kakowet, 52; Ken Allen, 64,
  76; King Kong, 92; King Tut,
  228; Komo, 79; La Petite, 48;
  Linda, 52, 191; Lisette, 62;
  Lucky, 221–23; Maya, 221;
  Mbongo, 183; Ngagi, 183;
  Pyorrhea, 230; Rocky, 179;
  Sally, 206; Sanetti, 54;
  Snowflake, 92; Timon, 96;
  Thelma and Louise, 93;
  Topper, 53, 210–11; Victoria,
  25; Yogi, 198; Zeya, 49

PHOTOGRAPHIC CREDITS
AND ATTRIBUTIONS

A. D. Bartlett, *Wild Animals in Captivity*, 1898: 18, 62

Author: xii, 42 (Susan Schafer), 80, 83, 130, 132, 140, 141 (Dr. Frank Lochner), 145, 167, 204 (Freddie Alexander, John Fairfield), 213 (Dick Sweeney, Huey Hannon, Bob Wild—Asian elephant, San Diego Zoo, 1987), and 224—African elephant, Kenya

Chief Henk Dop: 110—southern white rhinos, Botswana

Detroit News/Donna Terek: 268—polar bears at Detroit Zoo

Detroit Zoo: 95

Dr. Frank Lochner: 149 (John Fairfield, r.)

Hagenbeck Tierpark: 74

Jones & Jones Architects: 84, 85, color plate 2—Adam Jones

Martin and Osa Johnson Safari Museum/Martin Johnson: 245

St. Louis Zoo: 81, 82, 94

State Library of Victoria/ Samuel Calvert: 247

Telinject USA: 142

Woodland Park Zoo: Knudson Family Collection, 26; Karen Anderson, color plate 6; Agnes Overbaugh, color plate 7; Richard Wilhelm, color plate 5

The Wildlife Conservation Society: 24, 58, 71, 93, 134, 186

Zoo Atlanta: 76, color plate 8 (D. Beckert)

Zoological Society of San Diego: viii, 34, 120 (Abe, Dr. Phil Robinson, Dr. David Fagan, Harold Mitchell), 135, 196 (c. 1950), 236, color plate 1 (Joseph Jennings, r., 1977)

Zoological Society of London: viii, 23, 92, 137